February 14, 1994

" LR "

As Park's 1ST Workstudy
student at City Year not only
did you break new ground but
you made your old headmaster
aware of one of Boston's greatest
human resources. A resource I've
used many time this year in "plotting"
a grandparent-mentoring program....
Hopefully 1995-96 will find you at
City Year & me the beneficiary of
your interest & counsel.....
    I'm proud of you & very grateful.
        " DR "

A City Year

A City Year

**On the Streets and in the Neighborhoods with
Twelve Young Community Service Volunteers**

Suzanne Goldsmith

The New Press
New York

Published in the United States by The New Press, New York
Distributed by W.W. Norton & Company, Inc., 500 Fifth Avenue, New York, NY 10110

ISBN 1-56584-093-3
LC 93-83617
Photo credits: pp. 12, 33, 131, 150, 166, 172 (top and bottom), and 217—Jon Amsterdam
pp. 47, 52, 55, 61, 74, 80, 92, 95, 126, 176, 179, 187, 194, and 237—Farr Carey
The lyrics to *Song for America* on p.73 are reprinted by permission of Peri Smilow, © 1990 by Sign of the Dove Music.

Book design by Acme Art, Inc.

Established in 1990 as a major alternative to the large, commercial publishing houses, the New Press is the first full-scale nonprofit American book publisher outside of the university presses. The Press is operated editorially in the public interest, rather than for private gain; it is committed to publishing in innovative ways works of educational, cultural, and community value. The New Press's editorial offices are located at the City University of New York.

Printed in the United States of America.
93 94 95 96   9 8 7 6 5 4 3 2 1

For my parents,
William and Marianne Goldsmith

In Memory of Tyrone Gunn
1968–1990

Contents

On the night of October 3, 1990, twenty-one-year-old Tyrone Gunn attended a birthday party with his new girlfriend, Caroline. Because it was a work night, Tyrone and Caroline left the party shortly after ten, and after they kissed goodbye in the subway station, Tyrone headed for home, taking the number 22 bus to Waldman Avenue. It had been a hot day and it was a pleasant night, with just enough of a chill to persuade him to keep his jacket on as he strolled along with long, slouchy steps. As always, Tyrone wore a hat pulled down tight over his wavy, close-cropped hair and he walked with his hands thrust deep in his pockets. He bopped a little to the music playing through his Walkman headphones. Perhaps he was whistling—Tyrone had a gap between his front teeth and he liked to whistle. Or maybe he was whispering the lyrics of a rap tune along with the tape. In any event, he did not hear the footfalls of the person who came up behind him at the corner, just a few steps from the door of his apartment building, and shot him in the back of the head.

Tyrone's brothers, Jeremy, Sparticus, and Gemarre, were playing Nintendo in the living room of the family's second-floor apartment when they heard the two shots. Gunfire was not an uncommon sound in their neighborhood, but these shots sounded unusually close. Jeremy ran to the window and saw Tyrone lying on the pavement. He knew it was Tyrone immediately because he could read the lettering on the back of his red jacket: CITY YEAR. The jacket was part of the uniform that came with Tyrone's new job. The boys raced downstairs and into the street, but there was nothing they could do for their brother. He was lying face-down on the sidewalk in a puddle of blood. His headphones lay beside him, still pumping music into the night. He was already dead.

Tyrone Gunn was number 111 of the 132 men, women, and children who were murdered in the city of Boston in 1990. It was a peak year for killing in Boston. Like most young black males who are shot or stabbed to death on the streets of poor neighborhoods, he received little attention in the local newspapers the next day. There was a brief account of his death midway through an item on page 24 of the *Boston Herald*, and the *Boston Globe* carried a short article on the obituary page. The police made a routine investigation, but uncovered no motive and no suspect.

But unlike so many violent killings that occur on inner-city streets each day in America, Tyrone's death did not pass unnoticed outside his neighborhood. His funeral the following week was attended by over a hundred people—people whose skin was white and brown as well as those who were black, and people who came from wealthy suburbs and working-class neighborhoods as well as from Tyrone's mostly poor, black neighborhood of Roxbury. His death was discussed in hushed and angry tones by people in the mayor's office, and by the executives of a major international corporation. The friends who mourned him included the children of welfare mothers, college professors, poor immigrants, and wealthy bankers.

Tyrone was a member of a Boston-based youth community service corps called City Year. In City Year, young people of all races and from a wide range of backgrounds work together full-time for nine months on public service projects such as building playgrounds and community gardens, tutoring in schools, or doing chores for the elderly. They receive little pay—$100 a week—but if they stay for the full nine months, they are awarded $5,000, paid out over two years, to help with college tuition or other expenses as they make the transition to education or work. There are other benefits as well: the chance to learn work skills, and in some cases a chance to earn a high school equivalency degree, improve language skills, or gain other remedial education. They join, also, for the chance to give, to test themselves against a challenge, to take part in improving their own community, and for the chance to make friends with people whose backgrounds are different from their own.

I knew Tyrone a little; I was a member of his City Year team. Our team included, among others, a girl who had come to the United States with her family from Burma eight years earlier; a black former gang member who had recently been released from jail; a white girl from Cambridge who had graduated from a small alternative private high school; a black girl from a middle-class suburban family who aspired to go to Harvard.

We appeared to have so little in common that one team member dubbed us "The Misfits." In the second month of the program, when Tyrone was killed, we still didn't know each other well. But we all had memories of Tyrone, and I treasured mine: Tyrone sick with a cold but still working hard, shoveling dirt, a sparkling drop of mucus clinging to the tip of his nose. Or shouting angrily at a bus driver who had closed the door before a dawdling teammate could get on. Tyrone had a temper, which he told us he was working to control. He also had drive, discipline, and a finely honed sense of justice.

I knew that he was twenty-one and had completed two years in the Job Corps, and that he was working toward a high school equivalency degree. I later learned that he was using part of his City Year stipend to help his mother pay the rent—and that he had a four-year-old son.

For some of his City Year friends, Tyrone's death made him yet one more on an already painfully long list of lost friends and acquaintances. For others, like me, he was the very first victim of inner-city violence to be more than a sensational headline or a grainy newspaper photo. We had all shared something with Tyrone: sore muscles and sweat, a few jokes, lunchtime banter, satisfaction with work completed, and frustration with tasks more challenging than they appeared. Tyrone was real to us. We knew the sound of his laughter, the timbre of his voice, the way he walked, and what he ate for lunch. When Tyrone died, we cared. And now, when we read in the newspaper about another young man getting shot—whether the shooting occurs two blocks or two miles from our homes—we can no longer quickly turn the page, relieved that we are not a part of his world. We know that we are.

Introduction

first became interested in youth service in 1985, when I took a job as a team leader in New York's year-old City Volunteer Corps. I was looking for a way to do something about urban needs, and I wasn't qualified to teach or to be a social worker. I liked the idea of challenging young people to help, rather than counseling them to change. Leading youths in community service didn't require a graduate degree, and it would allow me to contribute, to learn, and to be with teenagers every day.

The City Volunteer Corps, known as CVC, was founded by Mayor Ed Koch as a model for national service—the idea of asking young people to devote a year or two to public service. CVC recruited volunteers between the ages of seventeen and twenty-one for a year of full-time community service. Their remuneration was a weekly stipend ($80 in 1985) and, at year's end, a scholarship of $5,000 or $2,500 in cash.

For a little more than a year I supervised a team of twelve CVC volunteers. It was an exciting job, focusing the time and energy of young people to accomplish needed work. My team gave swimming lessons to children with birth defects. We helped out as teacher's aides in overcrowded classrooms. We did chores and errands for old people who lived trapped and isolated in walk-up apartments. We painted the bottom of the third-largest outdoor swimming pool in the world.

But it wasn't always easy to focus on the service—for me or for the young people I supervised. Many of them had chaotic home lives. More than three-quarters of the volunteers were high school dropouts, 90 percent were black or Hispanic, and the great majority were poor or near-poor. Volunteers called me up or knocked on my door at moments of crisis, wanting to talk or to borrow money. I found myself advising pregnant girls, young mothers, teenagers who were living on the street, and boys who had been mugged on the way home from work.

My job involved not only counseling but discipline. Over time, I lost count of the number of volunteers I had to dismiss for misbehavior or poor attendance. One boy on my team stole $200 from an elderly woman while cleaning her apartment. Another beat a drug addict on the street with a stick. Some volunteers came to work high, their pupils dilated, and then stopped coming at all.

Just keeping my team members in the program was a struggle.

Mayor Koch had intended CVC to comprise a wide range of young people in its ranks: white, black, Asian, Hispanic, poor, middle-class, affluent. But despite both broad and targeted recruitment efforts, white and middle-class youths did not enroll in significant numbers. At the same time, many of the disadvantaged youths CVC attracted required more support and structure than the program was then equipped to provide. Two-thirds of the corps members were dismissed or dropped out before completing their year of service.

But studies showed that City Volunteers gained in many ways: they increased in empathy for the elderly and the disabled; many of them remained involved in community service work long after graduation; and they were far more likely to register to vote than their peers who had not been involved in service.

Furthermore, my own experience convinced me that community service was an emotionally intense and fruitful experience, even for those who failed to complete the year. Each week, my team members showed me the journals they kept of their day-to-day experiences, and almost all contained compelling evidence of their increasing compassion, awareness, and sense of their own skills and responsibilities. Even the negative experiences were valuable. When a popular member of my team was caught stealing candy at the school where we were working, and then lied about it, the team voted—after an agony of deliberation—to expel her from the program. She didn't graduate from CVC, but she and all the members of the team learned something valuable from the experience.

Clearly, there was much still to be learned in the areas of supporting and retaining "at-risk" youth in service. But ideally, I thought, "success" in such programs would be measured not only in the number of high school equivalency degrees obtained and the number of service-hours performed, but also in the quality of the relationships that developed and the life lessons learned, even when they did not lead to graduation. National service should not be seen as a way of encouraging (or forcing) young people to "give back" to a community that had in many cases failed to nurture them, but as an experience in which they can hash out values, contribute to the common good, build self-esteem and a sense of responsibility, and cooperate in seeking solutions to social problems.

In addition, I felt strongly that national service should not be only for the disadvantaged. The richness of my own education in CVC showed me that people with backgrounds similar to mine—middle-class or affluent, white, college-educated or college-bound—had much to gain by their participation.

It was because of that conviction that I was particularly interested in the national service model that was being developed in Boston by a privately funded youth corps called City Year. During a summer pilot in 1988 and a subsequent full year of operation, City Year was very successful, with most participants staying through to the end and speaking enthusiastically about their experience in a glowing series of local newspaper and TV news reports. City Year's structure was patterned after that of CVC. But the City Year corps was drawn from all racial and socioeconomic groups; it reflected the diverse population of the Boston area.

City Year's diversity set it apart from CVC and many other existing youth corps. Because City Year enrolled youth from all backgrounds, it was clear that it was not strictly a volunteer program, nor was it workfare. Its founders said they hoped to build an institution that would help complete the civil rights movement by removing social barriers to integration and provide the "missing link" in American democracy: training for citizenship. The core of the program was service and the education it would provide for a lifetime of civic engagement.

I wanted to know what serving in a diverse national service corps was like, and in City Year I saw an opportunity both to live the experience and to report it for others. While much had been written about the idea of national service, almost nothing had been written about the experience.

In August of 1990 I met with City Year cofounders Alan Khazei and Michael Brown, and they agreed to let me join City Year, not as a staff member or a corps member but as a participating observer. I would spend nine months working on service projects around the city with one team of City Year participants, and afterward would write a book about the experience. I would be open about my book project, and would seek the permission and cooperation of those I wrote about, but otherwise would try to blend in as much as possible. In addition, Alan and Michael gave me permission to attend staff meetings and document the operations of the program on a variety of levels.

This book is an account of what I observed and experienced in the nine months that followed. It is my hope that it will give those who have not had the opportunity to take part in such a program a chance to share my experience: to meet my teammates and read about the challenges we faced and the relationships that developed, to experience vicariously the arduous work, the moments of disappointment and pride, of boredom and passion. I wanted, through this book, to give readers a long and unflinching look at what can happen in the course of what President Clinton has called "a season of service."

The names of my teammates and supervisor as well as all other City Year corps members have been changed, save that of Tyrone Gunn, who died in the second month of the program. I also changed the names of the children we worked with at the Blackstone school. Everything else is presented as it happened.

This book is not a rigorous critical evaluation of City Year or of national service. I used no control groups and no random sample. My teammates are unique individuals, not archetypes, and their lives and choices, while suggestive, cannot supply the basis for broad conclusions. It is also important to note that my portrait of City Year—which, since the time I joined, has gained a national profile as a potential model for President Clinton's national service initiative—is a ground-level snapshot taken early in the history of an innovative and evolving program.

Still, I hope that this story can make a positive contribution to the national service debate by giving readers a little piece of the action—a chance to live out a year of national service through my experience. Perhaps one day the privilege of joining a program like City Year will be open to all, but today it is still a unique and rare opportunity. I took advantage of that opportunity, and with this book I hope to make others aware of it.

A City Year

The Team

My City Year team comes into being on a warm September afternoon in a rustic outdoor chapel by a lake in western Massachusetts. The chapel, a cluster of split-log benches and a rough-hewn rostrum huddled beneath a canopy of spreading oak and pine, is part of YMCA Camp Becket-in-the-Berkshires, where we have all come for five days of intensive orientation to the City Year program.

Glancing around at the seventy-two new recruits from my seat near the back, I am struck—as I have been many times already this week—by the patchwork array of physical types and styles that surrounds me. There is a broad palette of skin colors, ranging from dark, shiny brown through all the mulatto and Asian-olive tones to creamy, raw white. But racial differences are only the beginning. There are differences of style, of class, and of attitude. There are crewcuts, flattops, high-tops, low-tops, shags, weaves, perms, page-boys, shaven heads, and puffed, moussed manes. People are wearing hiking boots and party shoes. High-rise basketball shoes and high-heeled sandals. There are girls in baggy overalls and girls in skintight shorts; guys in nylon jogging suits and guys in tattered prep-school sweatshirts. Some sit ramrod straight; others are slouched or leaning against one another. One girl sits cross-legged on the bench. A tiny diamond sparkles in the side of her nose.

For three days we have all participated in activities ranging from games of introduction and late-night nature walks to serious discussions on topics such as urban needs and cultural diversity. We've had group calisthenics at seven each morning. We have eaten together, washed together, and shared our sleeping quarters. There is already a feeling of intimacy in this large group, and at this moment we are all excited.

The purpose of the gathering in the open-air chapel is to hand out team assignments. It is an important moment, one that every-body has been anticipating with pleasure and dread. We are to be divided into six teams that will serve together for nine months. For three days I have heard a lot of speculation among the recruits about what their teams will be like. How are they chosen? Will friends be put together? What will my team be like? Will we get along?

One thing everybody knows is that the teams will be "diverse." That, as we have all been told countless times since our arrival at Camp Becket, is the City Year way. The corps members don't know just how the teams were selected. They were not present at the staff meeting late last night. I was, and as I wait for the teams to be announced, I am remembering the scene.

"Who has Barkley Jones?" asks Tony, looking up from the yellow pad balanced on his knees. Tony is the team coordinator on whose team I plan to spend the year. He, like me, is a former CVC team leader and an old hand; Alan and Michael think he is an excellent supervisor, and since I have chosen to focus on one team, they want it to be his.

Tony looks at the other team coordinators gathered around him. "Barkley Jones! Anybody have him? Is there anybody you'll trade him for?"

It is after midnight and there are twelve of us crowded into the living room of a tiny two-room cottage near the edge of the camp, remote from the other buildings. The room is shabbily furnished but quaint, equipped with an old refrigerator, a couch, two armchairs, and some wooden seats. The windows are open and a bare lightbulb is swaying gently overhead. People are scattered everywhere, some on the couch or on chairs, some sprawling on the rug.

I am not here to participate in this debate, but to listen and watch. I am seated on the floor with my back against the refrigerator. It's vibrating slightly.

"Come on, you guys." Tony looks around, pleading. Like everyone, he is exhausted from three days of supervising recruits almost around the clock. The team-picking process has been going on for nearly an hour, but trading has reached a logjam. Nobody speaks.

Tony and the others are trying to put together teams that are balanced not only by race and gender but also by educational background, personality, economic status, and a variety of other intangibles. This trading procedure has developed of necessity as the quickest and most effective way to get the job done. But it is hard work, an emotional struggle. And it's a messy process.

"Okay, who has a guy they'll trade for Caroline Rein?" Tony tries again. Ernest, the oldest of the team coordinators, leans forward and squints at a large display of Polaroid photos glued to a posterboard, trying to identify Caroline.

"I'll give you Tyrone Gunn," he says.

"I might give you Caroline and a box of Havana cigars," says Tony, his mouth twitching, "but I don't think Tyrone should go on the same team with Charles."

"You're going to lose Charles anyway," says Alan, who is seated on a threadbare easy chair to Tony's right. "My guess is he's going to be gone in a week at the outside." He cranes his neck to look at Tony's list. "Ernest, you should give Tyrone to Tony."

Alan turns to his right to look at Gordon's list. "Wait a minute. You have four white women? Get rid of one."

"That's what I've been trying to tell you," Gordon says plaintively. "I can't seem to get a trade here."

"I only have one black woman," says Tony. "Look at Ernest's team. He has three."

The door opens suddenly and Jonathan, a staff member who works on recruitment, pokes his head in.

"What's this, the slave trade?" Jonathan is black, and his question draws a brief, awkward silence. But he is laughing good-naturedly. The screen door slams as he ducks back out.

"I have to trade one of my white women for someone on either James's or Mia's team," says Gordon.

"I only have three," says Mia. "But I'm a white woman. I think. Who knows anymore? I'm a woman, at least." Everyone laughs, and trading resumes.

The teams are not complete until nearly 2:00 A.M., when everyone is almost blind with fatigue. Later that night I find myself tossing and sweating on my narrow, swaybacked cot, unable to sleep. The team roster changed so many times during the trading that I can't remember for certain who is on the final list. I will be spending nine months with these people. Who are they?

Now, sitting in the outdoor chapel and waiting for the team announcements, I am still going over the list in my head, trying to remember who will be called for my team and what I know about each person.

The six team coordinators fan out in front of us, facing the corps. The ceremony begins, and as they take turns announcing the names of their new team members, each recruit stands when he or she is called and walks proudly or fearfully toward the front. I'm paying closest attention, of course, to Tony's—my own—team.

"Jacquelyn Jones!" announces Tony. Jacquelyn strides proudly to the front, flashing a dazzling smile to the right and to the left, Miss America greeting her public. She is black and beautiful. Jacquelyn was the first corps member I met, back at the City Year headquarters the day before we left to go to camp. That smile invited conversation. "I'm from Florida," she said. "I went to West Point after graduation, but I had to leave because we couldn't think. They wouldn't let us think. And I'm a thinking person."

Just yesterday, I remember, Jackie volunteered to read aloud a poem she had composed at our daily "community meeting." It was a very personal poem, about the unexpected death of her father, and she wept a little as she read it, yet managed to finish the poem with poise and dignity. Today, by contrast, she looks brilliantly happy. She takes her place by Tony.

"Charles Johnson!" Tony calls out, and Charles grins broadly as he swaggers to the front, both arms raised, making victory signs overhead. He is small and slight of build, with big eyes and high cheekbones, smooth brown skin, and a wide, flawless smile.

Charles loves attention, and he has a shifting, restless energy. Three days ago I watched as he spent most of the two-hour bus trip from Boston to the Berkshires on his feet, moving up and down the aisle. "Welcome to the Love Boat," he announced. "We'll be serving drinks on the promenade deck shortly." I also noticed that while many found Charles amusing at first, they soon grew annoyed and shifted in their seats, turning away from him as he tried to entertain them, and trying to sleep, their faces mashed against the windows and the woven seat-backs.

Charles's persistent antics have grown more than annoying in the past three days. He has been reprimanded three times for a variety of offenses: cursing, talking during meetings, wandering unauthorized outside his cabin at night.

Nevertheless, Charles can be charming; but sometimes his humor seems menacing. I am most fascinated by his eyes, which are bright—too bright, a team coordinator commented privately, wondering if Charles was high on drugs—and which often glitter and dance. But when you meet Charles's gaze, his eyes are as cold and as opaque as stones.

"Richie Dale!"

Richie plunges his hands in his pockets and lopes slouching to stand behind Tony. His skin is light, and he speaks, I know, with the flattened vowels and dropped *r*'s of Boston's white working-class Irish and Italians. By contrast, his style of dress is black, as are his gestures, his haircut, and his gait.

I remember a confrontation I observed yesterday between Richie and Tracy, who will also be on my team. About thirty of us were hiking through the woods.

We came to a fork in the path and stopped, uncertain which way to turn. After a moment's hesitation, Tony, who was leading, turned and ran back toward the camp. "I'll be right back," he yelled, but we'd already come a fair distance; we knew he would be gone a while. There were groans. A few people sat down in the path.

Richie began to complain. "They want us to work, or not? This is a waste of time." He looked around angrily and his gaze came to rest on Tracy, who was bouncing her head to some silent music. She seemed happy, oblivious.

"Why you try and act like you're black?" Richie demanded.

Tracy turned slowly and looked at Richie. "I don't try and act black," she said. "I'm white. That's my choice." She paused. "Besides, you ain't even black. You think you are, but you ain't."

Tracy shook her long black hair as she turned away. Richie glared at her back, his fists clenching at his sides.

"Tracy Danszka!"

I recall my first impression of Tracy as she, too, takes her place at the front. It was the day before we went up to camp, and we were all standing in the street outside the City Year headquarters, waiting for a brief introductory meeting to begin. Tracy was sitting on the hood of a car. She has long hair, dyed dead black and her lips were painted a shocking red. She was surrounded by a cluster of young black men, some of them leaning on the car, some leaning against a brick wall. As she chatted and looked about for new arrivals, she danced a little, her thick torso swaying to the rhythm of a silent tune. Every so often she threw her head back and laughed.

Later, inside, there was a meeting. A staff member reviewed the rules that would be enforced at camp. No drugs or drinking. No leaving the camp on your own. No sexual relations. No visiting with members of the opposite sex in their sleeping quarters.

"Can we hang out outside their cabins?" Tracy called out from her seat in the back. There was a burst of laughter. She smiled raffishly.

"Tyrone Gunn!" Tony continues his roll call. Tyrone walks to the front slowly. He takes his place and stands looking modestly at the ground.

My earliest image of Tyrone also dates to our first day together. The entire corps was waiting for the buses that would take us to camp, and our luggage was piled in a mountain near the curb of the alley-like street where the City Year headquarters is located. When the buses finally arrived and the announcement came that we could get on board, there was a confused crush as people tried to heft their bags and backpacks and stagger toward the underbelly baggage compartment of the idling buses. The drivers had undone the latches and raised the doors but were not there to help us load. Piles of bags were blocking everyone's way, creating confusion and frustrating the loading process. People began to yell and complain.

Suddenly Tyrone emerged from the mass, slender and a little older than the others, to judge from his taut, hollow cheeks. He was dressed in black and wearing black patent-leather shoes with gold crests. Silently, he began to load the bus, pulling bags from the pile and pushing them carefully to the rear of the compartment. Confusion turned to order. The crowd waited patiently as Tyrone cleared the way.

Some of the others I have had little contact with so far. There is David, who comes forward with a loping gait, hands in pockets, shoulders rounded. He has a scraggly beard and lank, longish, dark blond hair that has already earned him the name Shaggy, after a hippie character in a Saturday morning television cartoon. He wears a yin-yang earring and a silver peace sign on a leather thong around his neck.

June tries to hide her face when she is called. She is small and slight and seems always to be hiding behind a long puff of frizzy hair. I have spoken with her a couple of times and she speaks haltingly, with a heavy Chinese accent. She goes to stand almost directly behind Tony; only the side of her face is visible as she peers out.

Earl slinks forward with the smooth, undulating gait of a practiced ghetto street-corner denizen. He is tall and thin. The few times I have engaged him in conversation, he seemed quiet, almost gentle, his words bubbling up slowly in a deep voice. In group meetings he is passive, standing just outside the circle of action, saying little or nothing.

Alison walks confidently in her rugged country work boots. In style she is half punk, half pixie. Her hair, peroxide blond, sticks out spikily beneath the black wool fisherman's cap she wears each day, and her ears are rimmed with silver studs and hoops. Her manner is quiet and thoughtful, but she has an even smile that lights up her dimpled face. She surveys the team and looks a little pleased, a little shocked.

Amy frowns a little as she ventures forward. Her expression, as far as I can tell, is always one of intensity and introspection. Her long Asian hair is beautiful and shiny, straight, without adornment. As she stands looking out at those of us left on the wooden benches, it sweeps down like a curtain, shadowing her face.

Lisa struts to the front. She is pretty, with big eyes, light brown skin, and a sophisticated demeanor. I recall the day before when I sat with her at lunch and she haughtily cut short my efforts to make conversation, answering a harmless question with a single word, then shifting into Spanish with some others who were sitting at the table. She seemed to be dismissing me, perhaps in order to impress the others.

Brendan's face is stoic as he comes forward to take his place with the team. His dark hair contrasts sharply with the paleness of his skin. His T-shirt sleeves are rolled to reveal the youthful but well-developed musculature of adolescence. He appears wary. He looks around at his new teammates and shakes his head incredulously. I can just make out his words.

"We're the misfits," he says.

It's true, I think, looking at the team from my now lonely seat on an empty bench. All six teams, now chattering together, laughing and eyeing one another carefully, display the visible diversity that is City Year's trademark. It is difficult at first to say exactly why my team-to-be is different, but it is. Taken together, they are a little rougher, shaggier, and more streetwise than the others. Looking back, I can see why that might be. During the late-night selection process, when the trades were flying thick and fast and quick decisions were made as tired staff members longed for bed, Tony took one, and then another, and another of the corps members that others thought might be too hard for them to handle. Although several of the team coordinators had a good deal of relevant experience, and three were in their second year at City Year, Tony was seen as senior, the most experienced of the group. One by one, he took on the harder cases.

Despite our five years' acquaintance, Tony is still in many ways the most mysterious of all to me. One moment solemn and spiritual, the

next a teasing trickster, Tony delights in keeping everybody else a little bit off balance. He has a shock of long, thick black hair that, combined with his round, handsome face, makes him look much younger than his twenty-seven years; but years before, I saw him hollow-cheeked and bald, his head shaven in a gesture of self-purification. His expression is always lively, but also guarded. He stands like a soldier, leaning forward, feet apart, chin high, and muscles flexed. He writes like a monk, in a delicate, curly, floral hand.

I first met Tony when we were both team leaders at CVC; he welcomed me reassuringly into what was a hardy club of mavericks. One year at CVC had already made Tony one of the most experienced team leaders, and he had a reputation for competence and commitment. We did not become close, but we shared the bond of having been through something others cannot understand.

When Alan and Michael suggested I follow Tony's team, I was at first uncertain. Tony and I knew one another and we had friends in common. I was worried about the difficulties this might create as we tried to define a new relationship. But I also knew that Tony had the respect of everyone who had worked with him. He was totally committed to City Year and to national service, and he had a Zenlike intensity about him. He was intriguing.

As for Tony himself, he welcomed me onto his team, courageously accepting the scrutiny my presence would bring. "I trust you to be fair," he said. I was pleased by his trust, at the same time recognizing that he meant something else also: it was a challenge.

After all the corps members have been called, the newly formed teams go off in different directions to grill hamburgers together and have their first team meetings. I watch Tony and the others trail away into the woods; Tony has asked me to give him thirty minutes alone with the team before joining them. He wants to find out if anyone has serious objections to the presence of a writer on the team. My heart is racing a bit when, at the appointed time, I walk down the wooded path to a clearing where the team is having their barbecue.

Tony takes my arm and pulls me to the side, his face serious. "I'm sorry, Suzanne. I tried to convince them."

I feel the blood drain from my face.

He looks at me sympathetically for a moment, then breaks into a mischievous grin. "Only kidding. They're honored that you want to write a book about them."

I ask to tell the team in my own words just what the project will entail. They sit on the ground and look up at me with curiosity as I haltingly explain my reasons for wanting to write about them and their City Year experience. I try to be as honest as I can in telling them how intrusive my reporter's presence will at some times be and to emphasize that I do not believe in letting anything be "off the record." It is a difficult message to deliver. But their reaction seems mostly to be one of curiosity, as well as pleasure at the idea that their experience will be recorded. They agree: people need to read about this program.

Tony, too, has a speech to make. I take a seat with the others on the ground as he stands before us, his legs spread military-style and his hands clasped behind his back.

"I want to make one thing clear, right from the start," he says. "I'm not here to be your friend. You have each other for that. I'm here as the supervisor of this team."

The group, chattering a moment ago, is now at full attention. All eyes are fixed on Tony—except for Charles's. Charles stands behind us with a spatula, worrying a hamburger that is still sizzling on the grill.

"It's your performance, and your work, and your character here that counts," Tony continues, "not your relationship to me. There are rules here, and there are things I simply will not tolerate."

He lists them. Disrespect; laziness; violations of confidence; racist and sexist remarks. Tony paces back and forth before us, his voice gathering strength and conviction, his words picking up speed.

"What I do like is professionalism. When we walk around in the city and people see us, they're going to think, there is a group of people who are professionals and who are providing service. They're going to see it in our bodies and in the way we carry ourselves."

Jacquelyn and David are sitting up very straight. Tracy smiles and nods.

"While you're in City Year and on this team, I will do everything in my ability to support you. If you have any difficulty doing the work, any personal problems or struggles, or if you need help pursuing personal goals, I will be there to support and help you. I'll never tell you that I'm too tired or that it's too boring or that I'd rather be doing something else.

"At the same time, when it's time to do the job, my expectation is that you'll never say you're too tired, you're not interested, or you don't feel like it. We're going to be asked to do things we don't like. You don't have to say you like it. But I do expect that you will do it."

Charles slides the hamburger onto a paper plate and sits down with a flourish, smacking his lips loudly. Tony looks at Charles, eyebrows raised, and then goes on.

"The sacrifice you make coming into this group is giving up part of who you are. When you walk down the street, you're not going to see things the same way. Everything is going to look different. You're not going to be able to see an abandoned building and just walk by. You're not going to be able to see a homeless person and just step over him."

Earl is chewing on a tiny flap of skin peeling from his thumb. Amy's eyes are cast down, but she is listening intently.

"We're going to open up your heart. And it's going to make you vulnerable. You will come to a point where it hurts so much you will want to leave." As he speaks, Tony's eyes move down the line, searching out the eyes of everyone in turn to make his point.

"When I go to bed at night, I don't sleep very well. I read the newspapers and I watch the news and listen to the radio, and sometimes I get very scared for the world that things are not going to work out. But there is hope. I happen to believe that of all the things that are happening in this country, this is the one place that offers genuine hope." He pauses.

"Even after you graduate from City Year and from this team, I will be someone you can count on for the rest of your life, whether that means help with a résumé, a job recommendation or whatever. Sometimes the world is like a combat situation and you need a friend and ally. When the chips are down and you really need someone, I will be there for you.

"But while you are here, I want you to remember this. I'll be the first to support anybody when they need it, but I will also be the first to hold the door open and say goodbye to any one of you who is destroying what is good for the rest of the team. It's painful, but I'm willing to do it. I don't want anything to ruin the beautiful thing that we're creating as a team."

Two

It is the fourth day of orientation, our first day together as a team. We spend the afternoon in a series of exercises aimed at building unity and cooperative spirit. One activity in particular, "the spider's web," captures everyone's imagination. But we do not master it easily.

The spider's web is a sturdy wooden frame, a little more than six feet tall and just about as wide, with thick ropes crisscrossed and knotted together to form an irregular vertical net. It stands in the middle of a field. We stare dumbly at the taut rope web—Tony, Alan Khazei, an instructor, the twelve team members, and me. The late afternoon sky hangs gray and heavy overhead.

The instructor, a solid, earnest outdoors type in jeans and a faded flannel shirt, is solemn in his description of the task. We must get everyone from one side to the other of this rope barrier. We will have to pass through the holes without touching the ropes or the wood frame, using each hole once and only once. Some of the holes are four- or five-sided and large enough to go through with ease. But some are small, and many are high up, four or five feet off the ground. A couple of people slide their eyes uneasily toward Tracy, who is very heavy. We begin to argue.

"I don't want anyone to pick me up," says tiny June, sidling up next to me. "I hate that."

"I know how to do it," says Brendan eagerly, perhaps a little too eagerly. Brendan is only seventeen, the youngest on the team. Everyone else is talking at once, paying no attention to him, and his eagerness fades as quickly as it came. His face takes on a stony look.

Charles doesn't want to discuss procedure. Eyes glistening, he makes a break for the net, plunging his arms through one of the lower holes and grazing a rope as he goes. The instructor sends him back.

Tyrone too has a plan, but nobody will listen to him, either. His dark face bunches angrily and he walks away to stand alone, contemplating the horizon.

By now, everyone is arguing. People are beginning to raise their voices. "Shut up," someone says. "I can't believe this," says someone else. What looked fun at the outset is turning into a battle.

"Please, Tony. You're the leader. Show us how to do it," says Jacquelyn. She smiles at Tony with a look that is both coy and desperate. Tony shakes his head.

"The point is for you to figure out your own way," he says.

"Let's just do it," says Richie in exasperation. "Figure it out as we go."

Brendan puts his head and arms through a hole near the bottom and walks through on his hands as we lift his legs, wheelbarrow-style. Then the boys line up in front of Jacquelyn, who points her arms elegantly over her head like a diver and leans into their arms with her face down, her body rigid. They slide her thin body slowly through one of the smallest holes, just below waist high, and when she is halfway through, Brendan helps her to put her hands on the ground and crawl the rest of the way.

We argue over each new step. Tony goes through, then June (with much reluctance), then Tracy, who squeezes her eyes tight shut and whoops with excitement once she is safely through.

Then Richie turns to me. "Okay, now Suzanne. You ain't gettin' outta this." He cocks a scarred eyebrow.

I step forward and as I do my body tenses with shyness. Richie, Tyrone, Earl, Amy, Lisa, and Charles are standing in two rows facing each other with their arms outstretched. I turn my back to them and close my eyes. Then I lean back.

My body feels heavy and awkward and I struggle involuntarily as they lift me to a horizontal position. I seem to be coming up one limb at a time. My hair gets caught between someone's arm and my shoulder and my head is yanked back. My body rolls to one side, then the other. I think I'm going to fall.

Then suddenly I am up, straight, flat, weightless, and the team is passing me swiftly through the web. Someone on the other side cradles my head, then supports my shoulders, my back and finally my legs. I point my toes as my feet pass through, then bend at the waist and drop my legs to the ground. I am through.

Ten minutes later, after a total of forty minutes of wrangling, everyone has passed through the web. It seems as if the task has taken us forever. Following the instructor's directions, we sit down in a circle on the ground, looking at each other uneasily. There is no joy here. We have all heard the reports from other teams who went before us: "We finished the spider's web in twelve minutes!" "Oh yeah, it went smooth as silk!" Judged against the others, we have failed. And in the process, some harsh words have been passed.

Tyrone remains outside the circle. He gets down on his stomach and begins pumping out pushups, breathing hard through his nose, his thin muscular body drawn taut. Charles tears up handfuls of grass and casts them aside with disdain.

"So what do you think?" asks Tony.

"This isn't a team," says Richie scornfully. "It's just a group of people."

Lisa glares at him. "You got a attitude," she says.

"Everyone wanted to take control," says Amy, pushing back her long hair. "No one wanted to follow."

Alison disagrees. "No one wanted to take charge," she says. "If someone had been leading, we could have done it much quicker."

David looks troubled. He takes off his glasses and wipes them on his shirt. "We can't respect each other until we know each other. And we won't know each other until we do things together. I can't really get into this teamwork stuff yet."

"I don't think we all trust each other," says Richie. "You can't respect someone you don't trust."

Alan looks around the circle thoughtfully. "We accomplished the task," he says, "but nobody really feels good about it. There's a lesson to be learned there. It's not just getting it done, it's how you do it."

"I don't know about this trust thing," says Charles. "I trust him," he points at Tyrone, "and him," pointing at Earl, "and him." He points at Richie. "I been sleeping in a room with them. As for the rest of you, I think this trust thing is a lot of bull."

"I trust all of you here," says Jacquelyn.

There is a pause. Then David straightens and peers at the rest of us from behind his round glasses. "We run out too fast," he says, "and so there's friction and trouble. I think City Year's going to be hard, but I don't think we have any idea yet how much patience it's going to take."

"We're all still strangers here," says Tony. "Don't take the wrong idea from this. Don't think that we lost. We're just reorienting."

He looks around the circle significantly, as if he wants to will confidence into the team. We get up and head back toward camp, walking as a group but saying little. When we reach the edge of the field, Brendan hangs back. He picks up a stone and throws it into the woods, watching it arc through the trees and land with a rustle. A few moments later I look back and he is still standing there alone, casting stones, watching them fall.

City Year:
The Idea and the Program

City Year began as an idea shared by Alan Khazei and Michael Brown, friends at Harvard College and Harvard Law School. Between college and law school, Alan worked as field director for presidential candidate Gary Hart in his home state of New Hampshire; Hart had made national service part of his campaign platform. Michael worked to help launch the City Volunteer Corps in New York in 1984. He also worked on Capitol Hill as an aide to Congressman Leon Panetta of California, who sponsored an early, and unsuccessful, national service bill. Both young men had a longstanding desire to help promote social justice and were uninterested in joining corporate law firms when they finished school as so many of their classmates were planning to do. After law school they wanted to do something that would make a difference. They began talking about how they could help make national service a reality.

I met the two at a conference in the fall of 1985. They were in law school at the time, but had come to Washington for the day to network with practitioners and policymakers who had gathered to talk about national service. Two years before graduation, Alan and Michael were already hatching their idea of starting their own privately funded youth corps in Boston. Talking with them over lunch, I got a glimpse of the fiery idealism they would later bring to the difficult job of recruiting funders, advisers, and a core group of dedicated volunteers to join them as they built City Year from an idea to a reality. They were both clean-cut—Alan with a chiseled face and curving nose, and Michael a little more round-faced, with scholarly wire-rim glasses—and extremely well-spoken. Their excitement and commitment communicated itself in their words as well as in their body language. They leaned eagerly across the table as they spoke, and they seemed in perfect synchronization, even on occasion completing each other's sentences. They seemed almost to think in unison. The clarity and the passion they projected, as well as the synergistic quality of their friendship and their words, gave the two a powerful charismatic appeal.

National service, they said, was not just a feel-good scheme for encouraging volunteerism. Instead, it was a critical vehicle by which to engineer a revival of civic virtue in America. Alan later showed me a research paper he'd written in which he argued that a system of national service could help us "reach the full promise of American democracy." The Constitution, he wrote, set up a republican state that was fundamentally flawed. It rested on a compromise between the republican ideal of a state ruled by people who are willing to put aside self-interest in favor of the common good, and a pluralist state in which the common good emerges from the natural balancing of individual interests. Dependence on the second ideal had resulted in a failure to invest in ways of promoting the first. National service could help establish a truly republican state by infusing young citizens with a sense of the common good and teaching them the skills and habits of civic engagement.

The idea of national service grew out of a long tradition of service in America. Sharing and mutual aid were important components of life among Native Americans and colonial settlers; the Colonies were protected by a citizen militia, which played an important role in the Revolutionary War and remained in existence throughout much of the nineteenth century. The cherished "rugged individualism" that characterized notions of what is American was countered by traditions that emphasized reciprocity and interdependence, such as barn raisings, quilting bees, and volunteer fire brigades, as well as service in democratic governing bodies. Full-time community service, long a religious tradition, was secularized with the development of such institutions as urban settlements at the turn of the century.

The first government-sponsored, full-time national service program in the United States—apart from the military—was President Franklin Roosevelt's Depression-era Civilian Conservation Corps, which over nine years enrolled more than three million young men to clear mountain trails for national parks, build roads and bridges, plant trees, and take on other tough conservation tasks. The participants lived under strict rules in spartan backcountry encampments and were paid $30 a month, two-thirds of which was sent directly home to their families. Reflecting the social culture of the time, the CCC enrolled black and white men (no women) but deployed them in segregated camps. It targeted the disadvantaged and those who could not find jobs—a relatively broad group in the 1930s. The program was dismantled in 1942 in order to free up resources for the war effort.

President Kennedy gave new life to the national service idea in his 1961 inaugural address, when he called young people to action—"And so, my fellow Americans, ask not what your country can do for you: ask what you can do for your country"—and announced the creation of the Peace Corps, which to date has enrolled 140,000 Americans for humanitarian service overseas. VISTA (Volunteers In Service To America) and other plans for domestic service followed, but many of these programs lost momentum in the face of the Vietnam War. VISTA became politically controversial and was ultimately reduced to a tiny program during the Reagan years.

The early 1970s saw the creation of the federally funded Youth Conservation Corps (YCC) and Young Adult Conservation Corps (YACC), programs designed to provide summer and year-round jobs for tens of thousands of unemployed youth. These programs, which were administered by the Interior and Agriculture departments, were both eliminated in the early 1980s.

The creation of the California Conservation Corps in 1976 (in which more than 40,000 young people have already served for a year or two of backcountry conservation work) began a new era of experimentation with national service at the local level. Youth corps began springing up all over. In general, they targeted out-of-school youth who were looking for ways to gain skills and improve their educational opportunities through public service. The earliest corps focused on physical labor, in parks and wilderness as well as in urban contexts. A federally funded experiment mounted in Seattle between 1973 and 1977, the Program for Local Service, put young people to work in social service jobs, and in 1984 the City Volunteer Corps in New York piloted a youth corps model that mixed physical labor and human services work. The CVC was soon emulated in other cities.

These programs were usually funded by states and localities, with help from foundations and corporations, as well as in-kind support from not-for-profit agencies. Some received fees for the work they completed, typically mixing public service with remunerative contract labor. They also made use of federal job training and education funds.

Many of these seminal programs presented themselves as models for national service, in hope that the federal government would eventually create a national network of service programs and pick up some of the cost. Political support for the idea, however, though broad, was not deep. Though it had an undeniable superficial appeal—who was against community service?—among both policymakers and practitioners there was a lack of consensus about what form a national service program should take, and, more important, what its goals should be. Was it job training? Civic education? Cheap labor? Volunteerism? Rehabilitation? Who should be asked to serve? And what benefits should be offered? In the 1980s, ten different national service bills were introduced in Congress, and the idea of a federally funded and coordinated national service system gained some momentum among pundits and politicians; but the legislative initiatives failed to pass.

Meanwhile, experimentation continued at the local level. By the end of the 1980s, there existed nearly seventy youth service corps in states and communities around the country. Other kinds of service programs were flourishing as well: college students were getting involved in community service in record numbers; elementary and secondary schools (public and private) were experimenting with ways to integrate service and learning; senior citizens' organizations were starting intergenerational volunteer programs; college graduates were creating opportunities for post-college service, such as Teach For America; and youth-serving organizations in inner cities were beginning to involve disadvantaged young people in service as well as recreation and education.

Alan Khazei and Michael Brown both advocated federal funding for national service, but they too were eager to get started, with or without federal legislation. In any event, they were convinced that the best way to promote their vision was to seek private funding that would enable them to build their own program. Without the restrictions of government money and government rules, they could experiment more freely and build a model for others to follow.

And so, in 1987, working out of a borrowed ten-by-fifteen-foot office in Harvard Square, and joined by two other committed friends they had recruited (the number would soon swell to twelve, most of them working for no money at all), they began knocking on the doors of Boston-area corporations, charitable foundations, and other institutions. Their senior advisory board included Senator Paul Tsongas, who was a former Peace Corps volunteer; Matina Horner, president of Radcliffe College; Winthrop Knowlton, a retired book publisher and assistant secretary of the treasury under Lyndon Johnson; as well as the director of the mayor's youth services program in Boston, the head of a citywide school volunteer program, and the principal of a respected local public high school.

They were surprisingly successful for such a young and inexperienced group. Even as they were scrambling for money to subsidize the program, they were confidently recruiting for a nine-week-long summer pilot program to "test-drive" their ideas. By June of 1988 they had recruited fifty corps members (selected from 150 applicants) and raised about $250,000 to pay for the summer program. The money came from local corporations—the Bank of Boston, Bain and Company, General Cinema Corporation, New England Telephone, Equitable Financial Services—and from private contributions and foundation grants. A volunteer fundraising group sponsored a benefit dance for City Year in a downtown hotel.

The idea of a summer pilot program was an inspired one. It was in keeping with the plan Alan and Michael had made to start small for maximum flexibility, so that they could experiment and learn as they grew. It also allowed them to succeed in an area where earlier youth corps, like CVC (in New York City), had failed. Because they were not asking the volunteers to take a year off from school but rather to take part in an adventure for just one summer—a summer in which they would receive $60 a week and walk away at the end with a $1,000 scholarship—it was easier to recruit young people from affluent and middle-class families, as well as those from poorer backgrounds. Later, City Year would ask participants for a nine-month commitment; but in that first, critical summer, when they introduced their first City Year corps, they established a distinct public image as a diverse program. Most of the participants were high school students, but there were also eight college students and a number of high school dropouts. Any group photo—and many photos appeared in local newspapers that summer—brought home the fact that this was a racially diverse effort. City Year, clearly, was not a jobs program for minority youth. Nor was it like the Peace Corps, open only to college graduates. It was a *citizenship* program, and it was for everybody.

The summer pilot program had many of the same basic elements that characterized the City Volunteer Corps (which in turn had adapted program elements introduced in other youth service and conservation corps), elements that would later define the structure of the year-round City Year program: an overnight orientation retreat, daily group calisthenics, one day a week set aside for education and enrichment, and full-time service performed in supervised teams working in cooperation with existing nonprofit agencies.

At the end of the summer the program was roundly applauded as a success in local media reports, and City Year had planted seeds of goodwill in the nonprofit and corporate communities around Boston. The summer graduates, who talked to anyone who would listen about their exciting summer of service, proved an effective informal recruiting force.

But when the summer pilot program was over, City Year did not immediately scale up and begin a year-round operation. Instead, Alan and Michael and their core staff retreated to spend a full year mulling over the results, carefully planning their expansion, recruiting, and working to attract more money.

Eventually, all of the original corporate funders came through with new grants. All in all, they raised $1.2 million, and in the fall of 1989, City Year fielded a corps of fifty young people, enrolled for nine months of full-time service. The racial and economic diversity of the summer corps was replicated in this first small year-round group. I attended the graduation ceremony of that first City Year corps in June of 1990, and was thoroughly taken with the enthusiasm of the graduates and the compelling stories they told. I wasn't the only one. That day, Ed Cohen, of General Atlantic Partners, a New York–based venture capital firm, stood up and announced that his company would give City Year half a million dollars, spread out over three years. City Year was on its way.

Four

Two days after returning to Boston, at the end of our five-day orientation in the Berkshires, we gather at the City Year headquarters to begin work. By now City Year is operating out of the 8,000-square-foot second floor of a converted warehouse in South Boston. The building is old and a little cranky, but the space is airy and pleasant, well lit by a wall of windows facing east. The ceiling is high, the aged wooden floors are newly varnished, and the posts and beams are freshly painted.

The City Year logo, a shining sun in red, yellow, and black, bears a stylistic resemblance to Native American art—a visual reference to the City Year motto, which is from a Native American prayer: "Oh Great Spirit, grant that I may not criticize my brother or my sister, until I have walked a mile in his or her moccasins." Red, yellow, and black predominate in the furnishings and decorations of the City Year headquarters.

Despite its size, the headquarters offers a homey feeling. There is no receptionist; the staff members who do not wear uniforms are casually dressed; phones ring constantly (and sometimes endlessly); a pleasing sense of chaos pervades the office. There are few amenities—a couple of tattered couches, some homemade tables, a hundred folding chairs—but there is plenty of room, enough for the entire corps to gather there with ease. Alan and Michael each have a large office in front, where there is also a reception area and a single enclosed conference room that doubles as a classroom. The other staff members who work in the headquarters sit in makeshift cubicles located at the edges of the open room. The remaining vast expanse is for the corps.

On that first morning, we fill the space by setting up the folding chairs in a huge circle. This is the configuration we used for corps-wide discussions at Camp Becket. The arrangement allows for no hierarchy, nor for any giggling in the back. In a circle, everyone can see everyone else. In future, we will have a "community meeting" like this, we are told, every Friday morning.

The service work in City Year goes on from Monday through Thursday. Friday is called "enrichment day," and on Fridays the entire corps will gather in the headquarters to focus on the educational aspects of community service. Some weeks, teams will report to the corps on their projects. Other weeks there will be field trips and guest lecturers. Later, there will be activities intended to help corps members plan for the future.

On that Tuesday, the first order of business is the distribution of uniforms. Bright red jackets. Rain slickers. Khaki pants. One pair of sneakers and one pair of heavy-duty work boots. A red cap and a black knapsack with CITY YEAR printed on it in white. A black sweatshirt, also emblazoned with CITY YEAR.

The uniform distribution is a ritual, conducted with a sense of ceremony. Jon, City Year's field coordinator, the person to whom all the teams report, leads the ceremony. He is tall, thin and bearded, with piercing blue eyes, and he addresses the corps with an intensity that gives his words a sense of urgency. "The uniform," Jon explains, "gives you an extra piece of currency. It gives you credibility. The uniform helps us establish our group identity. It helps us build a community. It says that we're an exclusive group. It also symbolizes sacrifice. You are sacrificing part of your identity as an individual in order to be a part of the group."

Tony steps up next to Jon. "I've spent most of my life in one uniform or another," he says, "from Catholic School to martial arts to my first job, which was as a team leader in the City Volunteer Corps. My first martial arts teacher told me that when he was in the army and had to fit all his clothes and belongings in a small foot locker, it allowed him to free his mind. The uniform that we have to wear is a way to free our minds from all of those little details that we use to identify ourselves. The uniform makes us all equal on the outside. It will allow us to discipline our minds, to regiment ourselves, so that we can be ready for the work that we have to do."

At CVC, I remember, corps and staff members alike often directed tremendous resentment at the all-polyester, military-style uniforms. But the City Year uniforms are different. Many of the parts have been donated to City Year by name-brand manufacturers like Timberland, Gap, Reebok, and Patagonia. They are attractive, brightly colored, casual, and easy to wear. Besides, this morning the corps is filled with goodwill, the residue of five fun and challenging days at Camp Becket. Everyone is happy to be part of City Year. The corps members' names are called, one by one, and as each person receives the bag that contains his or her uniform, the entire corps applauds enthusiastically.

Part of each City Year uniform package is three T-shirts marked with the City Year logo in front and the name of a particular sponsor in back. The corporate sponsors are companies or organizations that have donated money to City Year—$50,000 to attach their name to a team for a semester, or $100,000 for the full nine months.

"City Year is entirely privately funded," Alan explains, standing in the middle of the huge circle of chairs and slowly rotating as he speaks. "We don't get any government money, although perhaps at some time in the future we will. Right now we are trying to send a message that it's important for private corporations and charitable foundations to get involved and make a difference. We call it corporate citizenship."

My team is pleased to learn that we will be the Reebok Team. A high-priced athletic sneaker manufacturer with corporate headquarters just outside Boston, Reebok has its own foundation and a reputation for giving money in support of human rights. The sneakers are wildly popular. The trademark has cachet among young people.

Tony talks to the team about our corporate sponsor. "Paul Fireman, Reebok's C.E.O., is one of the highest-paid corporate executives in America. He has a foundation that gives away twenty million dollars a year. Because of that, there's going to be a lot of attention on you. Video, TV, photographs, it's going to be an intense year. Millions of dollars could come to City Year if we do our job well.

"Everybody wanted to be the Reebok Team—but I pushed hard to get it for us. I thought that City Year would best succeed if this team were the Reebok Team. I think our group, under my leadership, can make it work."

"What do we get?" asks Charles. "Do we get extra sneakers?"

"All we get is the responsibility. We're going to have to be great."

We gather the next morning, as we will every Monday through Thursday for the rest of the year, at 8:20 A.M. on the brick plaza in front of the Federal Reserve Bank in downtown Boston. The Fed has several advantages as a morning meeting location. First, it is situated right next to South Station, a large and easy-to-reach subway station.

Second, it is just five minutes' walk from City Year headquarters. Third, it is a highly visible location, important for recruitment, fundraising, and for the corps' morale. In this spot City Year is squarely in the public eye. Commuters rushing from the train to downtown offices cannot fail to notice the small army of red-jacketed youths—especially if we have begun P.T.

We had our first taste of P.T., or physical training, at camp, at seven each morning. Now it will be part of the daily routine. At eight-thirty on this, our first morning of service, we line up by teams, facing the financial district with the early sun slanting in from behind us and glancing off the glass and steel buildings across the way. Tony and the other team coordinators stand in front of the lines, along with Jon, and they take turns leading us through a series of stretches and then increasingly strenuous exercises. The emphasis is more on vigor than on athleticism or conformity, and the cycle ends with a rousing set of jumping jacks, which we count aloud at the top of our lungs.

Our enthusiasm is high and several people stop to watch as we hustle proudly through the routine. From my position at the rear of the Reebok line, I can see that we make an impressive sight. With the staff, we are more than eighty strong, and our voices fill the plaza.

The idea behind P.T. is not only to encourage physical fitness but to give us all a launch for the day, a sense of cohesiveness and an upbeat beginning. Bringing the entire corps together in the morning before the teams fan out across the city is also intended to enhance corps members' sense of membership in the larger City Year community. There is a practical point, as well: latecomers are allowed a brief grace period, but a few minutes into P.T., Jon announces the time, and anyone who arrives after his announcement will be marked late. This will be the drill each morning all year, except when it rains, we are told, and no exceptions will be made. There will be no gray area regarding lateness.

That clarity is a hallmark of the City Year approach to discipline. The rules, as well as the disciplinary code, are laid out in a document called the City Year Contract. The contract focuses on ten areas of performance, and outlines the consequences of any possible infraction. The first incidence of lateness, for example, results in a verbal warning, as does the second. The third brings a written warning, the fourth a one-day suspension without pay, the fifth a two-day suspen-

sion, the sixth a three-day suspension, and the seventh results in dismissal. One can reverse one's advance toward dismissal by means of a "buy back": each week without a lateness removes the mark of one previous lateness. The same process is employed for incidents of "nonparticipation, disruptive behavior, or poor performance." A variety of shorter disciplinary timetables are used for more serious infractions, from threatening another corps member to using or dealing drugs.

Absence is treated a little differently; corps members are permitted ten absences during the year (no more than two per month); any time missed beyond that has to be made up with extra work in the evenings or on weekends; otherwise dismissal will follow.

Enforcement of the contract is to take place during weekly "contract meetings," where each team member is advised—in the presence of the rest of the team—of any contract infractions and penalties in the prior week.

The contract was described to us in an informational session at Camp Becket shortly after the teams were announced. We split into teams to discuss the rules.

"City Year is like a house, and all of the teams live in the house," Tony said. "While you're at City Year you're not allowed to break out of the house. Today, with the contract, we're building the floor and the walls of that house. "Does anybody have any questions?"

Charles's hand shot up.

"What if somebody brings a gun to work and it falls out of his pocket?" he asked. "Will you report it to the police?"

"I don't know about reporting it to the police," said Tony. "But he would be dismissed from City Year. Check the contract."

"What if you have a pack of cigarettes and it has one joint in it?" asked Earl.

"Let's not set ourselves up for negativity all year on this thing," said Brendan. "If you guys are really worried about this, maybe this isn't the place for you to be."

"What if you have to defend yourself because of where you live at?" asked Tyrone.

"Obviously, it's not possible to make a contract that accounts for every particular possible specific situation," said Alison, exasperated. "Let's let it go."

The City Year Contract does address most situations that might arise and includes provisions for leaving the work site without notice; using a Walkman in certain prohibited times and places; verbal or emotional abuse or harassment; vandalism; theft; possession of illegal weapons; and coming to work drunk or high or in possession of alcohol or drugs. Each rule violation has a specific and predictable outcome. Corps members can know at all times where they stand on the contract, and what they have to do to clear their record. The message is: staying in City Year is within each individual's control. Just read the contract.

After P.T. on Wednesday we go to Dudley Triangle in Roxbury, where we paint the exterior of a vacant storefront that another team will soon use to establish an after-school program. We also clear a nearby vacant lot with rakes and weed-whackers and set up folding chairs for the opening-day ceremony later that afternoon. Executives from many of City Year's corporate sponsors attend the event, as do a number of parents, Boston's police commissioner, and a few politicians.

"You are going to be a model for what I believe will be happening soon in most major cities across the country," says Bill Bain, president of Bain and Company.

The teams stand together during the ceremony. We have made enormous placards with the Reebok logo and we wave them around proudly during the speeches. Afterward, Tony introduces us to Jean Mahoney, the executive director of the Reebok Foundation.

"I'll be part of the team," she says. "Not just a funder, but another team member." She gives her business card to Tyrone, who is standing nearest to her. "I want you to keep this for the team, and every month I want you to have someone call me. Let me know what you're working on, what you're doing. Don't just share with me the happy times, share with me the tough times. Keep me informed."

"Damn," says Tyrone, a little later. "A hundred thousand dollars." The size of the corporate donations is mind-boggling to all of us, and the support boosts many corps members' sense that City Year is somehow special and its membership elite.

We have been told little about our first service project except that it will begin tomorrow, and that it will involve hard physical labor. As we separate that afternoon, I think of Tony's last words to us on Saturday, as the orientation was ending. "When you come in next week," he said with a solemn stare, "be prepared to die. Because you are going to die as a person and be reborn."

His words were dramatic, almost corny, but not one of us cracked a smile.

The Garden

After P.T. the next morning, the corps clusters briefly outside the Fed for a few announcements before we break into teams for our first full day of service. Tony chooses a space for us to meet on the plaza and we gather around in a circle as he hands out a one-page "Corpsmember Briefing Document." The photocopied document offers directions to the Virginia-Monadnock Garden as well as a description of the project. Our project sponsor, it says, will be the Virginia-Monadnock Neighborhood Association. Their role, like that of all of the nonprofit organizations that sponsor City Year projects, is to set up the work tasks and to provide tools, general supervision, and technical assistance.

"The Virginia-Monadnock Neighborhood Association was formed 11 years ago to fight crime and bring the neighborhood together to work on a variety of problems facing the community," the briefing document reads. "VMNA helped found the Dorchester Bay Economic Development Corporation, Neighborhood Housing Services, and sponsors the conversion of vacant lots."

The goal of our project is "to participate in Phase I of the reconstruction of the Virginia-Monadnock Garden in order to create a safe open space that does not encourage criminal activity and gives more local residents an opportunity to garden. City Year will also hopefully participate in springtime Phase II construction."

The task for our team will be to demolish the existing garden beds in the front of the garden, to move plants to provide a clear path for contractors to bring in heavy equipment, and to build a sample planting bed.

Tony gives us a moment to look over the briefing document. Several people—David, Jacquelyn, Amy, Alison—study it carefully, with full attention. Others quickly crumple or fold the paper and stuff it in their pockets without a glance.

"Now I'm going to introduce you to a tradition that I do with all my teams," says Tony. "Before we go out into the field to start our service work each day, I like to observe a moment of silence. You can pray, or meditate, or plan the day, or think about your girlfriend. Think about whatever you like, but please respect the silence. It's a chance to focus. Let's huddle up."

He bows his head and stares at the pavement. I follow suit, then look up to see Earl and Charles smirking. But Jacquelyn is standing very still with her eyes shut and others are beginning to follow. This little ritual is strange to us, but not altogether surprising. Tony cultivates a certain mystique, and the public act of group meditation might pass a little of that mystique on to the entire team. Everyone is silent.

The huddle lasts about fifteen seconds, then Tony looks up. "Let's go." We head across the plaza and down into the subway.

In sunny weather, Monadnock Street is pretty enough. It is located in Dorchester, a southern neighborhood of Boston far from the downtown area. The wooden triple-deckers that line most of the street are in relatively good repair. Their sturdy stone foundations follow the steep slope of the hill from which the street is carved. Front-yard chain-link fences are punctuated by occasional rosebushes and on this early September morning the slanting sun dapples the houses with leafy shadows from the trees across the street.

Across from the modest three-story homes, on the north side of the street, stand a number of beautiful Victorian mansions. Some of these old houses sag and tilt and have been stripped of their fanciful trim, but others have been restored to varying degrees of their original elegance. One house stands out from the rest, painted in tones of yellow, rose, and blue, with an elaborate series of repeated lines and angles, unexpected corners and appendages. The first-floor windows are trimmed with panes of leaded stained glass, and two rooftop widow's walks are framed with graceful wrought-iron curls and spires. This is the home of Bob Haas, founder of the Virginia-Monadnock Neighborhood Association.

The house at 29 Monadnock, next to Bob's, is quite a contrast. Its windows are sealed with sheets of plywood. In places, the cheap aluminum siding has fallen off, giving the house a wounded appearance. The front porch is partially collapsed, and a tangle of wires spills from an upstairs window. There is no house at all on the next lot over;

instead, there is a series of garden beds overgrown with weeds, some benches, and a scattering of play equipment. A sign in one corner reads: VIRGINIA-MONADNOCK PLAYGROUND AND GARDEN. Graffiti hieroglyphics dance across the sign's block letters. Three telephone wires stretch over the park, high above the benches and the arbors in the rear. A pair of black high-top sneakers, tied together by their laces, dangle from the wires, sending a message to all those looking to cop a quick deal: drugs sold here.

We have to take a train and a bus to get to the project, which causes some grumbling because the combined fare costs fifty cents more each way than a simple subway trip. When we arrive at the garden, we are met by two volunteers from the neighborhood association, who bring a wheelbarrow full of tools and guide us around the garden, pointing out what needs to be done.

"You will be part of the process of neighborhood revitalization," says one of the volunteers, named Betty. "We really appreciate the fact that you've come down here to help us."

"You bringin' us lunch?" asks Charles.

Bob Haas gives us a more complete orientation. We stamp the dirt from the garden tour out of the treads of our workboots as we cross his wooden porch and file into the house. We pass through a large hallway and into the dining room, where we seat ourselves around his big mahogany table. Light filters through a stained-glass window and spills a colorful collage across the table. We look around politely. Tony instructs the team to get out their journals—issued by City Year and considered "part of the uniform"—to take notes. Richie and Tyrone have not brought theirs; Tony frowns, and hands them each a piece of paper.

Haas is an exceptionally tall man, with longish, unkempt hair and thick glasses. He looks around awkwardly, as if he is not accustomed to speaking before a group. As he begins to speak, he takes on a curious, unsettling intensity, staring sadly out the window one moment, glancing into our faces intently the next.

"It still feels like yesterday when I came here," he begins. He tells us how he moved to Boston to work at one of the high-tech companies then springing up along the Boston beltway, Route 128, in the mid-sixties, and how around 1970, as recession loomed, he was laid off from his job. No longer able to afford a high downtown rent, he banded together with some friends to buy the house on Monadnock

Street, then an abandoned shell. It cost them $6,500. All the windows were broken and the wiring and plumbing didn't work. There was no heat and there were holes in the walls and bottles, garbage, and marijuana butts throughout. Initially they covered all the windows with plywood to protect their home from intruding youths and for months they lived like cave dwellers in the dank and dark.

But Haas was excited by his new neighborhood. It was a racially mixed area: about 40 percent white, 25 percent black, 20 percent Puerto Rican, and 15 percent Portuguese-speaking immigrants from the Cape Verde Islands. "We felt we were on the front lines," he says.

Haas describes to us the process of renovation, which took nearly a decade. During the first few years, the house was broken into every four months. Over time, many neighbors found the growing number of robberies frightening, and residents with small children began fleeing the neighborhood, leaving houses to stand empty or to be divided up and converted to substandard rental properties.

Haas's companions lost their faith in the neighborhood and by 1977 sold him their shares in the house, leaving him alone.

In 1978 he decided to try to do something to reverse the trend. He held a block party, and convinced neighbors to come to meetings at his house. Haas felt that a few local individuals were responsible for the plague of break-ins and suggested that people begin keeping an eye on one another's homes. One day, a neighbor observed two men entering Haas's house through a side window and telephoned the police. The thieves were arrested and convicted. They got only a light sentence, but Haas and his neighbors were invigorated by the victory.

What eventually ensued was a kind of strategic territorial war between residents and criminals that lasted several years. Slowly, the neighborhood began to stabilize. People stopped moving out, and the robberies grew less and less frequent.

The fledgling neighborhood association decided that to build on their newfound sense of community, they needed a common gathering place—a park. For a site, they chose a vacant lot halfway down the street, still filled with the charred rubble left from an abandoned house that had been burned down by squatters. They raised some small grants for materials from Boston-area foundations, and in the summer of 1984 a handful of volunteers built the park themselves. They leveled the ground, fenced in the area, planted trees and bushes, built beds for community gardening, laid in an irrigation system, built arbors, and installed benches and playground equipment. For five dollars a season, residents rented garden beds and planted vegetables and flowers. The park was a frenzy of color and a model for urban gardeners elsewhere in the city.

It wasn't more than a few summers, however, before things in the garden began to go awry. The funding to pay interns who supervised summer activities in the little park ran out, and the interns left. With the park untended, vandalism and deterioration quickly became a problem. Gardeners found their vegetables were harvested by others. The irrigation system broke down and was not repaired. The play equipment was covered with graffiti.

For several years, the neighborhood had been relatively quiet. But a new wave of problems was starting to settle on Monadnock Street.

The children who had been very small when Haas moved to the neighborhood were now teenagers, and some had begun loitering at one end of the street—selling drugs, Haas thought. Often at night illicit parties were held in the park.

One day, Haas had an angry exchange with a boy who made a habit of cutting through his backyard. Haas was repairing a gap in his fence and the boy was irritated at being shut out. Haas was surprised at the boy's aggressive insistence that he leave his yard accessible, but he went on with his work and the boy left, trailing a string of curses.

That night, Haas was awakened by a firefighter who led him coughing from his bedroom to where the neighbors were huddled in the street, watching flames shoot from his roof. The entire community watched in disbelief as nearly two decades of careful restoration work went up in smoke. What wasn't destroyed by fire was buried under six inches of water from the firemen's hoses.

When the ashes had cooled, investigators determined that the fire had been intentionally set, originating in a puddle of gasoline poured on the back steps.

Haas was devastated. He contemplated selling the house's remains and moving away. But where would he go? This was his home.

His neighbors on the street wanted him to stay as well. They offered him their couches and guest beds, and they organized a concert in the park that raised $2,300 toward repairing his house. He began the long work of bringing the house back.

Haas strongly suspected that the boy he argued with in his yard had set the fire, but nobody was ever caught and charged with the crime.

The following spring, a boy from across the street was killed in a gun battle at the bottom of Monadnock Street. Hundreds of youths crowded the street outside the nearby funeral home during the memorial service, and a shouting match nearly erupted into a brawl. From then on it was clear that Monadnock Street was marked on the unwritten map of gang territory. Haas weeps as he relates this part of the story.

"We are in a decline now," he tells us. "In 1984, I was willing to go out there and bust my tail, and my neighbors were, too. But I think that's something you can only do once in a lifetime. The presence of City Year is an answer to a prayer. We can't do it alone anymore."

When Haas is finished, nobody speaks for a moment. I see looks of sympathy mingled with incredulity. Who would have guessed the extent of the drama in which we are about to play a role?

We get to work around eleven, and by that time the early morning chill has given way to the cheerful heat of late summer. There are no drug dealers in sight, although we take note of a small cluster of men idling at the end of the street. Occasionally sports cars drive slowly past the garden spilling bass-heavy music from open windows.

Tony splits us up into small groups and assigns us to various tasks. There is plenty to do.

Lisa, Charles, and Brendan begin the difficult job of digging up the two benches near the front of the garden to make room for the playground equipment, which will be moved forward from the back of the lot. They work with shovels, a mattock, and a Pulaski. We were introduced to the tools at camp: a mattock is a two-sided pickax with one side sharp and the other flattened into a wide bill that can be used for loosening or prying up the earth, and a Pulaski has a chopping blade on one side and a pick on the other. We like knowing the names of these good, solid tools.

In the back of the lot, Brendan and Richie use crowbars and a small hammer to dismantle the standing wooden arbors.

I work with Amy, Alison, Jacquelyn, and June, pulling up weeds. The garden beds that are to remain in place have been neglected for years. The work is not hard, but it's slow and tedious. Some of the weeds have thick roots that reach deep and are tough to dislodge. Alison, I note, does not wear any gloves.

"I want to keep my callouses," she says, sitting back on her heels and ruffling her short blond hair. She pulls out an army-style canteen of water and takes a long swallow. "It took me a long time to build them."

The callouses are from farmwork, she says; she graduated last spring from a private "alternative" boarding school in Vermont where students have to milk the cows and such before class. Over the summer, she worked on a farm full-time. She is proud of the hardiness she has developed.

June shadows me as we work. Shy, she seems to be seeking protection. She doesn't accomplish much work. She complains that despite the gloves, the plant stems hurt her hands. She sits on the edge of one of the raised beds as she works and every couple of weeds or so she straightens and looks around, then rests a moment with her eyes fixed vacantly on some distant point across the street.

June tells me she is already thinking about quitting. "I didn't know the work would be like this!"

Tracy arrives in the afternoon, breathless. Tony tells her to work with me and we go to pull weeds in the shade at the rear of the lot.

"I had a fight with my boyfriend," she says as soon as we get started.

"Oh?" I respond. "What happened?"

"We had a fight and I told him to leave. So he hit me. I called the police." Tracy looks at me and I try not to look shocked.

"Did he hurt you?"

"Not really. I'm bigger than him! But he made me so mad. He thinks he's so tough."

At nineteen, Tracy is sharing a one-bedroom apartment in Malden, a working-class suburb of Boston, with her boyfriend. But lately he hasn't been paying his share of the rent, she says, and that is what they fought about.

"Someone told me, once a guy hits you, he's not gonna stop," she says, looking thoughtful.

Is he going to leave? I ask. Tracy isn't certain. But the apartment, she says, is definitely hers.

"He doesn't own one piece of anything in that house. When he moves out, the only thing that goes with him is his clothes. I got everything in the apartment for myself. I don't want to live with no man and he kicks me out or he leaves and I'm sitting there with one chair and a table."

Earl and David have been assigned to begin pulling up the railroad ties that make up the edges of those garden beds the neighborhood group has marked for removal or relocation. The ties are set well into the ground and held together with nine-inch metal spikes. It is a difficult job, and Earl and David are both a little awkward with the tools, but they approach the task with good spirit.

They make an odd pair, each exaggerating his image in contrast to the other: Earl the ghetto tough and David the beatnik throwback. Earl seems to have spent some of his first paycheck over the weekend freshening up his fade haircut, and David has embroidered on the hem of his pants a crude symbol that is part peace sign, part heart. "That's my sign: peace through love," he says with a grin.

At first the two stand looking at the garden bed, uncertain how to approach the task. Then David takes charge. "Okay, Earl, put that rock right there." He wedges a long spike into the crack between two beams and lays it across the rock. "Now grab the end, and let's push down." The two boys heave a moment and then the beams groan and separate and the air fills with the pungent, fresh scent of rotting wood. They slap each other a high five, move down along the beam, and begin the process over again. The routine continues throughout most of the day.

Toward the end of the afternoon, they reach a tie that refuses to yield to their efforts. After several tries, Earl and David are both flagging from the exertion, but the beam has not budged. Tony, who has been watching from across the garden, ambles over.

"Listen," he says, "there's only fifteen or twenty minutes left till we have to start putting the tools away. Why don't you guys go on to a couple of easier ones, and save this one to try again first thing in the morning when you're fresh?"

He walks away. Earl picks up the spike and looks at David. "Let's bust this out," he says in a conspiratorial tone. "Surprise him—do it before he gets back." David nods and they brace themselves for another go at the tie.

There is no rain over the next two weeks, and the work is demanding, day after day. As we swing our shovels and mattocks, heave against crowbars, and take turns bracing ourselves against the jarring vibrations of the jackhammer, there is time for thought, for conversation, and for taking one another's measure. The accumulation of spoken words, the rhythm of the work, the growing knowledge of each other's physical selves, all flow together to create predictable rhythms and patterns, a kind of heartbeat of the team.

People begin to settle into roles within the group. Jacquelyn and Lisa respond to taunts from the men on the team by setting out to prove that women are capable of hard labor. Alison works stolidly alone. June and Tracy seem always to disappear when big jobs come up. Amy's energy level rises and falls with her moods. Brendan throws himself into each backbreaking task as if it is a mortal battle, saying little and resting rarely. Richie and Earl watch him with resentment, but when Tony is watching them, they match his pace. Tyrone works hard, his sinewy arms surprisingly strong. David, too, is steady, occasionally entertaining the rest of us with humorous commentary on our progress. After much discussion and a vote, Tony permits him to bring in a tape player so we can listen to music as we work. Charles has sudden bursts of great energy; he likes to swagger over to a laboring teammate and wrest the mattock or spade from his or her stiffening hand. "Lemme show you the sure-shot way," he says, and sets to work, expending all his energy in five or ten minutes of furious activity, then dropping the tool and moving on.

Tony spends his time circulating restlessly, making sure everyone is occupied, has the right tools, is following directions. He intervenes when squabbles erupt, and he makes frequent notations in a three-ring binder that he carries everywhere.

As for me, I am intent on showing that I mean to pull my own weight on the team. I enjoy the work—we all do. At the end of each day, we take pride in the dirt that coats our sweaty arms and faces. It's like a badge of merit.

At first, I carry my notebook with me everywhere. I take notes during meetings and conversations, and, when my hands are otherwise occupied, I think about what to write when I get the chance. The most interesting conversations always seem to occur when I am busy working. I learn to store things in my head, taking notes only during team meetings and other more formal moments. When there is a natural break in activity, I jot down things intended to jog my memory later. I do the bulk of my writing at night, when I get home. Relations between me and some of my teammates grow more relaxed as the notebook grows less visible.

Most days we divide into pairs or threes to tackle different tasks. Tony assigns the groupings, changing them each day to encourage everyone to get to know one another. In bits and pieces we begin sharing details of our lives with one another. For the most part, however, people define themselves not by virtue of where they come from but by how they act and what they do.

At the end of the first week, Tony calls a team meeting in the garden. We gather in a rough semicircle, some seated on the last remaining park bench, some cross-legged on the ground. Tony stands a little to the side, hands behind his back, his attention coolly focused on Tyrone, who stands before us, fidgeting.

Tyrone has taken off his City Year cap and is holding it in both hands. Beads of sweat shine on his dark face. He fingers the cap.

"My name is Tyrone Gunn and I'm with the Reebok Team and I'd like to tell you about the project that we're doing, which is the garden at Uphams Corner."

He pauses and loses his train of thought. There is a long silence.

"We're doing very well and everyone on the team is enjoying the work," he continues.

"You're lying," says Lisa.

"Well, I gotta lie. I'm not telling these people the truth, that everyone's complaining."

Tyrone is practicing. He is to make the first telephone call to Jean Mahoney at the Reebok Foundation.

"You gotta speak louder," says Tracy.

"Give some details," says Alison. "Tell her how much work we're doing."

"Be confident. Or at least sound confident."

Tony goes to stand next to Tyrone. "Maybe the most valuable skill you can learn in life is to be able to speak in front of people," he says. "It's not easy. Tyrone knows what we've been doing. He's been here all week. But saying it in front of people is another thing. By the end of the year, you will all be pros at this."

At the end of the meeting, Tony asks each person to shake his hand. It will be another ritual, he says—people should not consider the workday finished until they have shaken his hand.

At lunchtime we usually head to the Dorchester House of Pizza, where we occupy a couple of the orange plastic booths, kid around, insult one another, and complain about the work. Sometimes it is the best part of the day.

One day, Charles is out of money. I'm sitting opposite him and he grabs my soda bottle, uninvited, and pours some into a paper cup. He takes a sip and puckers up his face dramatically.

"What's wrong with this?" he demands. "Why the fuck didn't you return it?" He fills his cup again, takes off his chunky gold ring and begins washing it in my Diet Coke. I'm too surprised to respond. From where she is sitting, in the booth next to mine, Jackie catches my eye and shakes her head incredulously. We both know that Charles has scored a point on the intimidation scale. Sometimes it seems as if he spends the better part of his time trying to rack up such points.

Suddenly a woman who has been sleeping with her head on the table in a booth across from ours slides soundlessly to the floor, like liquid running down the seat. She lands in the aisle, her twisted body extended halfway across the entrance, and lies still.

Amy runs over to the woman and picks up her hand to look at a hospital bracelet she is wearing, while Charles grabs her under the arms and lifts her back onto the bench. The woman comes to abruptly and looks up at him with wide, bloodshot eyes.

"She's lucky she isn't in my neighborhood," Tyrone comments. "Homeboys woulda robbed her, not picked her up."

The woman struggles to her feet and stands, swaying. Her eyes are wild and frightened. Lisa, Amy, and Tracy form a circle around her. Still seated at the table, Jacquelyn and June watch. The woman lurches and reaches toward Lisa, who grabs her arm. One side of the woman's face is purple and bloated. Her eyes roll back.

I look around and realize that Charles, Earl, and Tyrone have slipped out. I am standing helplessly.

The woman falls into Lisa's arms. "I'm going to look for a policeman or try to call an ambulance or something," I say, to no one in particular, and race out the door. Of course, no policeman is in sight, and when I reach the pay phone at the end of the block I find it is broken, the receiver gone, the cord dangling.

I go back to the restaurant and find that Amy, Tracy, and Lisa—with Jacquelyn and June still watching—have things well under control. They have walked the woman outside and propped her against the wall. An ambulance is on the way. Lisa hands the woman a cigarette, and Amy lights it.

"What's your name?" Tracy asks, poised to write the information on a napkin. "Where do you live? What's your phone number?"

"My name is Linda," the woman mumbles. She stinks of alcohol, stale and medicinal.

The ambulance arrives and the three girls step out of the way as two medics move in on Linda. They grab her just as her knees buckle and she melts to the ground.

Linda struggles as she is lifted into the back of the ambulance and tied to a stretcher. "Stay away from my pocket!" she yells. Lisa, Tracy, and Amy gather around the open rear doors and watch as the medics wrestle Linda down and take her pulse. June and Jacquelyn and I hover behind them.

Finally, the medics get ready to leave. Lisa waves as they begin to close the doors, but Linda has finally relaxed and let her head fall back, and she can't see. One of the medics touches her.

"They want to say goodbye," he says. "The girls who helped you out."

Slowly Linda opens her puffy eyes and tries to sit up, but her torso is strapped down. Tears roll down her face as she stretches both hands toward us. "I want to go home," she cries. "I don't know what's happening!" Lisa and Jackie wave, looking stricken. The doors close. All three girls have tears in their eyes as they watch the ambulance pull away.

Later that day, everyone reports the incident to Tony. "I never saw anything like that in my life," says Jacquelyn. "I grew up in my sheltered little suburb. I didn't know what to do. I couldn't touch her. I couldn't eat."

Amy writes about Linda in her journal. "Linda is the woman you see in the street and turn your head. She is the woman life forgot and society ignores. . . . I will always remember Linda because helping Linda was the first thing we did to help somebody as a team."

I am surprised how affected people have been by the incident. In the recounting, it takes on a mythic stature.

That Friday, Amy is asked to choose the "word of the day" at the corps-wide community meeting. "My word of the day," she says, looking gravely around the big circle, "is trust. In our project at the Virginia-Monadnock Garden my team has been doing a lot of heavy lifting, and we've had to depend on each other, trust that they're not going to drop the timber on your foot.

"We all have to trust other people as friends, trust that they're going to be there for you. Trust that the bonds we're making here at City Year are going to last."

Six

One Sunday afternoon, Richie takes me up to see his hometown of Amesbury, an hour north of Boston. We drive around town while Richie points out sites both of historic interest and of personal significance. He points to a parking lot: "That's where everybody goes. I come here first when I want to find someone." The public high school: "I was a freshman three years runnin'," he says. "You hadda have 180 days in school to pass the year and my combined attendance for two years was 160." We pass his middle school. "That's when I was still a good student. I was smart, but I wasn't a nerd. That's a rare commodity—a good student who's also cool."

It is only with great reluctance that he shows me the house where he and his grandparents live. It is a trailer, planted in a quiet wooded spot on a dirt road. I drive by slowly. "Okay, you saw it—let's go," says Richie, before I get a real look. He doesn't want to go in. "I don't want to see my grandparents if I don't have to." I want to meet his grandparents, to see the house, but I feel bad about making him take me to a place he is ashamed of.

There is no explaining Richie Dale's appeal. At age seventeen, he is already all crooked and broken: his wide, swollen nose, the product of too many fights, gives his voice a stuffy, nasal twang, and his face, too rarely washed, is freckled with blackheads. His eyes, too, look swollen, and his wide lips curl back over a broken front tooth that is often etched with brown from the tobacco he chews. He wears a small gold hoop in his left ear and a silver cross around his neck. He is tall and lanky as well as strong. Riding the subway, Richie invariably occupies more than one seat, and when I am sitting near him he sometimes places his long-muscled leg across mine or leans heavily against me. Once or twice he has even sat in my lap, like a little child.

His skin is white, or faintly olive-toned, but he wears his straight hair long on top and shaved up the sides in an approximation of a low-top fade, a popular black hairstyle. His mother is part white and part black, he explains. Other teenagers say he looks like Vanilla Ice, the white rap star. He is boyish, an enormous street urchin. A cross between a member of an inner-city gang and a member of Our Gang.

Richie is bright—he'll tell you so. "My I.Q. is 128. I have the papers to prove it." Maybe that's what makes him so appealing. Or maybe it is his affectionate nature and the way he puts his arm around you when he is near. Putting his arm around you is never enough for Richie, however. He leans on you, throwing his weight across your shoulders as if to say, "I'm here. Take notice. Carry me."

We drive to the next town over, which is a resort town, and we look at some of the fancy shops. "I wanted you to see this," he says. "It ain't like this in the city, is it?"

We stop for lunch, and over a pepper-and-onion pizza, Richie tells me about his life.

"My mother's a bitch. My mother left when I was like three years old—between three and five. She was fifteen when she had me. She did it to get out of the house.

"My father was wicked cool, he'd like give me the shirt off his back and everythin'. My father has an associate's degree. And he, back in 1980 or som'n', he got arrested. For murder."

Richie's father and two others, he tells me, killed a man and a woman who had identified them to police as drug dealers. His father only intended to threaten the couple, Richie maintains, but things got out of hand. He believes his father was only an accomplice, that he is not the one who stabbed the couple to death.

"Anyways, he went to jail. The end of my father, right?

"I got committed to DSS—the Department of Social Services.... They labeled me emotionally disturbed. Because all these things happened to me they figured this kid's gotta be screwed, right? So they pulled me in. That's when I started gettin' emotionally disturbed."

Richie describes for me six different foster homes, group homes, and juvenile detention facilities he has lived in since that time. He ran away from many of them, and committed a variety of crimes ranging from smashing mailboxes with a baseball bat to car theft. He has known any number of social workers and counselors, and from his account, many of them have worked hard on his behalf, but he is restless and lonely and he hates restrictions. A couple of the foster homes he speaks of with great warmth. "Best place in the world. I love that place. They care the most. They treat you like you're just havin'

some problems. Not like you're a criminal." Other places frightened him. "Maximum Security Detention Facility for Youths. Right? Jail for kids. I got sent there for mailbox baseball. Kept my mouth shut. Scared shitless. All the time I was like, why did they do this to me? I musta done something really fucked. 'Cause these kids—there's homosexuality goin' on and all this. Oh, my god."

He was drawn to City Year, he said, because he saw a team working in Boston one day near the group home where he was staying at the time. They looked like they were having fun and one of the girls was blond and very pretty. "And then I found out what they were doin' and I was like, shit! I wanna be a part of this. I felt like it would give me back a sense of, like, that I was a useful member of society."

We drive around some more. Richie points out his girlfriend's house, a tiny building with a red door. "I like to go there," he says. "There's a feeling there."

"Of what?" Silence. "Stability?"

"Yes."

"Love?"

"Yes. . . ."

One day Richie and I are transplanting rosebushes in the garden. The bushes look dead, but the roots are very much alive. Working with two spades—mine rectangular, flat, and square-nosed, Richie's cupped and pointed, we try to free each bush from the loose rocky soil without cutting too many of the roots. I slice a circle around each plant, feeling with my spade for the edge of the roots, then Richie follows, gently trying to pry the bush free. The sandy earth falls away from the roots easily enough, and many of the bushes still have a root ball left over from their potted days, their hard, woody roots spiraling tightly beneath the earth. But new roots have extended in a series of horizontal missions, creeping along the edges of the flower bed, penetrating the roots of other bushes, branching out and emerging here and there to send new shoots skyward. We work the tools gently into the earth to tease the roots apart. We stay with this task through much of the afternoon.

Amy and Tracy have dug a series of holes for the transplanted bushes. When there is just one hole remaining to be filled, Richie picks up a scrawny little bush with just a few roots and two or three shoots.

"That one's so small, I think we should just throw it away," I say. "I don't really think it's worthwhile." There are plenty of other bushes to choose from.

Richie picks up the tiny bush and carries it away, casting me a reproachful glance over his shoulder. "I'm gonna plant it anyway," he says. "To spite you."

For fifteen minutes he works diligently on his own, first watering the hole, then holding his little bush upright in the hole with one hand while he tenderly packs the red soil around its roots with the other. He waters around the roots periodically as he fills the hole.

"It's going to be the biggest, best bush of all of them," he says, looking over to make sure I am listening. Then, a little sadly, a little self-righteously: "Some of us got told once that *we* weren't exactly worthwhile." He turns his back and continues watering his little bush.

Seven

Tony stands at the front of the room facing eight white-clad dancers and starts the class by shifting his weight from foot to foot in a low, lateral, rocking motion. The dancers follow, spreading their arms and moving their shoulders, keeping their center of gravity low: right, left, right, left. Tony starts with a jaunty smile but his focus soon shifts inward and a mask of cool intensity slips over his face.

Here at the back of the room, David, Jackie, and I try to imitate Tony and the other dancers. Jackie's long arms and legs are all over the place. David has his eyes closed and is wearing a beatific expression as he sways back and forth. Right, left. The floor is gritty beneath my bare feet. The movement is awkward at first, but soon it becomes mesmerizing. Right, left.

Tony has invited the team to come and join his *capoeira* class for a night. The class is taught by a Brazilian *capoeira* master, but after years of study, Tony is one of the most senior students and sometimes takes over in the teacher's absence. We three, more curious about Tony than about this Brazilian art form, have taken him up on his offer.

According to legend, Tony explains, *capoeira* evolved as an art form practiced by slaves in Brazil, who deceived their masters into thinking they were only playing, then used their moves to break away to freedom. It's not hard to see why it appeals to Tony—a cross between martial arts and dance, *capoeira* is at once playful and deadly serious.

"*Capoeira* just connects with something primal and magical," he says. "It's a very profound experience. When you're in the game, nothing else exists except you and the other person. The *ginga* move [the rocking motion with which he began the class] is cleansing. It allows you to throw out your anger. It's healing. It gives me a sense of release.

"*Capoeiristas*, especially in Brazil, are happy-go-lucky. They're not that self-conscious about themselves. They don't filter their actions through an ideal, the way more educated people do. They cultivate *joie de vivre* and openness."

After the *ginga* and some group exercises, the game begins. Master Deraldo, a pixie of a man with a mop of curly hair and twinkling eyes and teeth, has arrived, bringing with him a number of musical instruments. There is a *berimbau*, a long, bowed stick strung with a single wire and painted in stripes, a pair of tall drums, a cowbell, a notched gourd. A few of the students take up instruments and begin to play, while the rest of us form a circle around them. The music begins slowly, then gathers volume and intensity. It is tuneless but rhythmic and joyful. Tony and Deraldo sing and chant in Portuguese. In the center of the circle, two students begin to joust. They dance in mirror motion, taunting one another with their bodies, kicking and recoiling, turning cartwheels and handstands and passing between each others' legs. The game is fast, with a quirky, rugged grace. When all the students have paired off and taken turns "playing"—both in the game and on the instruments—Master Deraldo looks at David, eyebrows raised. With eager, ginger steps, David enters the ring. He jousts with Deraldo, improvising jerkily while Deraldo smiles and taunts him gently. Then Deraldo looks at Jackie and me; Jackie shakes her head, so I move out and take David's place. I try to interlock my movements with Deraldo's and it goes well until he kicks me lightly in the stomach and I reel away. Then Tony is crouching, his dark eyes boring into Jackie's. She slowly makes her way to him and together they dance into the ring. Eyes sparkling, Tony leads Jackie through a series of spars, each a little more difficult than the one before. They play and play, and when they are through we applaud their game.

After class, Tony leads us through his own post-*capoeira* rituals: stretching, buying fruit juice at the convenience store across the street from the arts center where the class is held, and gulping it down in greedy swallows. He does this, we know, several nights a week. We stand together in the darkened street a moment, talking and laughing before splitting up. *Capoeira* warriors, bonded by ritual.

There is something about Tony that is larger than life. We see it each morning as he starts P.T., drawing a deep breath and throwing back his head so his voice will carry across the plaza:

"Today we're going for excellence! Total unity! Synchronicity!"

He struts up and down between the lines of corps members, the veins in his neck bulging as he strains for volume.

"I want to see high drama! This is an adventure! A cup of high-test coffee! This is art!"

Our performance doesn't quite live up to such a billing. On my team, as on others, some members are more committed to the P.T. ritual than others. Brendan's execution is militarily precise, for instance, and David's and Jacquelyn's is exuberant. But Charles stands at the back of the line, slowly rotating his hips and making suggestive noises while the rest of us do four-count waist bends. During toe touches, Earl gestures pathetically in the direction of his feet. Lisa flaps her arms lazily when the rest of us do windmills, and Tracy's jumping jacks are nothing more than tiny little hops.

Because of the relish with which Tony acts the role of drill sergeant, he has acquired the nickname "Boot Camp Tony." But his manner is more firm than harsh.

When someone on the team is not making an effort, Tony walks down the line and stands a moment by that person, watching. He might lean over and whisper into his or her ear. But that is all. If there is no improvement, Tony will bring the matter up later and treat it as a contract violation. He shows no anger; there's never any confrontation.

"I put a lot of effort into motivating the team," he says. "But I want them to be motivated not for me but for the situation and for their personal goals, so that their success is not totally dependent upon me.

"Detachment is important, because ultimately it allows a higher form of love to take place. If you can stay one step removed from certain details, you can get closer to the core of things."

Detachment. A higher form of love. The core of things. Those are the kinds of things that Tony talks about. On the one hand, he is a "happy-go-lucky" *capoeirista*, living in the moment; on the other hand, he is driven by ideas and ideals. Most people in the corps— including me—find Tony just a little baffling.

Tony tells me his life story over several lunches in a restaurant near the project. He is twenty-eight years old. He was born in Buffalo, New York, the fourth of six children in a Polish-Italian-American family. His father is a doctor, his mother a nurse and homemaker. Both sets of grandparents lived nearby. His maternal grandfather was

a mailman and his grandmother a waitress. Tony's childhood memories are of sitting with his grandparents hearing stories about the old days. His own childhood was comfortable, but he was aware that his grandparents, the children of immigrants, had endured severe privation and many years of numbing labor.

Tony was raised in the Catholic Church, attended Catholic school, and was confirmed, but after he left home to go to Cornell University, he discovered that he felt little connection with the Church.

Tony's major was painting and printmaking. He also studied martial arts. There, he says, he found a spiritual home. "I recognized a spiritual side of myself that is a very important part of my life and that I didn't want to throw away with my disaffection with the Church. My martial-arts teacher was religious. You have to study meditation, and it's very hard to meditate without involving spirituality—something greater than yourself that you can respect and be close to."

After graduation, Tony moved to New York City to work on his art. But things did not go well. Pressed for cash, he soon became disenchanted with the life he'd chosen. On the recommendation of a friend, he applied for a job as a team leader in the City Volunteer Corps. He knew very little about it—just that it involved working with kids and doing community service work. He found, however, that the work combined the spirituality, discipline, and physical involvement he had discovered in martial arts. He stayed at CVC three years.

It troubled him a little that his family did not seem to understand the work he had chosen. They could not see any career path there, and he felt they did not respect his choice.

"It was really exciting to me," he says, "and I just couldn't explain it to them. I couldn't relate the breadth of what I was going through.

"Time after time I've seen corps members go through the same thing. They want people to understand the power of what they're experiencing, but they can't communicate it."

After three years as a team leader, Tony felt tired and burnt out. He quit his job and drove to New Mexico to experiment with a more bohemian lifestyle: painting, working temporary office jobs, and studying *capoeira*. The idyll didn't last long. Again, he went into debt, and when a friend offered him a partnership in an ice cream business back east in Massachusetts, he accepted.

Alan and Michael knew Tony by reputation; he had earned considerable respect among his colleagues at CVC. When they learned he had come to Boston, they recruited him to help out as a consultant when they were planning the City Year program. After a while, they offered him a staff position.

He was happy to get back into youth service. His work as a team leader was for him an expression of his developing philosophy. "I saw this documentary on television about Mother Teresa," he says. "She told of a man she'd found lying on the ground who stank so badly that no one would touch him. She cleaned him. He said to her, 'Why are you doing this?' She answered, 'Because I love you.' And she really meant it. She was able to feel a deep connection to all people that transcended the physical limits of race, of appearance, of what they smelled like, so that she could go up to any human being and tend to them and say, 'I love you.' She could see through to the spiritual being. That's something I strive to cultivate in myself.

"I don't talk explicitly about these things with the team," he says. "I want to give people a chance to raise those questions on their own. Service can be a spiritual experience. Taking people out of their normal context and societal paths calls everything into question. A lot of what we do at City Year is create fertile ground for spirituality to grow."

Within the team, people occasionally chuckle at Tony's grandiosity. His talk of dying and being reborn; his talk of moral war. Such language sometimes makes us squirm a little. But sometimes it is also inspiring, and sometimes it makes people think about their lives in new ways.

Finally, it is our last day at the Virginia-Monadnock Garden. We have finished the demolition work and the garden is ready for new construction and planting in the spring. We gather for a team meeting in the spot where a bench once stood—it took Charles, Lisa, Tyrone, and Jackie two days to dig out the huge slabs of cement that anchored it.

"What did you think about the work?" asks Tony. "Too hard?" He pans the team with his eyes. "Too easy?"

"Too long," says Jackie. Her head is resting on Charles's shoulder. Next to her is Amy, with Tyrone kneeling behind her, playing with her long black hair. The rest of us are clustered around, except for David, who sits off to the side on a pile of rocks.

"What is this?" Tyrone demands. "Are we the only team that gets this kind of work?"

"To me, the physical work is necessary at the start," says David, who is emerging as a kind of team philosopher. "Because at first, we don't know each other, and in the human service projects we'll need to lean on each other."

"Is this the hardest work we're going to have?" asks Brendan.

"I cannot guarantee that," says Tony. "But I will say this. I have never supervised a project where the work was more physically demanding. This project is training for later projects where you will have more responsibility. When the hard work comes, they'll say, 'Call the Reebok Team,' because we can handle it."

Tony goes on to say that perhaps we can come back to the Virginia-Monadnock Garden in the spring to install the new garden beds and help to put in the benches and playground equipment.

Besides, he points out, nobody has yet figured out a way of getting those sneakers down off the telephone wire.

"Come back here?" says Charles, with a sneer. "I wouldn't even walk down this street."

"I want to come back," says David. "We've done the hell work. Plus, it's just, like, finishing the job."

Eight

We are assigned to two quick one-day service projects before starting our next long project. The first assignment is to repaint the jungle gym and other equipment at a playground in Roxbury. The second is to visit and perform chores for elderly people in a housing project in Charlestown. The neighborhoods are both poor; one is inhabited by blacks, the other by whites.

"You in the heart of it now," says Lisa, as we bounce along Seaver Avenue in the back of a city bus. "White folks don't belong here."

Charles looks at Lisa. "Ain't hardly even any Puerto Ricans here."

Lisa, who is Puerto Rican, nods. "And mulattos be wrecked in this neighborhood." She looks at Richie.

Charles turns to me. "I see you here, I'd say, 'Who's that sucker?'"

Charles and Lisa are having fun trying to make some of the rest of us feel uncomfortable. We stare silently out the windows of the bus.

It is a scary neighborhood. There are almost no people at all on the street. It is like a forgotten industrial zone. Everything is gray. The low, scattered buildings look closed, boarded up, and their walls are covered with graffiti.

Tyrone is sitting slouched in the middle seat at the back of the bus. Suddenly he straightens.

"That's where I live," he says, pointing. "Down there." He turns and points the other way. "Down that way is Egleston Square—home of the X Men. Puerto Ricans." Tyrone looks at Lisa for confirmation. She nods. "That's a gang," he continues. "Big gang. Goes all the way down to Humboldt Ave, to . . ." Tyrone's hand, which has traced a half circle in the air to show the extent of the X Men's territory, hovers a moment as he tries to remember the street name. "Chestnut," says Lisa.

"Yeah, Chestnut. And into the South End."

Tony stands up; we've reached our stop. We follow him off the bus.

Throughout that day and the next—painting the play equipment takes us into a second day—Lisa, Tyrone, and Charles lord it over the rest of us with their familiarity with the neighborhood. Earl stakes a claim as well, shaking his head with mock irony. "And to think we used to hang out and demolish this park. Now we trying to clean it up."

By lunchtime of the second day, we have nearly finished the job. We've given fresh coats of bright paint to two swing sets, a jungle gym, and a pair of stone turtles for climbing on. Tony sends us back to Virginia-Monadnock for the afternoon to finish up a few final tasks, sending us in two shifts. I go with the second group.

We take the bus back to Dudley Station in the center of Roxbury, where we wait for another bus to Uphams Corner. Lisa and Tyrone split off from the rest of us there, saying they want to have lunch at a place they know in Dudley Square and then walk to the garden. The weather is turning bitter and the rest of us draw our jackets tight about us as the bus terminal slowly fills with people.

Bus after bus draws into the station, discharges its load, refills, and departs while we stand forlorn beneath the sign for the number 15 bus. Twenty minutes pass. It's a bleak spot. Rusting overhead train tracks serve as a bitter reminder that once this neighborhood was served by trains as well as buses. The vestigial tracks form a sort of roof but serve more as a fumy wind tunnel than a shelter. Across the street I see an old painted sign advertising a five-cent cup of coffee and a sandwich for fifteen cents. It is the kind of sign that might be restored as antique in a more fashionable neighborhood. Here, it has simply been forgotten.

When our bus finally arrives, there is quite a crowd beneath the number 15 sign, and Amy, Jackie, Alison, Brendan, David, and I are separated in the rush for the doors. Somehow I get on and make my way to the back of the bus. I look out of the window to see if the others have made it on. I can see that David and Alison are still outside and the movement through the doors is slowing. At the front it is crowded, but where I am standing at the back there is ample space for many more passengers. "Move back," I call out impatiently. "There's plenty of room in the back!"

Nobody moves. I look around and everywhere, it seems, the eyes of the other passengers are planted on me with looks of scorn and suspicion. I am the only white person in sight, and for a moment I feel frightened. On all sides eyes are telling me I am unwelcome. I draw myself up and look away.

As the bus pulls out I see David and Alison still standing on the pavement. I wonder what they will do, and then I realize I don't know where to get off the bus. This is a different route to the garden from the one I know.

"Suzanne?" It's Amy, calling me from somewhere up front. "Are you here?"

"Yes!" I call back, relieved.

"We'll yell before we get off!" she reassures me.

Perhaps it is because of my experience on the bus that I feel such empathy for Tyrone when, the next day, we step off yet another bus onto a curb in all-white Charlestown. Charlestown has a longstanding reputation as a community that is closed to minority groups. This is the neighborhood where, twenty years ago, at the height of the unrest surrounding school desegregation in Boston, a black youth attending Charlestown High was shot during football practice by white youths on a nearby rooftop.

"No blacks or Puerto Ricans *allowed* in this neighborhood," says Tyrone with trepidation in his voice. "But it's okay," he adds quickly. "Just because I'm in a discriminating neighborhood doesn't mean I hate being here. I get discriminated in a lot of things. Doesn't mean I won't do it."

We spend that day doing household chores for old people who live in a low-income housing project. Nobody mentions race, but people are worried. Will the black team members be safe in Charlestown? Will the old people behave in an accepting fashion? When we gather for a briefing from the housing development's social services director, she addresses the issue obliquely. "I think you'll find these people are very anxious to meet you and waiting for you to come. I don't expect any problems. But I want you to feel secure and safe in Charlestown. Come see me if you have any security problems."

Later, Brendan complains privately that while black and Latino corps members are encouraged to talk about their fear of white neighborhoods, white corps members often feel they must keep quiet about their nervousness when working in black neighborhoods. Tony acknowledges that a subtle double standard does seem to exist, and promises to try to be sensitive to the issue in the future.

For today's project, Tony divides the team into racially mixed groups of three and four and sends us off with mops, sponges, and rolling buckets. I go with June, Alison, and Charles to the apartment of a tiny woman named Dorothy, who is perhaps in her early sixties. "All of you?" she asks, looking a little overwhelmed as she ushers us inside. The apartment is small and stuffy, but it is pleasant—no big cleaning job here.

Following the instructions on our assignment sheet, June washes the windows in the kitchen and the bedroom with Windex and Alison and I wipe grease stains from the kitchen walls. Charles genially joins Dorothy in the living room, watching *The Price Is Right*. We suspect that Dorothy might have asked for volunteers in order to have some company. Eventually we all go to sit with Dorothy in the living room. She and Charles are deep in conversation. Dorothy pulls out a wrinkled letter and passes it to Charles, who reads it, nods, and hands it back to Dorothy. She pushes it toward me. "That's from my daughter," she says.

> Hi Ma,
>   I only have 3 months left. I sit here think of a lot of stuff. And I'm glad that you can still love me. I'm so sorry for what I have done. . . . You were so nice and kind. And it wasn't you or anyone else. I just had to follow the gang. And it took me to learn from my mistakes. I had to come to a place like jail to see what I have.

I am startled that Dorothy would share something so intimate with strangers like us. I was wondering if this old lady would be intimidated by Charles, and here they were, chatting cozily, sharing their sad stories of the exotic world of jail.

At the end of the day we gather at the housing project's administration building, where the staff gives us a room to use for a team meeting. Tony wants to use the remaining hour of the day to meet with team members individually for informal evaluations, to listen to their concerns, and to discuss areas of their work that need improvement. He has been conducting such private conferences regularly whenever possible since the very beginning.

During this time, the rest of us are to talk quietly or write in our journals. We spend a pleasant hour. Spirits are high. Tyrone tells us proudly that one of the women he, Richie, and Amy visited was so pleased with their helpfulness that she wrote out a check for twenty dollars to City Year. We talk about the day, then move on to a general assessment of the team's performance. "Reebok is the best," says Tyrone. "Definitely."

"We had so many problems at the beginning!" says Jacquelyn. "Remember at camp? The spider's web? That seems like so long ago! I can't believe how far we've come since then!"

Nine

I am at home the next morning, still wearing my bathrobe and writing at my kitchen table, when the phone rings. It's Gordon, one of the other team coordinators. "Tyrone Gunn is dead," he says in a twisted voice. "He was shot last night. I thought you would want to know."

Hanging up the phone, I feel only disbelief. I stare down at the table and listen to the rush of blood between my ears. How strange, I think: his name was Gunn, and he was shot. Then I get dressed and drive to the City Year headquarters.

There, Richie greets me silently, his sweet, broken face solemn and heavy with significance. He slowly raises one hand, its back turned out toward me. On it he has written "I ♥ TRIZ." That is the boys' nickname for Tyrone. Charles is Chiz and Tyrone is Triz. Charles has written the same thing on his pants with a magic marker, the words running down one leg. His face is angry and cold. Neither of them speaks.

Reebok Team members are scattered about the office. June is huddled with a friend, a Laotian girl from another team. Amy is sitting by herself, eyes turned down. Tracy is comforting her friend Caroline, who was dating Tyrone.

I seek out Tony, who tells me, tersely, what he knows. It isn't much. Tyrone was shot outside his apartment building as he was returning from a party at Lisa's home. The killer approached from behind and escaped quickly. Tyrone's cousin, also a corps member, brought the news to P.T. this morning. Jon asked the T.C.s (team coordinators) to quickly round up their teams and tell them what had happened as gently as possible, then take them away somewhere so that they give each other support but avoid the mass hysteria that was possible if all the teams remained together. Already the news had spread out across the plaza and people were hugging and sobbing loudly. Some of the boys had begun shouting with anger and punching walls. Tony took the Reebok Team off to a diner and bought them breakfast.

"They were just shocked," he tells me. "A lot of people cried. Even Charles."

Now, two hours later, most of the teams have made their way to the headquarters. Work has been called off for the day. Corps and staff members drift about the room, talking softly and looking somber and confused. The buzz of the headquarters, usually frenetic when the corps is present, is muted. People seem to be moving in slow motion.

A while after I arrive the staff begins to round up the corps and we set up the folding chairs and sit down together. Alan's face is pale as he stands and begins to speak.

"This is our worst nightmare," he says, "that the violence we are working so hard to end could reach in and take away a member of our community. But I have to keep believing we are on the right path with the work that we are doing. . . . We have to try to make Tyrone's death bring us together as a community."

Following Alan, others speak. The mayor's youth adviser, who was with us at Camp Becket, admonishes us that no retaliatory violence will right the wrong that has been committed. Grief counselors offer their advice and services. A few corps members speak. I am not taking notes—I feel as if it would be inappropriate. Besides, my hands are shaking.

Tony asks the team to gather in the conference room. It seems important to be together. Most people do not yet want to talk, however, and Richie and Earl are not ready to join the gathering; they remain outside the room. Amy and Lisa weep a little, and for long minutes we sit together in silence. We are joined by a grief counselor, but the team resists his exhortations to talk. At this moment he seems like an intruder. Jean Mahoney of Reebok arrives and sits with us for a while. She tells us that the flag at the company headquarters has been lowered to half-mast and asks if there is anything else she can do.

"This kid did nothing, right?" she says, shaking her head. "There's no respect for human life."

Charles writes on the blackboard: "Triz is in here."

Tony asks us to gather at the office around six to have dinner so people will not have to spend the evening at home alone. Waiting for the others to arrive, Charles falls asleep on one of the couches, his face mashed against the cushions. Brendan sits on the edge of a chair, hanging his head forward disconsolately. Amy and Jacquelyn are quiet and David and I work a crossword together to pass the time. David has sewn a black knit headband around the sleeve of his jacket with long, clumsy stitches.

There is a rap tape playing low on the stereo, so low that it is just an insistent throbbing. We wait, and for long minutes nobody speaks. Earl and Richie are the last to arrive. When we leave for Chinatown, Alan joins us, along with a couple of other corps members who are hanging about the office.

It is a relief to get outside, and as we walk across the Fort Point Channel Bridge and past the tall buildings of the financial district, we are buffetted by a chilly, wet wind.

The Shanghai is almost empty, never a good sign in a Chinese restaurant but an advantage now as we don't want to wait. We want to get on with the busy-ness of pouring tea, unwrapping chopsticks, passing menus, ordering. We sit at a big round table and over dinner we laugh and joke, hollowly at first and then with increasing warmth. Almost as if nothing has happened. We eat ravenously.

But Amy is solemn and Jackie snaps at Earl. And when we are through with dinner, returning to the headquarters seems the best thing to do.

It's pouring now, and the wind drives the rain against us at a harsh diagonal pitch. We have no raincoats and we run almost blindly through the streets, becoming thoroughly soaked with rain.

Back at the headquarters, we dry off as best we can and Tony sets up the television and the VCR and puts in a tape he shot at Camp Becket. We watch the jerky shots of people walking, playing and clowning for the camera, searching for a glimpse of Tyrone. His face, his small head and gap-toothed smile, flits into the frame once or twice, so briefly we almost miss him. We pause the tape and crane forward to look at the disappointing, fuzzy image. Further along on the tape there is footage of the talent show we held on the last night, and we see Peri, City Year's education director, perched on a chair, playing the guitar and singing a song she has written. The song points out an ironic contrast between the joy surrounding Nelson Mandela's release and the rising murder rate in Boston:

Thirty-two dead on the streets of Boston,
their faces young and black.
They're screaming for somebody who will listen;
they're trying to fight back.

I drive Richie, Amy, David, and Charles home that night; Tony takes the others. Charles is the last one I drop off. All his mischief gone, Charles sits quietly, looking out the window and tracing patterns with his finger in the steam on the glass.

"Triz is in here," he writes.

The next day is Friday, and as always we begin with a community meeting in the headquarters. People talk a bit about Tyrone, and Tony plays a funeral rhythm for us on his Brazilian *berimbau*. The corps listens respectfully but most of the Reebok Team is not present to hear Tony's song. Amy, Alison, David, Richie, and June have stayed home; Earl has a date in court for something that happened shortly before City Year began. That leaves only Jackie, Brendan, Charles, Lisa, Tracy, and me.

The staff has canceled the scheduled activities for the afternoon and made plans to send the entire corps out to Fields Corner in Dorchester to work together for a few hours clearing a vacant lot. They have decided that it will be healthy for everyone to spend the day sweating together, sharing one big task. When we arrive at the site after lunch, Charles and Tracy are nowhere to be found. Lisa is angry. "They should be here!" she fumes.

Our team is assigned a large area to clear. The lot, surrounded by graffiti-covered brick apartment buildings and sagging, wood three-family houses, is thickly overgrown with tall weeds and bushes. Drug dealers and buyers hang out there, Tony explains, and parents fear what might happen to their children walking by on the way home from school.

We are given weed-whackers—long, angled scythes—as well as shovels, rakes, and plastic bags. We set solemnly to work. Jacquelyn and I pick up trash: broken whiskey bottles, fast-food containers, the front-left quarter-panel of a car. Lisa works alone, cutting weeds, hacking away viciously. After a while, Tracy arrives, wearing a sheep-ish grin.

Brendan, as usual, heads off by himself. After a bit, I notice him digging with a shovel, and I go over to look.

There is a piece of crumpled metal jutting from the ground. Unable to pull it up, Brendan has already dug a six-foot-long trench along the edge of what appears to be a metal sheet. He seems very determined. I begin to help digging, and Jacquelyn joins us. Soon we are joined by a few boys from other teams. We keep trying to pry the object out of the ground but have no luck. We are sweating.

"Maybe we should give it up, Brendan," I say. "Maybe there's a whole car down there."

"We're just doing the job we were sent here to do," replies Brendan, still digging.

It takes the better part of the afternoon to remove what turns out to be the entire rear end of a pickup truck, twisted, squashed, and mutilated. Six boys strain and heave to hoist it into the air, then place it on their shoulders and carry it reverently across the lot and lay it gently near the curb. Brendan looks at the resurrected wreckage with his hands on his hips. The set of his shoulders is proud, but the look on his face is bitter.

In the first week or so after Tyrone's death, I am often surprised by the responses of those around me, as well as my own. People who were close to him seem unexpectedly calm, while people who barely knew him weep often and openly, or show violent anger, or become suddenly remote and withdrawn. Perhaps those different early reactions are symptomatic not so much of the degree of each person's affection for Tyrone but of their own histories, their past experiences with death and violence, their sense of their own place in the world.

Those corps members who come from poor neighborhoods where violence and murder are not uncommon events are the first to show their grief and their anger. It was mainly they who cried and wailed or bristled with anger as soon as they heard about the killing. Tyrone's death has opened up for them an already existing pool of sadness and outrage about the harshness and unfairness of life, the evil that lurks always just around the corner. They know how to react to tragedy, because it has visited them before—if not within their own family, then at school, up the street, in the neighborhood. That's how things are in Boston. You don't grow up or hang out in Roxbury or North Dorchester or South Boston without knowing people who have been stabbed, shot, or killed. Those corps members are familiar with the rituals of death and mourning. And because they reacted the soonest, they seem to be recovering the soonest. They already knew how fragile life can be.

Those who have lived more sheltered lives—among whom I count myself—react at first with numbness and disbelief, and then profound confusion. How should we feel? How should we act? What does this mean? To have seen and perhaps even talked to Tyrone one day and then learn he is dead the next—such an event is disorienting and it blasts an enormous hole in the sense of security drawn from a comfortable middle-class childhood. People have found different ways to express or to escape the novel sense of fear and unsettlement Tyrone's death brought on. They are depressed; they withdraw; they sentimentalize their memories of Tyrone; they drink.

Within the Reebok Team, it is clear how each person's history affects his or her response to Tyrone's death. Amy is depressed, almost frighteningly so. Perhaps for her, this sudden loss has awakened buried and incoherent memories of the early loss of her parents. Charles is angry and wild, and even more uncommunicative than before. Richie is laconic. David and Alison seem shell-shocked—sober and a little confused. Jackie, usually so bubbly, is irritable and moody—her father died of cancer just six months ago, almost without warning. Tracy and Lisa are at once mournful and a little self-important—their friendship with Tyrone gives them greater status in grief. Lisa is especially troubled by her connection with Tyrone's death; he was coming home from a party at her house when he was shot. If only she had made him stay a little longer, leave a little earlier, remain and sleep on the couch. Earl's reaction is hard to gauge; he seems to take his cue from those around him. Brendan exaggerates and romanticizes his friendship with Tyrone, comforting himself by talking about the special respect they shared for one another. June comes in each day querulous and hollow-eyed. She's having trouble sleeping—every time she closes her eyes she sees Tyrone. "Why do the nice people have to die?" she asks.

Two days after Tyrone's death, I remember suddenly that I took pictures of him one afternoon at the Virginia-Monadnock Garden. The film is still in my camera and I rush it to a one-hour photo shop and wait while the pictures are developed.

Tyrone shows up clearly in two of the pictures. In one he is lifting a thick piece of lumber onto a stack. Lisa is helping him. The picture reveals nothing of special interest.

In the second photo, he is sitting next to June on a piece of wood, looking off to the side with a distant, almost languid gaze. He looks weary. But what interests me in the photo is June's expression. June rarely smiles, and when we were working in the garden, which she did not enjoy, her face sometimes twisted sourly. But here she is grinning, almost laughing. Was Tyrone responsible for that smile? What did he say to make her look so happy?

I go, both curious and apologetic, to see Tyrone's mother, Tiajuana. I am afraid she will resent my intrusion. But I want to see her—to know what kind of a family Tyrone came from and what kind of a place he lived in. I also want to share with his mother some of my good memories about her son, some memories I hope might be comforting to her. I go on a Monday, just five days after he died, carrying as gifts a zucchini bread still warm from my oven and copies of my two pictures of Tyrone. I feel timid as I drive down unfamiliar streets toward the Gunns' address. It is a stone apartment building, a solid, pleasant-looking edifice on a street where it coexists incongruously with ramshackle wood-frame homes. There are no names on the buzzers at the door. A little girl is sitting on the stoop and I ask her which is the Gunns' apartment. She leads me up a flight of stairs, through an open door and directly into Tiajuana's living room, where I stand blinking in the sudden light of an airy, comfortably furnished room and wonder how to introduce myself and explain my entrance without knocking.

Tiajuana rises immediately. She is tiny and delicate, like a little bird. I tell her I was on Tyrone's City Year team, and she hugs me. "I brought some pictures for you," I say. "I would like to see them," she says in a high, girlish voice, looking up at me with mixed excitement and dread. She smiles as she looks at the pictures and her eyes fill up with tears, then she hugs me again.

She shows me her own photos. Tyrone as a little boy in a matching winter jacket and hat. Tyrone as a teenager with a bushy Afro. The photos are arranged on a little side table, with flowers and other artifacts, including an enormous Mother's Day card from Tyrone, dated the previous spring. At Tiajuana's invitation, I sit down on a red crushed-velvet couch.

"I had no idea of all the work he was doing in City Year," Tiajuana says. Alan, Tony, Lisa, Tyrone's girlfriend Caroline, his friend Joe, and others from the corps have been to see her several times already; she is overwhelmed by their warmth and impressed by their accounts of Tyrone's efforts. "He joined to study for the G.E.D. and because his friend Joe was so hepped on it. He got very fond of the program."

I stay a while and listen as she talks about her son, whom she describes as a gentleman who enjoyed taking his mother's arm as they walked down the street. "I was more like his friend or his sister than his mother," she says, her eyes filling up with tears again.

Tiajuana left Tyrone's father when Tyrone, her second child, was only five months old. She had not completed high school, but once she was on her own she earned a G.E.D., an associate's degree, and a data entry certificate and now works as a secretary for the state. She has been with the man she now lives with for twenty-one years. He is the father of Tyrone's three younger brothers and has tried to be a father to Tyrone.

Tyrone was a quiet child, she says, but as a teenager he was popular and enjoyed music and dancing. He and his brothers earned pocket money by break dancing on the street for quarters. He earned A's and B's in school but dropped out after the eleventh grade because he was bored and joined the Job Corps, where he stayed for two years and earned a certificate in electrical work. She says Tyrone was ambitious but sometimes got sidetracked by his interest in girls and by his hot temper. She worried sometimes that he drank too much, but he didn't use drugs. Another of her sons does, she says, and he is no longer welcome to live in the house.

One item in particular comes as news to me: Tyrone has a son. Jamie, now four years old, lives with his maternal grandmother—Tyrone and the mother broke up before the baby was born. Tyrone saw little of his child save for occasional visits.

Tiajuana says Tyrone was as good a father as the mother's family would allow him to be. She is proudest of Tyrone for the role he played in the lives of his younger brothers. They looked up to Tyrone, because he took an interest in their lives.

Just before I leave, we go into the kitchen, where I see that Tyrone's younger brother, Jeremy, has placed my pictures of Tyrone side by side on the table and is staring at them, moving his eyes from one to the other as if he could somehow bring them into three dimensions, bring them back to life.

One morning, Tony announces that Lisa has moved away to North Carolina. She left without telling anyone on the team. We know she has a boyfriend at a military base there, and there's a rumor in the corps that she is actually married to him. Perhaps she is depressed and just wanted to get away. In any event, her departure is a mystery to most of us, and a source of some chagrin to Tony, who had approved an advance of $235 for her—for an "emergency"—just the day before she disappeared.

Losing Lisa is a little anticlimactic in the wake of Tyrone's death. She was not well liked by most on the team; her sharp mouth and a reputation for dishonesty kept people on their guard around her. Tyrone was her best friend on the team. She also was friendly with Tracy, however, who bemoans the loss of her "buddy." Amy says she misses Lisa's loud voice; David grieves over the further reduction in our numbers.

I feel more relieved than sad that Lisa is gone; she made me uncomfortable. But I wonder how the team has been changed by her departure. She and Tyrone are like two parts of a machine we never had a chance fully to assemble.

On the team and within the corps, I hear little talk or speculation about what precipitated Tyrone's murder. I sometimes feel as if to ask why it happened is to suggest that Tyrone did something to cause his death. Tiajuana thinks perhaps the bullets were meant for another boy who lived upstairs and wore a red jacket like the one Tyrone had on when he was killed. His brother Sparticus thinks it sprang from an argument over a girl.

The newspapers said police had "no motive and no suspect" in the killing. I go to see Lieutenant Detective Edward J. McNelley, head of the Boston police's homicide squad. Detective McNelley says he can't give me any information about a murder that is "under investigation." He reads to me from the police report: "11:27 P.M. . . . radio call . . . corner of Wardman and Westminster streets . . . bleeding from the head . . . taken to Brigham and Women's . . . pronounced dead at 12:05 A.M." All this information appeared in the newspaper.

"Do you have any leads? Any witnesses?"

"I'm sure there were a lot of witnesses," he says. "Nobody who will tell us anything. Obviously, people who know him, who hang with him, know why it happened. Things don't happen on the street without people knowing why."

Lieutenant McNelley has a lot of other information for me, statistics that he updates daily. Tyrone was the 111th person murdered in Boston so far this year. Seventy-three of the victims were black or Hispanic males; eighty of them were aged thirty or younger; thirty-nine were between nineteen and twenty-four.

The homicide department is understaffed and overworked, he says. And this thing—this rising tide of homicides—is overwhelming. I believe him. He does look overwhelmed.

He asks me what I knew about Tyrone. I tell him about City Year.

"City Year . . . City Year," he murmurs. "So that's what that is. One of their hats turned up in one of the cars. We were wondering what it was."

Tyrone's hat, I suppose, picked up by a police officer from where it lay on the pavement near his body that night. Shouldn't it have been held as evidence? I wonder. What if it had belonged not to him but to his killer?

The funeral is on Wednesday evening, a week after Tyrone's death. We are dismissed from work early that day, and Tony gathers the team quickly together before we part to encourage us to go to the funeral if we want to, but he also warns us that it could be painful. Nobody should feel obliged to attend, he says.

June asks me for a ride to the service and so, after going home to change from my uniform into a dress, I drop by the headquarters to pick her up. I find her sitting primly on a couch in a black taffeta dress, a look of terror on her face. "I never went to funeral before," she says. "I not know what to do."

"Don't worry," I tell her. "We'll stick together."

Taking along another girl who needs a ride as well, we drive to Bullock's Funeral Home on Blue Hill Avenue, at the edge of Roxbury. It is still light when we leave the office, but it is dark by the time we arrive. We are early and only a few of the others are there, Tracy among them. I want to wait a bit in the outer rooms of the funeral parlor until the place has filled up, but June is already tugging ahead. She goes into the sanctuary and marches right up the aisle as if drawn magnetically to the casket. I follow, and we kneel and look in together.

For me, as for June, it is my first glimpse into a casket. To see Tyrone again is strange, and comforting. A pink, gauzy veil, like mosquito netting, hangs across the open lid, creating a dreamy effect. Behind the gauze, Tyrone's face is waxy and his features seem heightened, exaggerated. His taut skin and his big eyes, closed peacefully, make him look far younger than I remember him. But seeing him there seems suddenly to bring my memories into focus. I want to stay there, to stare and stare and memorize each feature of his face. I glance at June, who also appears entranced, leaning forward over the edge of the casket. A line has formed behind us. I stand and turn back toward the rows of benches. June follows, with a regretful look back over her shoulder at Tyrone.

We sit near the front and watch the line of mourners creep by. Tony looks thin and shrunken but respectful in an ill-fitting suit. Tracy goes up twice. Charles swaggers but when he reaches the casket he hunches over and I can see his shoulders shake. Shortly afterward, he leaves with Amy, who has agreed to drive him home.

The photocopied program for the funeral has on its cover an old picture of Tyrone, apparently clipped from a prom photo—the hair of a woman standing next to him is just visible. Inside is a long obituary written by his mother. "He was a very loving and caring son, and every day seemed like a holiday, especially to his mother."

The funeral proceedings go by for me in something of a blur. Two City Year corps members sing a duet. A minister delivers a tirade about the scourge of violence in the city. Tiajuana sits up front, looking beautiful and fragile; she weeps and moans loudly and calls to Tyrone. With her is the man she lives with, Henry. One row behind her is a man who looks very much like Tyrone: his father, Charles. When Charles Gunn kneels before the casket, he sees his own likeness in his grown son's face for the first time.

Tyrone's four-year-old son, Jamie, is seeing his own father's face for the very last time.

Tony, Charles, David, and Brendan are among the pallbearers at the burial the following day. At Tiajuana's request, they wear their City Year uniforms. Like an honor guard, they carry Tyrone's casket solemnly across the grass through heavy mist. A preacher says some words, then pulls some roses from the flower arrangements beside the grave and passes them around. When Tyrone's casket is lowered into the ground, everyone takes a small, instinctive step forward to watch it sink into the earth. Then it is covered with cement slabs, and Tyrone is gone.

The Greenhouse

Taunton State Hospital is a remote, seemingly idyllic spot, a nineteenth-century institution constructed of brick and green grass, with quiet quadrangles and paths from one building to the next. It is the second-oldest mental hospital in Massachusetts and was occupied originally during the 1860s by a population made up largely of postwar morphine addicts. Now it houses a variety of patients, most of them committed to locked wards by doctors or the courts: people with long-term mental illness, people who are mentally retarded, drug addicts, and female criminals who have been found to be insane.

A place for healing, and yet a place of desperate isolation, it is both the perfect and the worst possible setting for our next project.

Our assignment is to fix up a dilapidated greenhouse on the hospital grounds: a simple structure, built, we are told, by a Works Progress Administration crew during the Depression. It consists of a small brick building with two rooms and a cellar, and two glass-paned hothouse wings. The hospital wants to use the long-abandoned greenhouse as a place where patients can grow flowers and vegetables for recreation and therapy.

During two decades of neglect, the greenhouse has greatly deteriorated. We are to clean out the brick house, wash it down, and paint the walls; putty the windows and scrape and paint their peeling frames; clear the debris out of the greenhouses, weed the garden beds, and remove the shards of glass from broken panes overhead; scrape and apply rustproof paint to all of the iron posts, ribs, cogs, and joints inside the two greenhouses. Professional glaziers will replace the glass.

We are scheduled to work there for three weeks.

While at the hospital, we are confined almost exclusively to one another's company. We cannot walk into town, and the only place to buy lunch is a small hospital canteen where patients who are well enough to have been granted grounds privileges sit watching television or staring into space. During the first week of the project, we have a series of guest speakers who meet with us at lunchtime in a small auditorium in one of the hospital buildings and talk about different aspects of mental illness and its treatment. The information is not directly relevant to our work, but the talks add a stimulating component to the project—at least for some. Charles, Earl, and sometimes Richie take these lunchtime lectures as opportunities to sleep, trying to hide their slumber from Tony by leaning forward in chairs as if simply resting their heads on their hands. But others pay close attention and take careful notes in their journals.

Sometimes what we learn in these sessions seems ironically descriptive of our own feelings and situation.

"Let's talk a little bit about psychosis," says Paul Silva, one of the staff psychologists. "Psychoses include manic-depressive psychosis, schizophrenia, and borderline personality disorder. All of these are major, major illnesses and they all produce major dysfunctions."

We learn, for instance, that manic-depressive psychosis is characterized by periods of extreme activity, fast talking, and feelings of power, followed by periods of depression and listlessness.

I think of Charles, who, just minutes earlier, was whirling dizzily about the room. Now he is utterly still, elbows on his knees, his chin in his hands.

Silva goes on to talk about other personality disorders. Brendan raises his hand to ask a question. "From what you just said, I could fit into all of these categories," he says. "I could be any one of these things." Some of the others nod anxiously.

Many kinds of mental illness, Silva explains, involve extremes of feelings or behavior that people who do not suffer from mental illness feel as well. The difference is in the degree. Brendan is reassured, if not entirely convinced.

In some ways the entire team appears to have been gripped by a kind of collective manic-depressive reaction. Both individually and as a group we suffer wide and sudden mood swings, and our performance at work is unpredictable. One day we seem to work smoothly and well, but the next will be filled with crises and setbacks—paint spilled, tools broken or lost, sudden angry outbursts. Our attendance rate is the worst in the corps. Tracy, in particular, is missing work with alarming frequency. "I just can't get up," she complains. I know the feeling. Since Tyrone's death, there have been several nights when I tossed anxiously in my bed, reluctantly alert. The day we learned Tyrone had been killed was the first day of work I skipped in five weeks, but in the two weeks since then I have missed others—three days or more, for no other reason than that I could not bring myself to come in.

Mourning is a complex process, and it is clear that missing Tyrone is only one ingredient in the murky swamp that has enveloped the team. For some, the grief was intense but short-lived; for others it brought on great swells of pain that rose like a dark midnight tide, relentless, urgent, and strong.

One reaction we all share is irritability. There are quarrels, and long silences. We play the radio to mask the need for conversation. We work, and work is often soothing.

I work, and watch, and continue to learn about the people on my team.

Alison seems to enjoy working alone best. She seeks out the more skilled assignments—puttying a large, latticed window, for instance—and works on her own for hours in a trance of concentration.

"I know I shouldn't avoid people," she says. "I wonder whether it's because we're all so different, or just because people who work together all the time are bound to irritate each other?"

Alison is from Cambridge, the daughter of an architect and a city arts administrator. She has been educated mostly in the public schools but transferred from the city high school to an artsy, private school in Vermont in her junior year because her parents were worried she had fallen in with the wrong crowd and her grades were dropping.

Alison was happy to get out of the house. Her father, now a recovering alcoholic, was still drinking in those days, and although she gives few details, she says her family life was painful. In response, she had become fiercely independent and rebellious.

"I became a skinhead," she says. "My head was shaved on top then, with a fringe around the edge. I wore it that way for a couple of years. I guess it was part of the teenage identity crisis. Joining something like that makes things easy. You shave your head, you wear boots, blue or black jeans and a flight jacket, and they accept you. You feel good."

She informs me that there are seven sects of skinheads. "I was in the mildest one—not the white supremacist kind, just the drug-taking kind."

After a while, she got bored. "When my identity crisis was over, it suddenly seemed stupid."

Now, at age eighteen, Alison wears her hair short and spiky, peroxide-blond. It gives her a waiflike look. She wears half a dozen silver earrings in each ear, and a Harley-Davidson wallet attached to her belt with a chain.

She joined City Year after doing a brief internship there during her senior year. She had been accepted at three colleges but wasn't excited about attending any of them. She wanted to take a year and do something productive while she thought more about the future, and she felt she needed some structure. Her parents were not happy about her choice, and told her if she wasn't going to college she was on her own. She moved out and took a cheap apartment in Somerville, which she shared with two other corps members. In addition to City Year, she had two part-time jobs so she could cover her rent and expenses.

She is happy with her choice to join City Year. She loves the diversity; she attended integrated schools but was frustrated by the voluntary segregation among the students.

So far, however, Alison doesn't feel that people on the team are really connecting. Maybe the team just needs more time, she muses, to finish grieving for Tyrone and overcome the chill left by his death. Perhaps then it will begin to feel more like a team.

Charles is not naturally forthcoming with me about his background, and when I ask him questions, he either ignores them, turns them back at me with an insult, or answers them with a studied exaggeration that has the effect of cutting the conversation short. He answers even innocuous questions—"How was your weekend, Charles?"— with an opaqueness that feels like aggression. "My weekend was filled with violence," he answers, casting me a menacing glance. Perhaps I am at fault, in part; perhaps he feels that I am uneasy with him and responds accordingly. But I notice that he is often the same with others on the team.

Still, over time, I learn a fair amount about Charles's background. He is twenty-one and lives with his grandmother in Kenmore Square, near Boston University. He never knew his father, and his mother is "out of the picture," he says. "I feel like she's just another person. That's all I feel about her."

Charles attended public school in Boston and was unhappy there. One day he describes how a teacher used to punish him for misbehavior by making him fill the squares on page after page of graph paper with tiny figure eights. As a child, he was diagnosed as hyperactive and was treated for a while with the drug Ritalin, but his grandmother was uncomfortable with the drug treatment and ordered it stopped.

Charles dropped out of high school sometime in his junior year. He has a three-year-old son.

Prior to joining City Year, Charles served two and a half years in jail for selling drugs. He entered City Year shortly after his release. He has another nine-month suspended sentence, which means he will go back to jail if he fails to check in with his probation officer or is ever arrested. He joined City Year, at the urging of his grandmother, in the hope that it would keep him out of trouble. For him it is a job, and a chance to earn a G.E.D.

I wonder sometimes what Charles would be like if his hyperactivity had been properly treated. Some days he is like a top, with only two modes of operation: inert or spinning out of control.

"Work, June," Charles whispers, sidling over to stand directly behind June, who is sponging dirt off a cement wall. "Work, my little June. My little Orient Express." I am sponging the opposite wall and, listening, I stiffen. Surely June will be offended? But she just giggles and moves away. Charles follows her. "My little wonton soup."

Tony has asked Charles to keep an eye on June today. It is part of his strategy to elicit responsible behavior from Charles. It isn't working.

"Here, let me help you," says Charles. He attaches a hose with a spray nozzle to the faucet of the greenhouse sink and begins spraying the wall June is cleaning. Water goes everywhere. June jumps back with a scream and flees the room.

"Charles!" I yell. "You're getting everything wet!" All our jackets and bags, heaped on a counter, are now drenched.

Charles turns to look and seems to deflate suddenly. He turns off the hose. "I guess I got a little carried away." He goes outside and sits on the stone wall in front of the building.

"We aren't on break, man," calls Tony from where he is at work scraping paint. Charles pretends not to hear. Tony waits for a bit, then walks over to where Charles is sitting. "It's not time for a break."

"I need a cigarette."

"Well, you can't have one."

"I'm tired. I'm pissed off."

"Well, you gotta keep working."

Anger washes across Charles's face. "C'mon man, I ain't a machine."

"If you can't work for an hour without stopping, that's just not acceptable," Tony says with finality and walks away.

Jackie is, by many measures, the most accomplished person on the Reebok Team. She is bright and imaginative and often charming, as well as striking—tall and slender, with clear skin, big brown eyes, and a brilliant smile. Sometimes she talks about modeling. She gets a lot of attention and has an active social life—she likes to recount her dating adventures, which seem to involve a different man each week.

Although her family is not rich, they are comfortably middle-class and Jackie does not try to hide this as some others do. She is proud of her heritage, and tells people that she will be the fourth generation to attend college in her family. Her mother is a dean at a community college, and her father, who died this summer, was retired from the army.

Jackie has always been academically gifted. "I left public school when I was nine," she tells me one day when we are working together shoveling debris from one of the hothouses. "I'd skipped the fourth grade and they put me in with the fifth- and sixth-graders, and even that wasn't challenging. So I went to private school, where I got my butt kicked—academically, that is."

She is planning to apply for admission to a variety of highly competitive colleges next year, and she seems to stand a good chance of being accepted. She attended an elite girls' boarding school, where she earned a straight-A average, scored high on the S.A.T.s, lettered in four sports, and worked for a summer on Capitol Hill. After high school she was accepted at West Point—her father was a career military man—but was unhappy there and dropped out after just a few weeks. She has spent the past year earning an associate's degree at a community college, something that takes most people two years.

But in spite of all her accomplishments, there are indications that Jackie is feeling a little lost and undirected. She has not recovered from the shock of her father's recent death; joining City Year was in part a way to take a year off and regroup.

It's not working out quite as she expected, however. Since moving up from Florida she still has not found a place where she can afford to live. She spent the first few weeks staying at the home of a City Year staff member, and is now staying with the family of another corps member. She complains that she is not getting enough to eat. She is broke all the time and is looking for a second job. She is homesick.

At first, Jackie seemed to be intent on experimentation. She went to parties and she actively explored the city. But Tyrone's death cast a pall on such activities and rekindled some of her grief at losing her father. She is frustrated, bored, and unhappy. Once effervescent and talkative, she is now sullen and sometimes rude to others on the team. She has begun to talk about quitting.

With Tony's permission, Jackie takes an emergency vacation to Washington to visit her sister for five days. Tony shares with me his concern that she might not return.

But the following Monday Jackie runs up, out of breath, and takes her place behind me in the P.T. lineup just as Jon is announcing that it is eight-thirty.

"You're back!" I whisper, surprised by my own pleasure at seeing her back.

"Yes," she says, smiling.

"We weren't sure—"

"I told you! I left my clothes here on purpose so I would have to come back."

The next week, Jackie finds an apartment in East Boston to share with two other corps members. She gets a part-time job as a salesperson in a clothing store. Perhaps she will stick it out, after all.

"Life is hard," June says one day as we work together cleaning debris from the hothouse flower beds. "It will always be hard. This work is hard. I not used to all different people. All my friends from high school are Chinese. They like to smoke, hang out. They don't like to work."

I am spending a lot of time with June these days. She seems to gravitate to me, perhaps because I am easy to talk to. I am drawn to her shyness, but others are not. They are a little offended by her brusque manner and apparent refusal to join the group. Within the team, she has come to seem almost invisible. I wonder how much of the behavior that makes her seem unapproachable—her reluctance to smile, or to look people in the eye—is culturally acquired.

June is Chinese, but grew up in Burma. She came to the United States with her family when she was six years old. She is the third-youngest of eight children. Her family lived for many years in Boston's Chinatown but moved several years ago to Quincy, a smaller city just south of Boston, and she completed high school there.

June cannot remember very much about her life in Burma, except that in a country where there was terrible poverty, her father, a jeweler, was quite well off. Here in the United States, however, he has never learned enough English to return to that profession; he is a cook in a Chinese restaurant.

June feels bound to her parents. They need her around the house, she says. But she worries about her security; her parents are getting old.

June applied to City Year directly after high school graduation. "I work because I need to have the money," she says. She would like to buy life insurance for her parents. She would like to buy a house.

"My mother tells me not to go shopping. I want to save money, but I keep buying things."

As for her life plans, June would like to go to beauty school and become a cosmetician. Or perhaps to work in a clothing store. "The airport is nice," she says. "I'd like to work at the ticket counter. I'd like to see the people who are buying tickets to go far away."

There are other immigrant youths in the corps; they join, in many cases, for an acculturating experience. June, however, seems not to have fully understood what City Year was about when she signed up in the office of her high school guidance counselor; it was just a job.

"June is like a satellite that flew into our orbit by mistake," says Tony. So far, June has given no indication that she likes being here. She says she hates the work. But she shows up dutifully, day in, day out, arriving early despite the long subway ride from her home.

Earl likes to brag. "Back in the old days," he'll begin. "Back in the criminal days, I was always the mastermind. When I was runnin' with the gang . . . we never got caught."

You don't have to be around Earl very long to know he is no criminal mastermind. He is not quick enough, or evil enough. That is not to say that he hasn't been involved in criminal activity; he's had his share of arrests for crimes such as attempted auto theft, breaking and entering, disorderly conduct. He has not served time, however—

he has always been protected by his juvenile status and by the intervention of his mother.

Earl came to Boston from New Jersey with his mother after she and his father were divorced just three years ago, when he was sixteen. She was motivated in part by a desire to remove her son from what she saw as a bad environment. They live in a small house in Mattapan, a mostly black, working-class neighborhood at the southern tip of Boston. Earl gets along with his mother, who works for a family planning agency and is going to law school at night. She lets him keep his own "crib" in the basement of her house, for which he pays her a nominal rent, but she keeps an eye on him.

Earl dropped out of school in his junior year. His mother wants him to earn a G.E.D., so she signed him up for City Year, which she felt would be a supportive environment. He isn't too enthusiastic about the work, but he, like June, is faithful and prompt.

Earl is about six feet tall and thin. He smokes Newports all day, drinks a lot of beer on nights and weekends, and never exercises. His uniform is too big for him and makes him look a little silly, but his face is beautiful, with a wide nose and velvety dark skin. He speaks slowly, in a deep voice. He considers himself a ladies' man. It was a while before I saw how he dresses off the job: fashionable, baggy, pleated pants; silk-looking shirts; top-of-the-line sneakers. I wonder where he gets the money.

People on the team make fun of Earl sometimes. He has grand fantasies of his own importance and he doesn't seem to realize when people are mocking him—he likes the attention.

"Remember that Friday, you know, a couple weeks ago? When I was absent? I bet nothing got done 'cause I wasn't here."

"Oh, yeah, you're King Shit," says Richie.

"Yeah, I am," says Earl seriously, unfazed by the dig.

There is something sweet and steady about Earl, and during these unsettled October days he is becoming, oddly, a kind of pillar of the team. He is always there, always on time, never too enthusiastic but never depressed. His presence has a kind of stabilizing effect on all of us.

Brendan often broods these days, selecting the hardest or most solitary task and then throwing himself into it. He works extraordinarily hard.

Brendan, who has just turned seventeen, is the youngest on the team. He was born in Cincinnati, the only son of parents who each have older children from previous marriages. Along with their Irish, Scotch, and French Canadian blood, both of his parents are part Native American, a heritage of which he often speaks proudly. His father is a jazz musician and his mother stays at home.

Brendan remembers his early years as a time when the family was "dirt poor." They came to Boston when he was two, taking an

apartment in a public housing project. His public elementary school was predominantly black, and the other children picked on him because he was white. He survived by becoming something of a punk, he says, and so he began having troubles in school. In his junior year of high school, his parents separated and he took advantage of his father's new address in the more affluent community of Brookline to enroll in the suburban school there. But his parents eventually reunited in the city, so Brendan had to leave Brookline High. Disgusted at the prospect of changing schools yet again, he dropped out, although he was only three credits from his degree. Like the others on the team who lack diplomas, he goes to the City Year headquarters twice a week in the afternoon for G.E.D. classes.

There are only two people on the team with whom Brendan has good relations. Amy and he are close, and they can often be seen talking earnestly together. And Tony is his hero; Brendan is already standing and walking like Tony and borrowing his phrases. Others on the team, however, regard him as a know-it-all. He is often moody and unapproachable and a little self-righteous. At the same time, he seems vulnerable.

When I first try to get to know him, Brendan says, "Pretend there's one less person when you write your book." Later, he takes it back, but I can't help wondering what made him say it. One less person?

Richie's behavior, never exemplary, is getting worse. His attendance is terrible, and he seems to challenge Tony at every opportunity. Tony doesn't get angry; he just lets Richie know with each act of defiance or insubordination that he has descended another notch on the contract. The contract offers a long leash, and the disciplinary dance is an elaborate one.

"I hate Tony," Richie says vehemently. We are watching a basketball game between corps members and staff. Richie has just come out of the game, breathing heavily, and has flung himself down next to me. He punches my arm, musses my hair, and then gives me a "wet Willie"—a spit-slick finger inserted in my ear. When I ask him why he is abusing me, he replies that he has to do it now because he won't see me tomorrow; he's been suspended. "I hate Tony," he repeats.

"Really? Do you really hate Tony? Or are you just mad you're suspended?"

"I love Tony as a person," Richie answers. "He's a really cool guy. I just hate him as a boss."

"Do you think he's a bad boss?"

"I just hate having a boss. I've had people telling me what to do all my life."

David is from Medfield, a suburban town south of Boston. He went to a private high school with the help of a scholarship granted him because his mother is a secretary at the school. He wants people to know that so that they won't think he is a rich kid.

In fact, he doesn't like to think he fits into any category. He talks often about what it means to be "middle class": growing up in the suburbs, going to the mall or the movies on Saturday nights, going away to camp in the summers. These are all things he looks back on with nostalgia, but which he also thinks are limiting and boring.

David is proud of almost anything that sets him apart from the crowd. He has eccentric tastes. He wears a jacket with a Chinese symbol—the character for "love"—painted on the back, and a silver peace sign hangs around his neck. Tall and slightly awkward, he wears his straight brown hair long, with little attention to style. He listens to reggae music, and he carries with him to work each day an enormous anthology of world poetry, as well as an American Sign Language manual. He dabbles in Eastern religions and philosophies. He has an enormous and seemingly indiscriminate curiosity about the world and an enthusiasm that sometimes bubbles up at odd moments. He is an oddball, but his amiable sincerity and goodwill, as well as the comic relief he sometimes provides, make him liked and accepted, both on the team and in the corps.

David wanted to be friends with Tyrone. He looked up to Tyrone and saw in him an opportunity to learn about a world different from his own. Now that Tyrone is gone, David has turned to Charles. The two are spending a lot of time together, not only at work but also in the evenings and on weekends. They talk on the phone; Charles takes David to parties.

"There's something I really like about Charles," he says, his words tumbling out eagerly as they always do when he is talking about something important to him. His desire to express himself sometimes makes him almost incoherent. "It's something I really can't understand. There's nobody on the team like him. I really respect him and his view of the world. I've learned so much from him. It's gonna split my reality in a lot of ways."

Charles, by now, is in jeopardy of dismissal because of his challenging behavior and poor attendance.

"I'm worried Tony is going to fire Charles," says David. "He's so central to the team. He represents something. A class, I guess, and a kind of person. It bugs me that he could get fired. City Year has set up an idealized system, and before City Year, my world view sort of fit theirs, but Charles's didn't at all. He was in jail a couple of months before City Year. He really wants to escape whatever he was doing, you know. But to expect him to give up his values right away is nuts. I feel, like, him being here is showing that he's changing."

David wants to help Charles avoid dismissal. When Charles is absent or late, David telephones him at home, encourages him and sometimes remonstrates with him. There is a lot at stake for David—not only his friendship, but his hopeful view that someone like Charles can change enough to achieve success.

Tracy has the worst attendance on the team, and one day when she is suspended from work, I visit her in her apartment in Malden, a white, working-class city north of Boston. She lives on a quiet side street of plain, shabby three-family homes. There is trash strewn on the sidewalk in front of her house and a jagged hole in the window of the front entry.

Her apartment is small and tidy, with worn, overstuffed chairs and a bookcase filled with dolls and records in neat rows. There are games—Checkers, Parcheesi, Monopoly—a big TV, with a cable box on top. A kitten is asleep on the couch.

Tracy is a character: big, brash, and outspoken. She is funny and often startlingly honest. But within the team, she has antagonized people with her absences and her nonchalant attitude, and she knows it. Her two friends on the team, Tyrone and Lisa, are long since gone.

"I'm used to having a buddy, you know? It feels like the team is deteriorating. And everybody's got a buddy—except me."

Tracy never knew her father. "My mother was nineteen when she had me," she says. "They were gonna get married. But when he found out she was pregnant, he didn't want to have anything to do with her.

"Me and my mother, we lived everywhere. We moved like twenty times. I was a little brat, a little terror. And when I was eleven or twelve, I started going to foster homes."

Tracy says her mother voluntarily put her in foster care because she was skipping school. She had a series of placements, both with families and in group homes. She ran away from some, and she got into trouble for truancy and shoplifting. When she was old enough to be allowed to live on her own, she dropped out of school.

"I messed up. I coulda graduated from high school. I really want my high school diploma. I want to walk across the stage. That's why it's gonna be good to graduate from City Year. I want everybody to be there."

In September, Tracy had a second job at a nursing home, changing beds and answering night calls. But after missing several days of work, she was fired. Now she is having financial troubles, which she says makes her depressed and causes her to miss work, resulting in even smaller paychecks. She doesn't mope, however—she goes out almost every night, driving the beat-up car she calls her "hooptie" into Boston, where she likes to go to nightclubs. Of course, she is often tired and has difficulty getting up for work in the mornings.

But Tracy says she is determined not to be fired from City Year. "I have to make it through something." She pauses thoughtfully. "They probably think I don't care. They probably think, 'She's been suspended, she don't care, she'll be outta here next week.' But I'm gonna shock everybody. Things are gonna turn around."

Amy has no memories of her Korean birth parents, and no knowledge of her first three years. She was living in a Seoul orphanage when she was adopted by an American couple from Andover, a wealthy suburb to the north of Boston. Her new parents were deeply interested in world affairs, and they had learned to speak a little Korean to help make their new child feel at home.

But it wasn't easy for Amy. She felt she was very different from the other children in her family's wealthy, WASPy town—and from her parents' three natural children as well, who are tall and Germanic-looking.

"My town is a white, yuppie town," she says, "so I was very much in the minority. I grew up feeling very ugly. And a lot of the time I thought I was ugly inside to match."

In reality, Amy is beautiful to look at: small and slender, with regular features and thick, gleaming hair.

Amy's parents separated when she was in high school, and Amy tried to numb herself with over-the-counter drugs: diet pills, sleeping pills, alcohol-laced cold medications. When, during her senior year, her parents divorced, she became frightened about her health and quit the drugs. After graduation she enrolled at Boston University, a large private college.

During her sophomore year, a personal crisis she prefers not to discuss led Amy to become depressed and begin drinking again and smoking pot. She decided to quit school for a while and try to get her life back together.

So far in City Year she has stayed sober. But she has not been happy. Her mood is often gloomy and she sometimes wears a pained expression.

Rather than talking about her troubles, however, Amy listens to those of others. Within the corps, she is popular as a confidante.

"I enjoy making people happy," she says. "I make them happy at the expense of myself."

Right now, she is upset with the team. "Tony, I want off this team," she says. "People aren't coming to work. If they don't care, why should I?"

She vents for a while, and Tony listens patiently. Finally, when she is finished, he offers some advice.

"Look," he says, "this is war we're involved in. It takes total involvement. Not everybody is at your level of maturity. You can be a leader and help them. I know you're already doing a lot. Maybe you just need to pace yourself a bit."

"I can't talk to my family anymore," says Amy. "I can't talk to my friends. Nobody understands what I'm going through."

"This is a kind of death," says Tony quietly. "You're losing a part of the relationships you've been used to. And I know it hurts. But death and life are interconnected. City Year is set up so that personality change can happen. People can remove their protective external sheath. You come here with problems, and you deal with them. And that's painful. But it's worth it."

Tony looks earnestly at Amy, who is rapt at attention. "If I could change one thing about you, you know what it would be?"

"What?" asks Amy, worried.

"Nothing. You're terrific. Don't panic."

"I know," she says. "I'm panicking. I'll try."

"I have a plan," Amy says, a few days later. "We're going to bring the Reebok Team from last place in attendance to first place. I'm going to call Tracy up every morning at six-fifteen and wake her up so she has to come in. She says if I do that, she'll come."

"Do you always get up so early?" I ask. Amy lives much closer to the Fed than Tracy does.

"No. But it'll be good for me. Tracy may not be my favorite person, but if she's willing to try, I'm willing to help her."

When Amy telephones Tracy the next morning, Tracy thanks her. Then she crawls back into bed. She doesn't make it to work at all that day.

Eleven

It's Thursday of our third week in Taunton, and the weather is still warm, so we hold the weekly contract meeting on the grass in front of the greenhouse. Tony begins reading his list of the team's absences, latenesses, and other offenses, a litany that lately has grown longer every week.

"Earl gets a verbal warning for returning to work late from lunch on Friday," he starts off. It is an annoying, common offense. Friday is payday, and many corps members cash their checks at lunchtime and go on shopping sprees before returning to work. On a few occasions, Charles and Tracy have failed to return at all.

"Richie will be suspended for one day tomorrow," Tony continues. Richie is absent, but Tony still spells out his offenses for the team. Part of the purpose of the contract meeting is to encourage group responsibility for preventing individual infractions. "He was out of uniform twice this week. He hasn't brought his journal all week. And I've had some other problems. I've asked him to do things and he's just said no. Plus, he was late twice this week."

With a one-day suspension, Richie is clearly getting off easy.

"Charles gets two written warnings. He came back late from lunch with Earl. He's been falling asleep in lectures, which is rude and unprofessional and reflects poorly on the entire team. And he has not been doing P.T. well in the mornings."

Charles, too, is absent. Perhaps he stayed out today in order to miss this meeting.

"Tracy will be suspended one day on Monday, because of her attendance. She has already missed six days in the month of October. She's on the edge." He casts a stern look at Tracy.

"There isn't really a good reason I've been out," says Tracy. "I've just been very depressed. I don't want to put it all on Tyrone, but there was that, and then there was me and my boyfriend splitting up and him moving out. That's made me pretty depressed. I'm sorry for not being here, and that the rest of you had to do extra work."

No one says anything. Six days in three weeks is a lot of missed time.

"I have something I want to share with all of you," says Tony. He pulls a black book from his bag. "This is Tyrone's journal. His mother lent it to me so that I could read it—and you could read it. Does anybody object if I read some of it aloud right now?"

We shake our heads.

And so Tony solemnly begins to read from Tyrone's journal. I am surprised and moved by Tyrone's words, and it is clear that the others are, too. The words, carefully printed in a slanting hand, have a sweetness and an innocence that jar strangely with my image of Tyrone's weary, hardened face.

> September 24, 1990. Thursday first day of P.T. at 8:30 in the morning in front of the Federal Reserve Bank was wild, crazy, fun, exciting and embarrassing for a lot of people. . . . First day of work. To me we moved . . . rapidly with the energy of 12 mustangs moving through a garden and playground. People walked bye asking us what, where we doing, why and are we getting paid for it. I like my job alot and I'm very proud to have Tony as my T.C. for the Reebok Team. Being on the Reebok Team has been alot of fun for me so far and may every day be fun for myself and my team.

> October 3, 1990. Wensday the day is almost over for us, some of us have to leave to go too GED. The day has been fantastic for us working out in Charlestown. The people we was working for were so nice and kind to us.

> Befor I had left to go to GED we all sat around talking about different teams and comparing them to the Reebok Team. There was know comparison at all. We are not the perfect team nor are we the worst team but at least we accomplish are goals.

"That was the last thing that he wrote," says Tony. "'We are not the perfect team nor are we the worst team, but at least we accomplish our goals.' Those words can be like a motto or a credo for us. I'd like to feel that we as a team are carrying on a legacy for someone who lost his life in this crazy world. I'd like to think that in those moments when we are tired, those moments in the morning when we want to roll over and turn off the alarm clock, those moments when we want to criticize each other, that we will remember Tyrone and that we will think of those words. In the spirit in which Tyrone remembered us, I'd like you to be available to each other when you see each other in moments of weakness. If someone needs a wake-up call, let's help them out. If someone needs help cleaning up, help them out. It's a cold world out there, but if you have five or six people who can help you out in moments of weakness, it will make a difference."

I can see from the looks of contrition and resignation around me that Tony's speech has found its mark. Cast against Tyrone's hopeful words, our troubles and trials seem petty, our ill humor selfish. I think about my own behavior: I have skipped my share of days, nursing my own confusion and anxiety. It is time now to pull ourselves together, both individually and as a team, and begin to move forward.

We sit a few more moments, talking reverently, talking about Tyrone. Then we get up quietly and return to work.

The School

In the course of nine months, each City Year team is to complete a number of short-term service projects, like our work at the Virginia-Monadnock Garden and at Taunton State Hospital, and two longer service projects, one in the spring and one in the fall. These longer projects are known as "flagship" projects and they generally involve "human service" (working with people) as opposed to "physical service" (labor). Each team expects the flagship will be their most challenging project, an opportunity to meet a real human need and to expand one's understanding of the world and of oneself.

The staff tries to build up anticipation for flagship projects. "How can I tell Alan that you're ready for a flagship, when attendance is less than 80 percent?" Tony chides. "Look at your shirt! Would you come in to work that dirty if this was the flagship?"

Tony also tantalizes the team by declining to give us any information about possible project assignments. Everyone knows he has been meeting with the head of project development, Lisa, to discuss plans, but he gives no hint of what is under consideration.

Finally, one day in late October, Tony announces that a decision has been made. We will be assigned to work in the Blackstone School, a public elementary school in Boston's South End.

His announcement causes an excited murmur on the team, as well as a few groans. Some welcome the prospect of working with children in a school. But there are others on the team for whom a school is the last place they want to work.

We have two days of orientation and training to prepare for the Blackstone School project. We spend much of the time in seminars provided by the staff of Boston Partners in Education, Inc., a non-profit organization that has oversight over all volunteer efforts in the Boston public schools.

First we meet with a longtime school volunteer, who tells us about her stultifying experiences attending the Boston public schools as a child in the 1950s; several on the team respond by relating their own school experiences. Amy remembers playing on the slides at her school; Charles remembers sneaking out the back door during class.

We also have a session with an education specialist who hosts a local television show about education and parenting. She is energetic and engaging, and in a couple of hours she covers a lot of territory, discussing issues such as low self-esteem among urban minority children, different learning styles, and the reasons children misbehave, and offering advice about how to deal with certain kinds of misbehavior. It is a fascinating session, and some on the team take careful notes, though it is really too much to absorb in such a short period of time.

Finally, a former school administrator gives us some background information about the Boston public schools. In particular, he describes the changes that have occurred since 1974, when an attempt to integrate the schools through forced busing resulted in massive white flight to the suburbs and a sharp increase in Catholic school attendance, and reduced the public school student population by more than a third.

"Today we have a school system that is seventy-seven-percent minority in a city that is seventy-five-percent nonminority," he says. He goes on to tell us that more than half the students are from low-income families, a fifth require remedial, or "special," education, and 15 percent come from homes where English is not the first language. He describes the political instability in the system, which has seen ten different superintendents in the sixteen years since 1974, and where public trust in the elected school committee is at an all-time low.

The Blackstone School has 900 students, making it the system's second-largest elementary school. It draws its students from neighborhoods with large black and Hispanic populations. The student body at the school is 47 percent Hispanic, 40 percent black, 10 percent white, and 3 percent Asian.

Standardized tests show Blackstone students achieving in the lowest quarter of their age group in the city, we are told. Two years earlier, 20 percent of Blackstone fifth-graders failed to score at or above the third-grade level on reading tests, the cutoff for advancing to the sixth grade. He warns us to beware of thinking that test scores are the only indicators of a successful school. But the school, he says, is up against enormous odds.

"There are tremendous needs out there. And so the schools are asked to do more and more. They have become the social service providers of last resort."

At the end of the orientation we meet back at headquarters with Peri, City Year's education director, for a review.

"What did you learn this morning?" Peri asks brightly. She is sitting up high on the back of a chair; the rest of us are gathered around a large table made from two doors balanced on wooden sawhorses.

"I learned that there are no swing sets in the schools here," says Amy. "No jungle gyms."

Charles scoffs. He is leaning languidly across the table, resting his head on one hand. "Tell me something I don't already know. Maybe *they* learned something," he says, dismissing the rest of us with a sweeping gesture. "I didn't learn nothing. Nothing." He straightens his arm and lets his head fall to the table with a thud.

"You didn't learn anything?" Peri repeats.

"Kids," he mumbles, his face pressed against the table. "I love kids. Got one of my own."

There is a silence.

"Okay," says Peri, getting up and moving to the blackboard. "Let's talk about the project. What are the communities you will be inter- acting with to make the project happen?"

"Teachers," says Jackie.

Peri writes the word on the board and underlines it. "Who else?"

"Parents," says Amy.

"I don't think we'll be meeting too many parents," says Richie with a note of disdain.

Peri ignores the comment. "Okay, what do we know about teachers? Or what do we think we know?"

"Not diverse," says Richie.

"Don't teach," says Earl. "Just concerned about money."

"Poorly paid," says Alison.

"Overpaid," says Charles. "Racist." He begins spitting out words like projectiles. "Selfish. Mean. Uncaring."

Peri cuts in. "I want you to think more broadly now."

"How can you just cut people off like that?" asks Richie, frowning.

"Yeah," says Charles. "You going to apologize?"

"I'm sorry if you felt cut off, Charles. Now let's go forward. Teachers."

"They're nosy," says Earl.

"What kind of teachers did you guys have, anyway?" asks Amy, her voice rising.

"Inner-city teachers," says Richie.

"I liked my teachers," Amy says. "You guys are making me feel like a teacher's pet."

Charles is now resting his entire torso on the table. In one hand he has an apple and in the other a small piece of cardboard that he has folded into a point. He stabs the apple with the cardboard. Then he does it again, and again, and again. From where she is standing, Peri cannot see what he is doing. But Amy and Jackie frown in consternation as they watch him.

The room is getting hot.

"Okay, let's find out what we know about parents," Peri says, pushing on valiantly.

"Irresponsible," says Jackie. "They make the schools do the things *they* should be doing."

Charles jumps to his feet. "Don't say nothing bad about parents." Suddenly everybody is talking, struggling to be heard. Charles backs toward the door.

Peri puts on her most soothing voice. "On this project, there will be strong feelings, because each of the issues that will come up has to do with the entire way we grew up."

"Charles, this is for you," says Amy. "None of us knows what it's like to have a kid. We're talking about experience of our own parents. Our experiences with our parents may be very different from the way you are to your son."

"I don't know how people here can talk about something they don't know nothing about," Charles mutters, sitting back down.

"What you are to this group, Charles, is a resource," says Peri. "Your experience can—"

Charles cuts her off. "I don't want to be a resource. I ain't sayin' nothing more."

There is a dead moment. "Maybe we need to take a break," says David.

Peri looks at Tony, who nods. "Okay," she says. "Ten minutes."

"Charlie's mad at me, I know," says Jackie, when we are standing outside the room. "But it's true! A lot of young parents are irresponsible. My sister's a kindergarten teacher, and sometimes she has to bring home children who are neglected."

We reconvene, and after some initial squabbling, things seem to settle down.

"What are some of the things that could go wrong with this project?" Peri asks, after a while. The question provokes a burst of interest.

"We could hit somebody," Richie says. "Or we could get hit. Those kids are gonna be little hoodlums."

"The kids might not like us," says Alison.

"Sexual abuse," says Charles. The whole team begins shouting things at once. "Teacher resentment." "Our teaching could be in vain." "We could teach something wrong." "Kids could manipulate us." "Not enough to do." "Burnout." "Disrespect."

"What would constitute success?" asks Peri.

"Praise," says Amy. "Or the program continues."

"We could make a difference to someone," says Brendan.

"Kids learn something," says Jackie. "Or *we* learn something."

"It's not like we're going to get a medal," says Richie. "But if we walk through there after we're done, and they remember us, that'll be cool."

The anxiety the team feels over this project is almost overwhelming. Five team members have dropped out of school themselves, and some have strong memories of school as a place where they felt unsuccessful and inadequate. This project could be an opportunity to reconnect with learning, to teach young children something new and have a school experience they can be proud of. But even for those who were successful in school, the idea of teaching is scary. To be caught by schoolchildren in an embarrassing error—to discover that one has confused a trusting and vulnerable child, or has given him incorrect information—how will that feel?

Thirteen

The Blackstone School, a two-story, modern brick structure, occupies most of a city block. When we arrive, it is encircled by yellow school buses—sixty-three in all. They look exactly like the buses of my childhood. Massed on the pavement outside the entrance is a crowd of perhaps a hundred small children. They part for us as we head for the door, and suddenly I feel very tall. Our uniforms make us doubly conspicuous.

A little boy looks up at us and points. "City Year!" he shrieks happily. Others begin to nudge and smile and point. "The City Years! They came back!"

We will benefit, it seems, from the goodwill left by City Year teams who have worked in the school before us. Our uniforms, which have begun to seem tiresome, now make us important.

We are met inside the school by Principal Bill Colom, a small man with a gentle manner. He leads us to an empty classroom and offers us encouragement, and a warning.

"You must demand respect, right from the start," he says. "It will be harder to gain later if you do not demand it at the beginning. Be consistent. If you say something, mean it. If you make a mistake, own up to it. And most of all, learn to say no. It will be hard, because the children are so cute. But it is very important."

"These kids are going to look up to you," adds Casel Walker, the vice principal. "Pretty soon they're going to look like you. They will talk like you. And you have to remember that decisions you make will affect all the children."

Each person will be assigned as a teacher's aide to a specific class. Some will stay with that class for much of the day, and others will leave the classroom for special assignments, such as helping to supervise in the gym, library, computer room, or swimming pool. We will also help out in the cafeteria at lunch, and on the playground. Before school starts, at nine-thirty, we will perform "bus duty," escorting children from the buses to class. The school day is over at three-thirty, which leaves us time to meet as a team at the end of each day.

Tony has provided the school with information about each team member, as well as the ages and subjects each would prefer to teach. Vice Principal Walker used that information to make class assignments. She now leads us through the school, introducing each team member to his assigned teacher and class, and leaving him or her there as the rest of us move on. "Say good morning to our new helper, Jacquelyn Jones," says the teacher in Jackie's class of kindergarteners. "Good morning, Miss Jacquelyn!" the children call out, looking up from their glue and construction paper with curiosity. Amy's class breaks into spontaneous applause when she enters the room.

An hour and a half later, I am in the cafeteria as team members begin to arrive with their classes. They each have to lead their class to the lunch counter, then to the class's assigned table, following the directions of the elderly "lunch ladies"—part-time workers who control the cafeteria with fear and bellowing. The corps members are to remain with the class throughout lunch.

Earl stands a little away from his group with his hands in his pockets. His class appears to be all boys, many of them quite tall. They are unruly and wild. Earl doesn't appear to interact with them yet at all. He calls me over.

"See that kid?" He points to a tall boy who has the three-leaf Adidas symbol razor-carved into the hair on the back of his head.

"He's a hood. I know, because he's just like I was. It's like looking in a mirror." Earl smirks.

Jackie's tiny kindergarteners are swarming around her legs. "No climbing on Miss Jacquelyn!" she says, in a proper teacher voice. She smiles wearily. "I'm alone with these little devils! My teacher's disappeared, they don't have their coats for recess, and I'm supposed to be on lunch now but I left my money in the classroom and it's locked! Help!"

Brendan stops to talk with me on his way into the cafeteria. His eyes are bright with pleasure. "My teacher is really cool. He's not really strict, but the kids respect him. And they like him. There's one kid in the class who's supposedly"—he pauses, searching for the word—"a little loose upstairs. But he's really smart! It's just that nobody's ever paid any attention to him." He walks away with a swagger.

Richie comes in followed by a pack of girls. "Oh, my God," he whispers to me. "One girl was climbing all over me! They asked me if I was one of the New Kids on the Block." Richie grins proudly.

June looks harried. "I want to work with younger kids. These fourth-graders are almost as tall as me." Indeed, a few look taller. "They're too hard," she says, drawing out the word. "I want a different class."

Tracy arrives alone. Her schedule calls for her to take her own lunch break before bringing her class to lunch. "At first I wanted a different class. I went right back to Tony and asked him to change me 'cause I don't speak Spanish and I'm in a bilingual class. I couldn't understand what they were saying! But now I like them. They were all hanging on me. They were like, 'Don't go to lunch! Please stay!'"

David is pushing a boy in a wheelchair. His class includes kids who speak only Spanish and children with disabilities. David is fluent in Spanish, and he is excited about the challenge the class will present. He has often said he might like to be a teacher. He looks at me over the heads of his small crew, grins, and shrugs. "What can I say? This could be my future."

We are given our own office at the Blackstone School. It is not a comfortable room—actually, it's a large stairwell that has been used for storage—but it is for us alone. The Reebok Team office. We gather there at three-thirty, after the children have left.

"How'd it go?" asks Tony.

"I have no problem," says Brendan. "It was cool. My teacher is great. Charlie, Earl, and I did gym. That was good, too."

"June?" says Tony, turning. June examines her painted nails.

Richie speaks up. "Her kids are little hoodlums."

June straightens suddenly, her eyes flashing. "I know!" she says angrily. "Someone threw the corn on my hair at lunch. That made me angry!"

Tony nods sympathetically. "How did it go with your teacher, June?" he asks.

"She's okay, but the kids. The girls are fine, but the boys. They say they don't have any Chinese people in there. I'm the first Chinese people in there. That made me angry."

Amy cuts in. "My teacher just sat me down with kids who don't know how to read and said, 'Read with them.' Then the lunchroom!

I didn't know what I was doing! They're not supposed to talk at the table?"

"Not after the bell," says Brendan.

"Then I had to work in the library. The librarian—he is so rough with the kids. They have assigned seats. Who ever heard of assigned seats in the library? He told me it wasn't worth going after a running kid because then you'll have to go after all of them. It's not my place to say, 'You're completely wrong,' but I'm going to have trouble working with him. And I love reading."

"I would have liked to meet with the teachers beforehand," says Alison. "My class in the morning just played. The teacher was just like, 'Why don't you just . . . play!' My afternoon teacher was really good. Lots of structured activities. They did sign language, talked about the first letter of their name, they had a snack, they had a routine."

"David?" says Tony.

"It was fun," says David. "A lot of the kids are hyperactive. They have at least one fight a day, the teacher said. And there's only ten kids."

"My kids are overall good maniacs," says Earl. "They even smoke in the bathroom."

"Is there any information you need?" asks Tony.

"What's the policy on smacking the kids?"

"Don't. What about you, Charles?"

"I'm the boss."

"Yes, but how's the class?"

"Oh, the class is a zoo. But they'll know better soon."

"How'd it go, Richie?"

"They're wicked cool. I love the kids. The first thing my teacher did, she told me some kids don't know the alphabet. She gave me a piece of paper and said, 'Richie's going to play a game with you.' And left. So I made it up. 'Is there an f in elephant?'"

"That sounds good," says Tony.

"At recess, they played tag," said Amy. "Richie was it. But they were all chasing Richie! Oh, Richie was in his prime."

"I don't know how I'm going to leave this place," says Richie. "I can't even wait to come in tomorrow."

Already the school has lifted everyone's spirits. I find myself smiling as I walk the halls, bending occasionally to talk to a child or stopping to let a class pass by, the littlest ones walking two by two, holding hands, the bigger ones moving through the school as if it were an exercise in Braille, reaching out to touch the walls, the corners, tables, and doors as they walk by. It's impossible to be idle inside the Blackstone School. Everywhere I look, children are calling out for adult attention. The place is utterly absorbing. Perhaps that is just what we need: absorption in something that will take us all outside ourselves. There is no time for reflection here once the first bell rings.

Fourteen

Tracy exhales before sitting down, trying to shrink herself so that she can fit her large knees beneath the tiny desk. No such luck. Unable to scoot the chair forward, she remains seated two feet back from the desk. She sighs and looks at the blackboard.

"Hoy es martes," the teacher writes on the board in a neat, round, teacher's hand. "El día está soleado. Hoy salimos temprano."

At their desks, the children bend their heads and copy the words, slowly pulling their fat, first-grade pencils across the paper. Tracy watches them. She has no idea what the words mean.

"What am I doing here?" she mutters.

A little girl gets out of her seat and pads down the aisle between the desks toward the back of the classroom. As she passes Tracy, she reaches out furtively and touches Tracy's thigh. Her expression is coy, adoring.

Tracy brightens. She leans over to whisper to me. "They're so cute in their little clothes. Look—her little pants are ironed."

The teacher, a plump and friendly woman, claps her hands twice and the children stop talking immediately. "Today we have Miss Danszka again. Can you say good morning to Miss Danszka?"

"Good morning, Miss Danszka," the children sing. Tracy blushes.

"Tracy," she says aloud in her raspy voice. "'I don't like 'Miss Danszka.'"

"Good morning, Miss Tracy."

"Daisy, I'd like you to work with Miss Tracy this morning," says the teacher. The plump girl stands up, beaming, and the teacher turns to Tracy. "Miss Tracy, will you pick one other child to do math with you this morning?"

Tracy rises awkwardly. "Everybody put their head down on the desk." She folds her arms in front of her and puts her face down, to demonstrate. The children obey, but as Tracy walks up the aisle between the desks one little boy keeps peeking, turning his head to look at Tracy excitedly, his eyes pleading. She touches him on the neck and he springs up, grinning. Tracy puts her arm around his shoulders.

Tracy takes a seat between Juan and Daisy at a round table in an alcove at the side of the classroom. The children open their books, which are different. Tracy glances at each book, then turns to Juan.

"Show me how high you can count," she says, pretending to count silently on her fingers. Juan follows suit.

"One, two, three, four, seven."

"No," says Tracy. "What comes after four?"

"Nine," he says, and smiles winningly. His two front teeth are missing.

"No, no, no. Five comes after four. Try it again."

Tracy turns to Daisy, who is trying to add three and two. Tracy holds up her hand and counts off the fingers. "One, two, three. One, two. Now, how many is that?" Daisy stares, then nods excitedly and rushes to write the number in her book as Tracy peers over her shoulder. "Why you write the five backwards? Silly!"

She turns back to Juan, who is counting pictures of baseballs in his workbook. "One, two, three, four, six."

"We're going to get this," she says. "Count again." Juan tries again, several times, never making it correctly past four. His energy and good humor are boundless, but his look is uncomprehending. Finally Tracy decides to show him. She holds up both hands and counts loudly. "One, two, three, four, five, six, seven, eight, nine." But Juan is now looking away, distracted.

Tracy leans over and whispers in his ear. "Come on. What comes after five?" She is pointing to her little finger. He stares at it, frowning, then smiles.

"Five, six, seven, nine!" says Juan.

"Nooo," Tracy is smiling. "Five, six, seven, eight, nine."

"Five, six, seven, eight . . . "

"What comes after eight? You've got it on the tip of your tongue! Spit it out!"

There is a long silence.

"Okay, let's skip the baseballs. How many oranges are here?" Juan successfully counts the five oranges.

"There! You got it! Circle the five." He puts his head on the table and circles the five.

"Okay. Juan? I gotta help my little friend here." Tracy turns to Daisy, who has been sitting quietly. She smooths Daisy's book open and peers at the problem: pictures of beads on sticks. "Which number is less?"

Daisy points to the beads and begins counting. "Uno, dos, tres—"

"No. English."

"One," says Daisy, almost inaudibly. "Two. Three." She looks up at Tracy adoringly. Juan begins to sing, his eyes wandering around the room.

"Four. Five. Six. Seven," Daisy continues.

"Eeeiii . . ." says Tracy, eyebrows raised encouragingly.

"Eight! Nine. Ten."

Juan is stroking his open mouth with his stubby pencil, staring across the room. Suddenly, the pencil becomes a plane taxiing across the workbook page, then taking off and circling around Juan's head.

"Count those balloons!" Tracy says and turns back to Daisy, who is now slumped in her chair, deflated. "You're doin' so good!" says Tracy. "Look! You done two pages already!"

Tracy continues to work with Daisy for a bit, but Juan keeps tapping on Tracy's shoulder. Each time, Tracy takes the bait.

"You're so cute!" She chuckles at his toothless lisp. Juan can't pronounce the number six. "Thip!" She laughs.

Daisy is speeding down the page of her workbook, circling answers in rapid succession. Tracy leans over to take a look. Daisy has answered four to every question. "Why you doing that?" Tracy asks. Obligingly, Daisy erases the answers and circles new ones: four, five, six, seven, eight. Again incorrect. She turns the page and circles all the answers on the left-hand side of the page.

Juan is playing with the pencil again. "Come on, I picked you for a reason!" says Tracy. "You gotta finish!"

She turns to Daisy. "Wait! I gotta help you! I don't want to erase the whole book!"

Juan is counting to himself. "One, two, three, four, five, seven, seven . . ."

Tracy touches his shoulder. "Start again." He stretches and yawns. Tracy frowns, then tickles him. "The next number is eight."

"Eight, eight, eight, eight, eight," he says. "One, two, three, four, five, six, seven, seven, seven . . ."

"What number did I just have you say over and over?"

He shakes his head.

"Come on, honey. All you have is one problem left. You have to do this one problem."

"*No*," says Juan. Tracy turns to Daisy, who is trying to balance her eraser on her head. Juan begins counting again.

"One, two, three, four, five, six, nine."

Suddenly Juan turns to his workbook and begins circling answers, cruising down the page. Tracy steals a peek. "Oh, my God, he's getting them all right!"

Juan finishes and looks up.

"Go like this!" says Tracy. She claps her hands.

On our second day at the school I have lunch with June and her class in the cafeteria. They do indeed appear to be hoodlums, as Richie said. One hefty boy named Theodore keeps jumping up on the benches and yelling, imitating one of the teachers.

June is afraid the class will make her lose her temper. Her strategy for avoiding this is to pretend they don't exist. She sits quietly at the table, a good distance from the children, eating her lunch placidly.

Theodore jumps off the bench, knocking me inadvertently with his elbow. When I ask him to sit down and be quiet, he does not even acknowledge that I have spoken. The class, seated at two adjacent tables, is growing so loud and unruly that I am tempted to stand up and try to do something, but I worry that might make June uncomfortable. Besides, I have a feeling it wouldn't do any good.

I see June again in the afternoon, leading the children out to the buses. "June," says Theodore, the troublemaker. "I didn't finish my math."

I watch closely, wondering how June will respond to this opening, but she doesn't respond at all. She ignores him. This project isn't going to be any better for June than the last, I think.

Tony tells me he is worried about June. He shows me some newspaper clippings she brought him from the want ads. "BROKE???" reads one. "International marketing company seeks 2 CRAZY individuals. If you like $$$, music, and having fun at work, call . . ."

"She asked me to help her make the calls!" he says. Tony has offered to help June find a part-time job to boost her income, but the jobs she wants are full-time jobs. He tried to explain to her that with her City Year stipend raised to $150 or $175, which he can arrange, she will be taking home more money than at a minimum-wage job. And if she quits she will forfeit her Public Service Award. She was unmoved by his arguments.

"She says her parents and her brothers don't like City Year. They don't understand." A couple of days later, June is absent and, for the first time, does not call in. "This could be her quitting," frets Tony. He goes by to speak with her teacher, a short, round, jolly woman with a bad leg that impedes her mobility in the classroom (she has had hip-replacement surgery, she explains).

"She's very shy," the teacher tells Tony. "But she does help them with the math. She likes to do that." Tony brightens.

"I think she's intimidated," he says. "Especially by the boys."

"Yes," she replies. "I can't believe I would get someone shorter than me! And me with my leg . . . " She shakes her head.

It's a Tuesday morning and Earl's class is having a lesson on capitalization, and it's going well. Most of the boys are engaged, raising their hands often to volunteer to come to the blackboard and fix a sentence that is missing a capital letter.

They are more boisterous than most classes; they turn in their seats to talk, they yell out answers, and occasionally a boy leaves his seat unasked and wanders about the room. This is a class of boys with learning disabilities and histories of behavior problems, but the only boy who does not participate in the lesson at all is Daquan, who has pulled his shirt up over his face.

"Mr. Henderson," says the teacher, a young and attractive woman with a businesslike manner. "Would you please go over and make sure Daquan stays with us?"

Without getting up, Earl uses his feet to propel his wheeled chair over beside Daquan. Slowly, the sweatshirt comes down, revealing the signature three-leaf Adidas symbol shaved into his hair. He's the boy Earl referred to in the cafeteria as a "hood."

"I'll beat you up," says Daquan. Earl is silent. "I'll beat you up," Daquan repeats.

"Nobody gets on me," hisses Earl, leaning close. "Especially not you."

"I'll beat you up. I'll beat you up at recess. You just a child."

"I'm a man," says Earl under his breath. Daquan is tall for his age, but Earl is twice his size.

"You a child. How old you? Nineteen? You a child." Daquan continues his taunts. "You been down south? Spend some time in the sun?" Daquan is dark-skinned, but Earl is darker.

"I think I better change classes," says Earl. "Too many nappy heads here for me."

The two continue sparring throughout the lesson. Whenever the teacher looks their way, they act as if they are concentrating on the blackboard, or on Daquan's worksheet. But as soon as she looks away, they start up again, insulting each other under their breath. "You got wide nostrils," says Daquan.

"People say, 'You've got only eight kids, a paraprofessional, and now a City Year volunteer?' " says Earl's teacher. " 'What do you need with all that help?' But what they don't understand is that I could use eight assistants in this class. These kids need a lot of one-to-one attention."

Four of the boys in the class have been in learning-disabled classes—a catch-all term that encompasses behavioral as well as learning problems—since second grade. Others have been bounced from school to school in search of a placement where they will thrive. No teacher wants them. Earl's teacher, in fact, has recently joined the class as a replacement; the teacher who began the year in this classroom has already moved on to a more choice assignment.

The teacher looks at Earl, and comments, in an aside to me, "Sometimes it's more like having another student than an aide, but I like the fact that Mr. Henderson can look at these boys and understand them. They can relate to him. They need a black male."

We meet to review our first week at the Blackstone.

"I want to go away, Tony, I want to go away," moans Richie, slumping back in mock exhaustion. "Make them go away!"

"My class is so rough," says June. "They won't line up. They always pushing. I don't think I can take it." Nevertheless, she is hanging in. I wonder if she has been bluffing in her threat to quit.

"I have a nightmare about this place every night," says Brendan. "A little girl smacked me today."

"Daquan smacked me today, too," says Earl.

"What did you do?" Tony asks.

"I got him in the bathroom!" Earl chuckles evilly. Tony's eyebrows shoot up. "No, no . . . I told him, 'You hit me again, and I snap.'"

"You have to be really careful what you say," Tony admonishes. "These little kids have no allegiance to you. They may seem to like you, but they'll turn you in for something you didn't do.

"I'm really happy how people are dealing with the kids, holding together when they are hitting you, yelling at you, and things you wouldn't tolerate from an older human being. But one of the teachers told me that City Year kids—she didn't know who—had called the children punks. I don't want to get those kind of reports. You have to control yourself all the time."

We go on to discuss Tyrone's birthday. We plan to celebrate what would have been his twenty-second birthday tomorrow with a cake for the whole corps. But what to write on it? Everyone is a little uncomfortable with the event. "This is pretty morbid," says Richie. Nevertheless, it seems like the right thing to do. We decide on "Thinking of you, Tyrone."

Tony goes over contract issues. Alison, David, and Jackie each get a verbal warning for lateness, and Amy gets three. There has been a rash of lateness throughout the corps, coinciding with the arrival of cold weather. The temperature has dropped below freezing, and each morning a crowd of people conveniently arrives just as we are finishing P.T.

Charles gets a written warning for nonparticipation; during a team meeting this week he lay down on the floor and refused to speak. One more warning and he will get a suspension. Earl gets a written warning for cursing in the school. And Richie gets a one-day suspension for leaving work early one day without permission or an explanation.

I'm with Tony later on when he is finishing up some work in the headquarters. He's seated at a computer, typing out a letter to Charles's probation officer. "This letter is to notify you that Charles Jones continues to be a full-time member in good standing at City Year." He thinks a moment. "To date, Charles's performance has been satisfactory, and has met all basic expectations."

He turns to me with a wry smile. "Of course, you say 'all' instead of 'only,' which is what you really mean." Tony recognizes that Charles's probationary status depends on his continued employment. If Charles leaves City Year he will probably go back to jail.

Good, better, best!
Never let them rest!
Until your good is better
and your better is your best!

The children in Charles's third-grade class begin each day standing at their desks and chanting in high-pitched unison. Charles lounges at the back of the room and watches the proceeding with an expression of disdain.

Later, when the teacher, a tall man, is lecturing to the class, Charles ambles up to the front and takes a seat at the teacher's desk. Within minutes, he falls asleep with his head in his arms. The teacher ignores him, although the children stare with curiosity at their sleeping classroom aide. Every so often, Charles awakens, lifts his head, and looks around the room through half-closed eyes, and then goes back to sleep. I wonder why the teacher doesn't awaken Charles, and then reflect that Charles is probably less trouble asleep than awake; with the children, he acts primarily as a bully. Charles does have a role to play in the classroom: when the bell rings for lunch, he stands, yawns, and walks to the doorway to wait while the children line up; then he leads them to the cafeteria and departs for lunch.

Everyone finds his or her own challenges in the work at Blackstone. For some, like June and Earl, it is sometimes a struggle just to get through the day. Others who take more easily to the tasks of teaching and shepherding children find greater satisfaction in the work, though it is equally stressful for them. The children suffer from a wide range of obstacles and problems: learning disabilities, physical handicaps, language barriers, hunger, neglect, and abuse are just some of the things they face each day. Many are emotionally needy and they soak up greedily the extra attention the City Year volunteers offer. Even without a classroom assignment of my own, I come away each day feeling drained, sucked dry by the children's insatiable need for attention. The feeling is stronger among my teammates, who must be available to the same children hour after hour.

But we all feel, as well, the exhilaration that comes with being liked, admired, and needed. Some team members take real satisfaction in watching their pupils improve, or in learning that their teachers value their contributions to the class. Some are fairly blossoming in their new roles as teacher's aides.

David often reads in Spanish to his bilingual special education class of third-, fourth-, and fifth-graders. The teacher has also trained David to carry a boy in the class who is confined to a wheelchair by cerebral palsy.

David spends a good deal of his time working with a boy named Roberto. I visit one day when David and Roberto are working on pronunciation. Roberto, a pudgy, fidgety boy, keeps trying to change the subject. Pockets of activity around the room keep claiming his attention. David gently directs Roberto back to the lesson.

Finally, frustrated, Roberto frowns and looks down at the page. "My name is Stupido," he says.

"No, Roberto," says David. "You are not stupid."

"I work with him until he starts yelling at me," David explains. "In the morning, he liked me. By the end of the day, he'll hate me. Then tomorrow, he'll like me again."

"David is very good with the boys as a male figure," says the teacher, a young woman who has training in bilingual education and in teaching children with learning disabilities. "I can depend on him. I treat David like a little brother. I think he wants to be a teacher later on."

David takes a seat next to a group of girls and begins working with them on multiplication. "How many sets of five do we have? Yes. Three sets of five."

Roberto is not interested in multiplication—only in reclaiming David's attention. He looks at me. "What's his name?" he asks, pointing at David.

"David."

"David!" Roberto yells. "Help me!"

David frowns. "Don't play with me, Roberto. Don't ask her my name. You know my name. And if you weren't fooling around, you wouldn't need help."

"Help me!"

"Try first. If you try for a while, and you still need help, then I'll help you."

When David leads the class to lunch, Roberto shadows him, trying to match David's stride. He doesn't want to let David out of his sight.

On the playground, David breaks up a fight between two boys from another class. "Chill out!" he yells, holding tightly to a little boy who is whimpering and flailing with anger. David holds the boy until

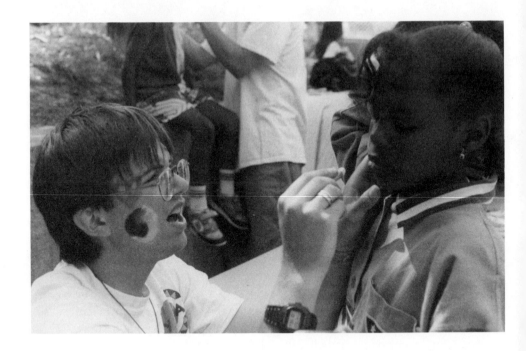

he is calm, then locates the other boy and sits with the two until the dispute has been sorted out.

In the afternoon, the teacher asks David to read to the class. She hands him a book in English, which he quickly exchanges for one in Spanish when she turns away. The children move the desks to the side of the room so they can pull their chairs up close to David as he reads. They talk and are distracted a little at first, but soon all are drawn into the story. David reads with gusto, holding the book up so they can see the pictures. He follows up with questions. "Es una tragedia? Una comedia?" Sitting on a desk before the class, all David's tentativeness and rambling inarticulateness seem to fall away.

Finally he leads the class in a song, "De Colores." He sings joyfully, and the children follow his lead, lifting their voices tunelessly, with spirit.

Alison is assigned to two different kindergarten classes, one in the morning and one in the afternoon. The teacher of her morning class is an older woman, handsome and well dressed (although somewhat disheveled) but with a look of fatigue and a tendency to begin yelling as soon as things start to get out of hand in the classroom. I go along as Alison and Mrs. Gallivan take the class to breakfast—provided free by the school—in the cafeteria. Alison circulates calmly among the children, collecting their cardboard trays and conversing quietly. She is gentle and friendly but not overly solicitous. As we walk back to the classroom, the children compete for a chance to hold her hand.

"I like the boys better than the girls," Alison confides. "Some of the girls are so clingy, you feel like you could be anybody. The boys test you more—they want to find out who you are first."

Over the course of the morning, Alison reads to the children and the teacher leads the class in a drawing exercise. The day finishes with a song. After we have helped the children wiggle into their jackets, hats, and mittens, the teacher calls for quiet and places a record on an old portable phonograph. She drops the needle carelessly in the middle of the song, but the children know what to do. They hold their hands out and follow the directions of a friendly man's voice which tells them to "open them, close them, open them, close them. Give a little clap! Open them, close them, open them, close them. Fold them in your lap."

"I hate these records," Alison whispers. "They're so patronizing!"

Later, Alison shows me an entry from her journal.

Dec. 6. On Monday Cheryl—a very quiet, sad girl with perpetually cold hands in my morning class—and I took a trip to the nurse's office. On Friday she showed me a large cone-shaped swelling on her stomach. . . . I didn't do anything at the time, but on Monday I asked the teacher if she was aware of it. She didn't know about the lump, but told me that she had been badly beaten by her step-mother. She told me about one incident in particular where she was hospitalized last month for a week. Her step-mother burned her really horribly because she couldn't recite her ABCs. . . . I saw her back which is also very scarred and pretty nasty. It turns out the swelling is a hernia. She's only five. The teacher said that after the ABC incident she was placed in a foster home.

The nurse called her foster-mother to ask about the hernia. She told the nurse it was going to be reduced in April. It seems odd to me to wait four months, but the nurse didn't say anything when I questioned this. I feel very badly for Cheryl, and I'm also very angry. It's so disgustingly unfair. I don't know what I can really write about my feelings concerning all this. It's just very sad and I feel extremely helpless and hopeless. . . . The nurse's apathy really pisses me off, as well as her attitude as if I were wasting her time. "Don't bring them to me unless it's an emergency." Well, maybe it wasn't an *immediate* life or death situation, but if I didn't take her there—where? She has a social worker who knows what's going on, but hell I didn't know what a hernia looked like, I still don't really understand what it is, and who's to say a social worker has a clue? Medical advice was needed. Who will advocate for these children?

Alison likes her afternoon class a good deal, and she watches the teacher closely, in order to learn from her. Still, she confides that she feels a little useless; her help is needed more in the morning class. The afternoon teacher, a younger woman, doesn't use records with the children but sings aloud herself, encouraging the children to look at the words, which are handwritten in big letters on a flip chart. The pages are appealingly decorated with hand-drawn illustrations. Unlike the banal, store-bought decorations in many of the classrooms, the walls here are made lively by innovative handmade displays and many drawings by the children themselves.

During a period of unstructured playtime, Alison helps a group of boys make figures on the floor by arranging colored sticks. Another group of boys is playing in the toy kitchen. One offers me "coffee," pouring me cup after cup of the invisible elixir.

There is one boy who plays in total isolation. He extends his small body across a toy truck and carefully inches it around the room, his head down, for the entire play period. We watch him with consternation.

"I wish I could communicate with him better," says the teacher. "He speaks an island dialect that I don't understand. It does appear that he can speak the proper King's English, but he doesn't seem to understand very much."

Alison looks at her. "Even without a language barrier, I don't know how much he would understand," she says. "He doesn't seem to be quite all there."

The teacher is silent for a moment. Then she takes a deep breath and lets the air out in a sigh of relief. "I think I really needed to hear that," she says.

Richie can often be found in the Reebok Team office at Blackstone during breaks, his long legs stretched out with his feet up against the wall, head bent low, reading or writing in his journal. He is very active in the school, and has been assigned two lunch-duty periods each day, which is wearing him out. He lets me see one of his journal entries from that time.

> I got closer to a kid in my class today and a little feeling of reality and futilism from another. One kid, Dave, stole two toys from two other children—one was a toy that a kid, Jon, had borrowed from his brother. And when I approached Dave he hid it and said he didn't take the toy. When I turned, Dave took off running. I went lookin for him and found him on one of the upper floors, I brought him back to the cafeteria and the vice principal came and took the toy and said he was going to keep it 'till tomorrow. Jon started crying that his brother was going to hit him I tried to calm him down but he wouldn't. Finally I just hugged him and he sobbed harder then he just hugged me tight.
>
> I feel that this child has a very unstable home life and that there is something underlining his crying, something besides the toy. Maybe I'm just reading into it to much maybe he is just a kid—but I don't think so. I looked into his records and it is exceptional, his homework is always done and in on time and he gets straight A's.
>
> Dave gave me feelings that $\frac{1}{2}$ of these kids just won't overcome the pressures of the city and the way of life that comes with most who grow up here—screwed values—not much incentive to do the "Right Thing"—and just all around kaos. I mean they see homeless sleeping on streets, drugs being sold and tremendous amounts of violence. When I was that young growing up I never saw a homeless person in the street or a friend killed or hurt over a mistaken shot from a dealer or someone after someone else. It really hurts to think of what those kids have to live with. It takes a hell of a lot more than I had when I was young to overcome this.

I often run into Jackie and her swarm of tiny charges moving from one place to another in the school. She reminds me of a straight and slender young tree among the creeping brush as the children cluster around her.

"Arms out to the side!" she calls out to her traveling band. "Now up in the air!" Twenty-four four- and five-year-olds march along behind her with their arms stretching toward the ceiling. "It's the only way I can keep them from hitting each other!" she giggles.

At recess, I watch her introduce a game of "Duck Duck Goose." She starts with a small group, but soon a horde of forty or fifty children have joined in. She knows what children like and is good at entertaining them without appearing to play favorites.

"I'm referring to these monsters as 'my' kids," Jackie writes in her journal. "This is becoming scary."

> It's funny, but I love my kids. I'm actually going to miss these terrorizers when we leave. . . . Thursday at recess, Javier and I played a secret game of chase. I would walk towards him . . . and he would take off. He's such a sweetie, very intelligent, but often gets into trouble because he is a busy body. Jamie is always good. He listens, participates, a teacher's dream. My little chubby baker. Dora is not quite as moody as she was. Davonne is even tolerable, but she is very fresh/fast. I know she'll be one of the first in her class to do the nasty. . . .

Amy works in a second-grade bilingual class. The teacher, a native Spanish speaker, shifts back and forth between Spanish and English in the lessons. Most of the children understand some English.

Amy is assigned to pay special attention to two boys who are behind in class. José and Antón are both newly arrived in the United States from the Dominican Republic, and neither has ever attended school before. They joined this class in October. They know almost no English at all.

"It's hard for them," says the teacher, "but it's also hard for me. I don't have the time to give them special attention. That's why I asked for a volunteer."

Amy works with José and Antón every day and has become very attached to them. While the class works silently on an assignment at their desks and the teacher sits at her desk preparing a lesson, Amy takes the two boys to a side table to work with them on English. José and Antón are both excited at the special attention. They smile with gap-toothed grins. Amy, usually so solemn, lights up with delight in their presence.

Using a set of handmade flash cards, Amy quizzes the boys on color names. José and Antón race through the flash cards—they know the colors cold and are pretty comfortable with a few other words: *mother, father.* They bounce in their seats and drum their pencils with excitement.

When they are finished, José grabs the cards and points to Amy. "You want me to do it?" she asks. "Okay."

José holds up the flash card with a blue circle on it. "Yellow," says Amy. José looks at the card and shakes his head. He holds it up while she feigns confusion a little longer before giving the correct answer. He holds up the card with the word *mother* on it.

"Father," she says.

José smiles. He puts the card down and shows her the next one, the one for *father.* "Muy bien!" says Amy, laughing.

Of everyone on the team, Brendan seems to me to undergo the greatest transformation in the classroom. He loves the responsibility and absorbs the children's admiration like a sponge.

He begins the morning by correcting math papers from the previous day. Today most of the children get all the answers right, but one boy has four mistakes. Brendan studies the paper to see where Hugo is going wrong. He calls Hugo up to the front of the room.

"You go too fast, you know?" he says, looking at the boy with benign consternation. "You got this one down here right. How come you got it wrong up here? Silly!" Hugo says nothing, but smiles. Brendan works with him for a bit, then sends him back to his seat. "I know you know these, so I don't want to see you up here again!"

Brendan circulates about the room. He is animated, tender, fatherly. He has developed a perfect teacher's voice: kindly and a bit exaggerated. "Let me tell you a secret," he says, bending over two girls who are struggling with a word puzzle. He has charge of a reading group for half an hour each day.

Brendan is also assigned to give extra attention to a boy in the class who is hyperactive. Brendan takes Matt to the nurse each day for his dose of Ritalin, and keeps an eye on him throughout the day. He has developed an arsenal of strategies for helping Matt stay calm and focused. The two have an ongoing arm-wrestling championship match. Out of every few contests, Brendan lets Matt win one. Winning makes Matt happy and seems to have a calming effect on him.

Eventually, June adjusts to her class as well. When I visit her she is helping with a vocabulary lesson. She grabs some paper and a couple of dictionaries and leads three students to a table at the side of the room. They take turns reading aloud and if they don't know a word, June makes all three look it up and write down the definition.

"They need a lot of help," she explains. "I help them, correct the papers. Most of them, instead of 90 percent, they get all wrong. They need extra help. And most of them live with just one parent. It hard for them. They need me."

When we have a quiet moment, I ask June if her thoughts on City Year have changed.

"My parents, they don't understand. They say, 'Why you work for City Year? It takes a long time to save the money for yourself.' But now my father says it's good for training. I worked before at Kentucky [Fried Chicken] but I not work like social worker. At least in City Year you get a chance to know what's going on. I don't know. Maybe I stay until the end."

Fifteen

Charles bursts into our stairwell office, where the rest of us are waiting for Tony to arrive and begin a team meeting.

"Fuck this! I don't care about this program. They be tryin' to dip me."

"Who?" asks Richie.

"Tony. He's doggin' me. I don't even like that dude anymore." Charles catches sight of his cap and dons it with a flourish. Hats are not permitted in the school.

"I don't give a fuck about this shit. I ain't gonna be no kiss-ass, 'cause that's not me."

Charles takes a seat. We are passing around a card for Vice Principal Casel Walker, who has just had a baby. David signs the card and tries to pass it to Charles, who shakes his head and pushes the card away.

"I'm about to steel on Tony," he mutters.

"You'll get busted," Richie warns.

"Those suckers can't put me away," said Charles.

Tony comes in through the passage under the stairs, followed by Alison. Alison is T.C.A. (team coordinator assistant) this week, and Tony has been preparing her to run the weekly team meeting. Each week a different person is appointed T.C.A. All the teams use T.C.A.s, not only to relieve some of the team coordinator's burden, but also as a way of giving all of the corps members a taste of increased responsibility. The job description expands a little with each rotation. Until now, being T.C.A. has primarily meant taking attendance in the morning and running errands for Tony. Taking charge of a meeting is a new assignment.

Alison sits on the floor in the middle of the room. "How are you?" she says, looking around. Nobody answers.

"How's it going, Charles?" Alison and Charles have always gotten along well. Now he stares at her aggressively.

"Why you want to know?"

Alison flushes and her shoulders droop. She looks down at the handwritten list in her lap and goes on with the meeting, trying to ignore Charles. As she talks, Charles leans forward, head in hands, and appears to fall asleep. Finally Alison turns the meeting back over to Tony for a contract discussion.

There is good news for Richie and Earl, who have come in on time each day for a week, erasing the written warnings they received last week. But Amy gets a verbal warning for lateness, and Charles gets a one-day suspension, also for repeated lateness.

"What's up with Tracy?" asks David. Tracy is absent again. Even her interest in her class doesn't seem to be resulting in improved attendance. "Is she almost gone?" We are all aware that Tracy is perilously close to the point of mandatory dismissal on the contract schedule.

"If she's late two days next week, she'll be dismissed," says Tony coolly.

Charles has been brooding in his corner, but now he jumps to his feet.

"I was late because I had something important to do, and I called in, and I get suspended? That's bull."

Tony waits a moment before responding in a calm voice. "If you come in on time, you won't have any problems. It's all within your control."

After the meeting, Charles and Tony go into the next room to hash it out privately. From where I am sitting in the team office, I can hear snatches of their conversation.

"I'm not going to jail," says Charles.

"That's what you think," says Tony.

"If I walk, I walk, Tony. I'm not going to lose sleep over this. Or commit suicide."

"I'm not holding you, Charles."

"I know you ain't holding me. When I want to leave, I'll leave. Why you keep pushing that?"

"Just this, Charles. If you can find a community that is more caring and supportive than this one, then you should go. My time is too valuable to waste on someone who doesn't want to be here."

"This is unbelievable," says Charles. "Seems like you always pick on me."

Charles is waiting to borrow some money from Tony. Charles has been borrowing money from all of us—a quarter here, a dollar there—on a daily basis. Tony puts him off for a bit, but finally hands him the two dollars. As soon as Charles finishes signing for the money, he is off, up the stairs two at a time. Tony calls after him.

"Charles? You're on the edge, man."

The very next day, Charles spends most of the afternoon talking to friends on the school pay phone, missing all of his classroom duties.

"This meeting is coming to adjourn."

"That means it's over!" says Jackie.

"I know what it means," says Charles irritably. He is the T.C.A. this week, and it is his turn to run a team meeting.

"Okay, how are we doing?" he asks. "Go around the circle." Everyone gives a brief report on how things are going in his or her class. "I love my class," says Tracy. "I wish we could stay longer."

Charles keeps the interviews going. But his expression is mock-serious and his voice sarcastic as he asks each team member, "Do you think you made a difference in at least one person's life here?" It is clear he is just playacting, and by this time nobody wants to play with Charles. People offer one-word answers.

When his turn comes, David simply mumbles something under his breath.

"What's wrong?" asks Charles.

"Maybe it's the radio," says David, raising his head suddenly and looking Charles full in the face. David has a small boom box that he used to bring each day so we could listen to music when we were working at the Virginia-Monadnock Garden and at Taunton Hospital. Charles offered him sixty dollars for the radio and David agreed. Charles took the radio home to "try it out," but that was two weeks ago and so far he has not brought the radio back, nor has he given David any money.

One Friday we go with the rest of the corps to attend a program at the Suffolk County Jail. At the entrance to the jail, a fresh new building dedicated just six months earlier, we have to remove all jewelry, hairbands, and hairclips, empty our pockets, and put our things in lockers before passing through the metal detector. Charles hangs back, lingering outside until the last minute.

Once inside, we hear from Bob Rufo, the county sheriff, who offers some statistics on local crime and imprisonment. He shows us a video of a program called "Jailbrake" in which school kids endure mock arrest in an effort to deter them from future crime. Then Rufo brings out two real inmates: enormous, menacing-looking men, armored in muscle. One is white, one black. Both have been in jail a year, Rufo says, and are still awaiting sentencing.

The white man, Eddie, begins to speak, loudly, belligerently, looking around the room and impaling us with his eyes.

"You can't never imagine what it's like in here," he said. "It's violent. I see men every day, big men, crying on the phone to their mothers to get them out.

"Some of you guys have been in trouble. But if you think you're a bad-ass and you can get over in here, just try it. I don't think you'll get over."

"Excuse me," says the other man, James, as he walks over to Charles, who is slumped as if asleep, his eyes half shut. "This ain't your bedroom, man."

Charles does not move.

"You a tough guy," says James.

"Yeah, I *am* tough," says Charles. He smiles a cocky grin, his eyes bright. James stares down at him, then walks away. James keeps his eyes fixed on Charles as Eddie continues.

"We have no pride in here. And what pride we do have, we swallow. Look at me. I'm facing twenty to life. I'm never going to go out on a date. I'm never going to be able to go to the refrigerator and get a Pepsi. I can't even remember what Pepsi tastes like. You see that water out there?" He points to the window, through which we can see the dull-gray water of Boston Harbor. "I'd give anything to be able to go over and touch it. And I never will. You know what I get for doin' this? For comin' out and talking to youse? A couple of bologna-and-cheese sandwiches. And I do it. Because those sandwiches are money in here. You see my sneakers? I didn't buy these nice sneakers. Some dude who was getting out on bail came in wearing these and went out wearing my cruddy old sneakers." He pauses to let us absorb the implication of what he has said.

James is now pacing, walking around the tables where we are sitting. He is so close we can smell his stale sweat odor. Suddenly, he swings around and looks at Charles.

"You think you can come in my house and sleep?" he bellows, then looks around at the rest of us. We are on the edge of our seats. He seems crazed. Charles giggles nervously and James whirls around.

"I ain't laughin' at you, man," says Charles in a small voice. James leans toward him.

"You want to do it right now? Because we can settle it right here. I can break you up, man, and I won't think twice about it. I got nothing to lose. What they gonna do? Put me in lockup? I ain't gettin' outta here, anyway." Charles squirms. "You think you a hard guy. I can tell. But you'll find out. You gonna end up here and I'll be waiting. You think you hard on the streets 'cause you got friends, but a little 110-pound guy ain't nothin' in here."

"One-thirty-five!" squawks Charles.

Finally, Rufo cuts it off. "That's enough," he says, and he and several guards escort James and Eddie out. As he leaves the room, James looks over his shoulder at Charles. "I'll see you in here, boy. Break you up. Punk."

The sheriff comes back. He gestures toward Charles. "James said he sees that young man as a younger version of himself," he says. "And that's sad. Because James is not going home."

One day, Tony surprises Charles asleep in class. This is the last straw. "I'm not inclined to cut him any slack anymore," he says. "He's not trying at all. He's just doing time in City Year to stay out of jail. He's slept through virtually everything important that we've done."

Charles is not only dragging down the team, says Tony, he is making the entire corps look bad. And he is unpredictable. Tony is worried that Charles might do something terrible—hit a child, or worse. "I don't like to send him to jail, but he can't stay here," he says. "I'm going to urge him to resign. If he will resign, I'll let him stay on for a little to look for another job. I can't honestly recommend him, but I can help him look."

Tony decides to take Charles to lunch and delivers an ultimatum. Afterward, he describes to me what happened.

"'Look, Charles,' I said, 'talking to you not as your supervisor but as your friend, I've got to tell you that you're just not making it. I've been getting a lot of complaints from the school: you're sleeping in class, you're talking on the phone too much. This just doesn't seem to be your kind of thing—sitting in class, wearing a uniform. I don't think you're going to make it here. And I think it would be a lot better for you if you resigned than if you got fired.'"

Tony says Charles took it calmly but disagreed. "I'm going to be a totally different person on Monday," he said. "You watch."

Tony is not expecting any big changes.

The following Monday, Charles brings David's radio back. David is ecstatic.

"I think he's changing," he says. "I think in the beginning he was thinking that, you know, I'd forget about it, and one way or another he'd get my radio without paying for it. But he changed and it renewed my faith in him. I think he decided that it wasn't worth it. We had a major breakthrough. He decided that our friendship was worth more than sixty bucks. I think that's really good—you know what I'm saying?—really important. I don't think he's ever done that, given something back."

When he gets home, David discovers the radio is broken.

Richie and Charles give different accounts of the incident that started outside the school cafeteria. Richie says Charles was trying to start a fight because he knew he was on his way out of City Year and wanted to drag someone else with him. But maybe Richie was the one looking for a fight.

It's difficult to tell how it began, because nobody on the team witnessed the initial confrontation. But several on the team were taking lunch in the team office, where the confrontation ended. Tony asks everyone who was there to help piece together an account of the incident.

"Charles came running down the stairs yelling, 'Richie's gonna kill me,'" says David. "Then Richie came. I remember they were swearing a lot."

"They were arguing and arguing," says Earl, shaking his head. "There was *f*'s, *f*'s and *BS* flying. Kids were all coming over and getting in the middle and they kept arguing. I was hoping to see some fists flying, I'll be honest with you."

"The children were asking, 'Why are they fighting?'" says Alison. "I didn't know what to say."

"Charles had a pencil, no, a pen, and he ripped it apart so the ink part came out," says David, his words slowing. He seems mesmerized by the scene that is playing back in his head.

"He said, 'I'm gonna stick you through the throat,'" says Jacquelyn, with excitement.

David goes on: "Richie was like, 'Why do you always have to use tools? You're too small to be talking so big.'"

"Then Charles got very serious," says Jacquelyn.

"Charles took Amy's fork," says Alison. "I remember Amy said, 'I really want to eat my lunch.' He held it like he was going to stab Richie with it. That's when Richie picked up a chair."

David cuts in. "I tried to grab it, but he was strong. Then he threw it, a little to the side, and Charles took off."

"Richie wanted to go after him, but we stopped him," says Jacquelyn. "We were all telling Richie not to worry about it, just forget it, Charles's gonna be out of here, don't worry about it, let him screw up for himself."

So far, everything that Tony has heard paints Charles as the instigator, the more guilty party. Tracy takes a more moderate course.

"That's all that happened," she says. "There was no hitting. It was an argument. There was no fight."

"Really?" asks Tony. "No fight?"

"I think as soon as someone picks up something like a knife, a fork, or a chair, it's a fight," says Brendan.

"The contract prohibits verbal, physical, and emotional violence," says Tony.

"Don't you think you're making this into bigger than what it really is?" asks Tracy. "If we weren't all around, it probably wouldn't have escalated. They were showing off, both of them."

Tony thinks for a moment before responding. "For people to be standing, cursing, brandishing a fork and a chair in the middle of an elementary school with kids watching, that's serious. And I have to take it seriously."

Back at the City Year headquarters the same evening, Tony describes the incident to the rest of the field staff. It is Thursday, and they have gathered as usual for their weekly meeting.

"I went to get a sandwich, and when I got back, I found out the whole roof had caved in while I was gone," says Tony. "There was a lot of cursing, it was ugly, and little kids saw it. It's, like, serious damage control."

Around the table, heads are nodding in sympathy.

"I don't know. They have this image of being the disaster team, of everything happening to them."

"They were just getting over all the other stuff," says Stephanie, another team coordinator. "What are you planning to do?"

"In the case of Charles, I'm leaning more toward dismissal because he was facing suspension already. He's been suspended four or five times already. He could have been dismissed before if I was willing to push it."

"People on the team aren't willing to work with him anymore?" asks James, another T.C.

Tony nods. "Even Earl told him today, 'Why don't you get a job?' when he tried to bum a cigarette. David called him at home because he was absent and they're kinda buddies. He said, 'What are you doing with your life? You're going to get fired.' Most people would get a sense of relief with his absence. The last two days have been good partly because he wasn't there."

Jon, the field director, is already planning a strategic response. "It rubs me slightly the wrong way, the idea of you treating the two of them differently when you weren't there to see it happen," he says. "But with the three days' suspension Charles was already going to get, if you suspend them both two days, it'll take Charles out of the program." He raises his eyebrows and looks at Tony.

Tony answers slowly without looking up from the table. "The thing is, from the stories I'm getting, they say that Charles was more the instigator. It could be a problem if team members feel I'm treating them the same for doing different things.

"Also, I have a problem with saying, 'You're going to get two days off and because of that you're dismissed.' I'd rather say, 'Because of the things you did you're dismissed.'

"I asked them both to come back here and meet with me. I talked to Richie. He said, 'I know I did something wrong. If you're going to fire me, fire me. If I'm going to be suspended, let's get it over with quickly so I don't miss any more days at the Blackstone School.'

"Charles, on the other hand—Charles didn't even show up."

"There's no way Charles is going to make it in this program," says Jon. "It's a foregone conclusion: he's not going to be here after the Christmas break. He physically cannot make up the time he's missed, plus he's a totally loose cannon and he's jeopardizing the entire program."

Charles enters the headquarters, visible through the glass windows of the conference room. Tony heads out to meet him.

"Why are we still taking this guy out with us in uniform?" Jon asks, shaking his head. "He doesn't care about anybody."

Twenty minutes later, Tony returns to the meeting. When he enters, discussion stops and everyone looks at him expectantly. He walks to his place and stands there, gripping the chair.

"The story Richie gave me is corroborated by what everybody else says, and the story Charles gave me is not," he says, looking at Jon as he speaks. "So both Richie and Charles will be suspended for two days. But since in addition it appears Charles is being dishonest, he's going to be dismissed."

"Are we all together on this?" asks Alan, who has joined the meeting. "Do we have a consensus?" Tony looks around the table. Charles is popular with a certain crowd within the corps, and he will be the first person dismissed from City Year this year. Some corps members will likely be angry to see him fired. It is important that all the staff members support the decision and be prepared to explain it to their teams. Each person meets Tony's gaze and nods his or her assent.

Tony breaks the news to Charles a little while later in the privacy of Alan's office. As soon as he utters the word "dismissed," Charles jumps up and runs out of the room to where Richie is lounging with some other corps members.

"Okay, Rich, let's do it!" he says in a hoarse voice. "Let's take it outside!"

Richie rises slowly, as if in a trance, and without looking at anyone he follows Charles down the stairs to Stillings Street. There they finally land their fists on one another with huge, resounding thuds that reverberate up and down the now dark, empty street. "Half-breed!" Charles yells, over and over. They fall and roll together on the pavement.

It takes Tony, Jon, and two others several minutes to break it up. Tony gets his arms around Richie and walks him away, up the street. Charles is still flailing, trying to escape from the men who have him pinned against a car. Finally they capture his arms and twist them behind his back. Charles heaves and wails into the night, his voice breaking into a desperate whine.

Finally Charles is calm and they let him go. He heads off on foot down Congress Street toward the subway, followed by Tony, who wants to complete his explanation to Charles, to make him understand exactly why he is being dismissed. He wants to sit with Charles and give him a chance to vent his feelings and then to calm Charles down, to discourage him from finding a destructive outlet for his anger.

He catches up with Charles. "We need to talk," he says. "Go away," says Charles. "Come on," Tony persists. "Let's go get a pizza. I'll buy."

Silently, Charles assents. "Listen," Tony says. "I had to fire you but I'm not your enemy. I want to help. If there's anything I can do, help you get a job, whatever, let me know. I'll be there."

I end up driving Richie home that evening. He is sure he will be fired for engaging in this second altercation with Charles.

"Just the day before yesterday I was lecturin' this kid in my class about violence. I told him fighting's never the answer. I told him it takes a bigger man to walk away than to fight. And I didn't just say it. I explained it to him and we talked, so I think he understood." He shakes his head.

"What am I going to tell my grandparents? What am I going to tell myself? There goes my chance of being a lawyer. Who wants a kid with nothin' but a G.E.D? I just fucked it all up."

Tony and Jon remain in the headquarters far into the night, talking things over. Charles started the fistfight, they decide. Richie had no choice but to fight. Besides, the fight occurred off City Year property, outside of City Year work hours. No action is required. They know it is a rationalization. But they do not want to fire Richie.

I am relieved by the decision, as is everyone else on the team when they hear the story the next day. We all want Richie to stay in City Year. He is doing so well at the Blackstone School, and working so hard. Conversely, while some on the team regret Charles's loss, they do not protest his dismissal. He has become more than annoying. The morning of his confrontation with Richie, someone stole forty dollars and a bus pass worth an additional thirty dollars out of Jackie's purse in the team office and everyone suspects Charles was the thief. Nobody can trust him, and we are all relieved that he is gone.

"I think Charles decided to go," says David. "He took himself out. During the fight, I think he could tell we were all against him, on Richie's side. Maybe that's when he decided."

At the community meeting the following day, two important events are announced: Charles's dismissal, and President Bush's signing of the National and Community Service Act of 1990.

The National and Community Service Act is the result of years of discussion and debate. It will provide grants to community service initiatives around the country, including youth corps like City Year.

"City Year is a gigantic part of what's going on around the country," says Michael Brown, addressing the corps. "There is no other youth service program like this. There are job training programs but not programs that put young people to work as citizens full-time for a year. There is no program as diverse as this.

"The thing to remember is that you're doing two things at once. The service we're doing is substantive. It's the heart. But we're also leaders for the country."

Perhaps Tony is thinking about the ironic contrast between the two events up for discussion in this meeting: a big step forward for the cause of national service, and a decision to leave behind someone who was unwilling to get with the program. The meeting goes on for more than an hour before Tony finally brings himself to stand and make his announcement. He has already told the team, but it is important to inform the corps of what happened.

"I have some not-so-pleasant news," he says. The corps, buzzing a moment earlier, immediately falls silent.

"As many of you probably know, there was an incident at our work site involving two corps members. They were threatening each other, brandishing various instruments, and it was very ugly. Some of the children in the school observed it. It was a very serious incident.

"Because of that incident, Richie Dale was suspended for two days and Charles Jones was suspended for two days. Based on where he already was on the contract, that suspension resulted in Charles being dismissed from City Year."

A murmur runs through the group. One boy, a friend of Charles, shoots his hand into the air. Tony gestures to him to wait, and continues.

"It's a terrible thing when the poison, the disease of violence comes into this community, especially when some of us are working on violence-prevention education. It's also unfortunate when somebody has to be dismissed."

Alan, seated next to Tony, stands up and cuts in.

"This is a very, very difficult milestone," he says. "We made this decision very carefully. We made this decision based on Charles's overall performance in the corps and not only yesterday's incident. We have standards here, and what we do is of great, even of national significance. We have to maintain high standards in order for this group to function."

The boy who wanted to speak drops his hand. We go on to other topics.

Seventeen

In the days following Charles's dismissal, Richie becomes irritable and moody; his personality seems changed. All along he has relished the role of disciplinarian, and could often be seen trotting some young miscreant from his classroom or the cafeteria to the office. "Maybe Richie should consider teaching," Vice Principal Jim Kirk said one day. "He seems to like it, and he's just firm enough. There's no nonsense." But now Richie is harsher and less forgiving toward the children. Sometimes, I think, he is too firm.

One day Richie's teacher asks him to help supervise another class on a field trip. I go along, as well. We lead the children out of the school and up Dartmouth Street to Boylston, where we all get on a Green Line train. We are headed for the weather station at the airport. By the time we reach Government Center, where we change trains, Richie is fed up with the class. "These kids have already put me in the worst mood," he says.

Richie does his best to maintain order. But it's an impossible task; the class is terminally unruly. The teacher is a friendly, kind woman, but she lacks authority, and the children have grown used to running wild. The day is one long series of disciplinary problems, and each time a child misbehaves, Richie takes it as a personal affront.

"I'm the adult, you're the child," I hear him telling one little boy. A girl asks him about his fight with Charles. "It wasn't a fight, it was an argument," Richie says. "Now go over there and stand with the group."

The team has given some thought to the question of whether we ought to explain to people at the school what happened between Richie and Charles. Some children witnessed the altercation and we thought it might be best to report it to the principal. But after a couple of days passed without any apparent fallout from the incident, it seemed better not to stir matters up with the school administration. Still, the children know about the fight and are curious about it. And what they know is seriously undercutting Richie's—perhaps the entire team's—authority in the school. Richie feels his power slipping from him and doesn't know what to do about it.

Inside the weather station, a technician gives us a tour of the equipment. The children huddle around the banks of video screens as the man describes what each one is for. With twenty-five children in the class, it is nearly impossible to see anything, and it is hot inside. Finally, the guide suggests we go up to the roof to see the rain-gathering apparatus.

"Yea!" the children shout.

"I'm too tired," says one little boy. Richie takes him aside.

"Come on, Kareem. You gotta stay with the class." The others are already heading for the elevator.

"No," says Kareem, and lies down on the floor. The class is out of sight. Richie looks panicked. He glances up and down the hall; nobody is in sight except me. He picks up Kareem and carries him, struggling and shouting, to the elevator.

"I hate this class," says Richie, when the field trip ordeal is finally over. "Bunch of hoodlums. They must be the worst class in the school." And while I know that the class was difficult, I also know that just a couple of weeks ago Richie would have handled them quite differently. He seems angry and demoralized. I can't help wondering if he feels guilty that Charles was fired and he was permitted to remain. In any event, his enthusiasm for our work at the Blackstone School is almost entirely gone.

The week before the winter holiday, City Year holds a big Christmas party in the headquarters. We all dress up for it, and the office is decorated with winking Christmas lights and streamers.

For Richie, the evening of the holiday party begins with a fight with his girlfriend, Diane. They make up and come to the party together, but both are still feeling bruised and angry, and when Richie dances with other girls at the party Diane becomes jealous and leaves on her own.

Richie finds himself standing alone in the street outside the City Year headquarters, angry and a little drunk. He kicks a car that is parked in the street. Then, in a sudden spasm of fury, he begins running down the street, kicking other cars, jumping on top of them and running across their hoods, beating on them with his fists and tearing off antennas.

A man returning to his car spots Richie in the midst of his rampage and summons a policeman, who grabs Richie, berates him, and takes down his name. When the officer has left, Richie returns to the City Year headquarters, where the party is still in progress.

"I don't know why I gave him my real name and address," he mutters. "As soon as they put my name in the computer they'll find out I got a record and they'll put me in jail."

Richie writes out a letter of resignation from City Year and takes it to Michael Brown. Later, he recounts to me the scene.

"He said to me, 'It's been nice knowin' you, and I wish we coulda worked together longer.'" Richie's voice shakes with indignation. "Then I went to Alan and turned in my uniform pants. You know what he did? He asked me for the jacket, too! They were so cold! They want me to quit! . . . I'm gonna be in jail next week, anyway," Richie says with a note of finality.

The next morning, Richie returns to the City Year headquarters and asks to retract his letter of resignation. Alan and Michael consent. He is suspended for a couple of days in punishment for his vandalism. Oddly, no criminal charges have been lodged against him for the incident.

Eighteen

Our last day at the Blackstone School falls on a Wednesday. Tony is tired and pale with exhaustion. It has already been a long week: first there was Richie's rampage and then, on Tuesday, Tony accompanied Tracy to a court appearance on a charge of driving with a suspended license. She had been pulled over while driving her "hooptie" to work. At her hearing Tracy was issued a fine, and Tony helped her gain some time to pay up.

"I'm fried," he says, rubbing his swollen eyes as we gather in our office at the end of the day on Wednesday. "I need a vacation."

The team, on the other hand, is ecstatic. There is a little party in the principal's office, with a cake, and each corps member gets a pin-on star that says "Blackstone Estrella"—Blackstone Star. Most are carrying presents from their teachers, some from the kids themselves. "It's heavy!" marvels June, staring excitedly at the wrapped gift she has received from her teacher. Brendan has a whole bag of goodies: a mug, a calendar, a card, a Smurf, pictures of reindeer colored by the children, and a note, which reads: "Have a merry Christmas and a good life to Bren Dan."

On Friday the team is scheduled to make a presentation to the rest of the corps about the flagship project. Each flagship ends with such a presentation, through which corps members educate one another about social problems and remedies, share ideas, and help other teams profit from their successes and their setbacks, as well as gain experience in public speaking.

Our presentation combines a slide show and other visual displays—including artwork by the children—with individual speeches by the team members in which they describe what made the experience unique for them. In addition, the team has arranged to bring several of the Blackstone children to the City Year headquarters to show them off.

The night before the presentation, Amy, Alison, David, and Brendan stay late with Tony at the City Year headquarters putting together the slide show and the visual displays. Tony leaves at midnight, and Amy stays until three. Alison and David are in at seven-thirty the next morning to finish editing the musical tape that will go with the slides. Jackie and Earl and I also come in early to set up.

Tony takes Tracy and Brendan with him in a borrowed van to the Blackstone to pick up fourteen children. It takes longer than expected, and when they arrive, the entire corps is already seated and waiting for the presentation to begin. When the children finally stumble into the room, many of them dressed in their best clothes for the occasion, the entire corps spontaneously rises to its feet and applauds. The children's eyes widen and they halt in their steps, overwhelmed. Brendan and Tracy urge them forward and the presentation begins.

It is a huge success. Amy begins the presentation by reciting some facts about the school and the neighborhoods surrounding it, and describing in general terms why the team was there. The slides are fun, if a little fuzzy and dark, and the pop music Alison and David have selected ("Young Americans" by David Bowie, to start) goes over well. The children and the team together sing the Blackstone School song ("Oh yeah, I go to Blackstone, / Oh yeah, just watch my style . . . ") to huge applause. Finally, team members take the floor, one by one, to tell their stories, some with children from their class standing at their side.

"The most important thing I dealt with was providing stability for the children," says Jackie. "You had to be with them one-on-one and be their friend as well as be a mentor, someone they could look up to."

"I learned how much of a social service school has become," says Alison. "In the time I was there I had to take kids to the nurse because they were badly beaten, we had to call up parents—it was really upsetting, but it was nice to know that people in the school are trying to do these things."

Earl is embarrassed. "Well I was workin' in the fourth grade and when I was there I helped 'em out, you know, with the reading and the math. They'd always run around. It was fun . . ." He pauses, then sheepishly unrolls a ten-foot-long poster the children made for him. "THANK YOU MR. HENDERSON," it says.

Brendan has one arm around his protégé, Matt, as he speaks. "You can see the hope in the kids' eyes," he says. Matt rolls his eyes and circles a finger near his temple, as if to say, "He's crazy." "You can see it in their eyes when they get that math problem right that they couldn't get.

You can see it in the teachers' eyes when City Year comes in the school—they pop a smile when they see us."

June has two little girls with her, each dressed to the nines. "They love me," she says excitedly. "Everybody call, 'Help, help,' and raise their hand. All want me at one time! They didn't want me to leave!"

David goes last. He reads a passage from his journal:

It is the last day at the Blackstone. The principal came and gave us Blackstone stars and certificates of award and a huge cake. I'm sick from the cake. Another chapter closed, pages we can't go back to. . . . We're all burnt out from here, yet within most of us, hearts want to remain. The road divides, and we are longing to remain with the kids who now know our names.

And so our team goes on. Amy goes to get film developed. Jackie and Alison go to talk with a reporter. Brendan pulls out his noodles and begins to eat. Tony quotes *Scarface*. Richie reads his book and misquotes *Scarface*. Earl lectures us on the non-safety of violence and drugs. June laughs in her own way. Tracy is up at lunch duty dealing out discipline. And so it is for us at the Blackstone: thrown in by our lonesomes, not knowing anyone, forced to make a reputation. And I personally am proud to be among the Reebok Team because the kids respect us. We tell them to stop fighting, and they stop. As long as we speak the truth, the kids gain and foster their respect for us. They respect us because we

have grown to understand their hope and filled their needs and wants.
Thus we and they grow and thrive.

David bows shyly and sits down—to thunderous applause.

I can see from the looks on the team's faces that they know they have done a good job. The presentation was informative, well planned, and heartfelt. Everyone took part, and for some that meant facing down strong fears about public speaking. They are proud of their work at the Blackstone. For a moment, the Reebok Team no longer seems like a group of misfits, magnets for bad luck. Just the opposite: it is a group of winners.

Later, when they are saying goodbye in front of the Blackstone, Brendan's student Matt hands him a picture he drew during the presentation. It is a drawing of a school. At the top of the page, Matt has written:

City Year
Reebok
I love you
Matt

Transition

The month of January is set aside for individual internships, much the way some high schools and colleges have an "intersession" between the fall and spring semesters. During November and December, corps members are encouraged to select from a list of internships compiled by City Year's education director, or to cast about for internship opportunities in a field of their choice. They are required either to work in a public or not-for-profit agency, or to find work that will help them advance toward a career or educational goal. City Year continues to pay their stipends during January.

Reebok Team members spend the month in a wide variety of jobs:

- David chooses to return to the Blackstone School to teach in his old class for one period each morning before going on to a full-time assignment in a men's shelter where he does odd jobs—and collects colorful stories about the people he deals with each day.
- Jackie works in a church, where she does organizational work for a soup-kitchen program, trying to locate resources and wangle donations, making telephone contacts, and setting up meetings.
- Amy works with an organization called Teen Empowerment, Inc.; she helps coordinate programming with people who are running youth organizations across the city.
- Alison works in the children's room at the Cambridge Public Library.
- Brendan works at a recycling program; he is made an "honorary member" of the board of directors.
- Tracy goes to work for an agency that provides home care to elderly shut-ins.
- June works at Tello's, a women's clothing store; she learns to use the cash register, to keep the clothing displays in order, to wait on customers.

- Richie and Earl both failed to do the research necessary to choose or set up their own internship and are assigned, along with several other corps members, to work at an after-school program in Roxbury. The program was started in the fall by a City Year team, and other teams will keep the program running through June. Richie, Earl, and the others staff it for the month of January.

During January, there is no P.T. in the mornings and there are no afternoon team meetings. Everyone reports directly to work at his or her internship site and Tony works in the City Year headquarters. Friday enrichment days continue as usual, so we see one another and have a Reebok Team meeting once a week, but in general January is a period when people think little about the team or the corps and spend time pursuing individual goals. For many, that is a good thing; for some, the loss of peer support is difficult to weather. As a team, we lose a good deal of momentum.

We also lose two more of our members.

Tracy reports that she likes working with old people, and she tells us at a Friday meeting that she's really enthusiastic about her internship, but it turns out that she hasn't been going to work at all. Sometime midway through the month, Tony discovers that Tracy has not shown up since the second or third day and has been forging her supervisor's signature on her time sheets ever since. Tony confronts her, and after hedging for a bit, she confesses. Instead of going to her internship, she says, she has been working at McDonald's, collecting a second paycheck. Tony knows, as we all do, that Tracy is behind on her rent and other bills—she saw this as a chance to catch up. But there is no avoiding the fact that she must be dismissed.

"It's a sad thing for me to fire anybody," Tony tells her. "Even though I am sometimes harsh with you, I will miss you. I hope you understand that what you did was wrong. Maybe you should reassess a little. Think things over. You have a history of problems in jobs. Think about why that is. Think about money. Maybe you can't afford to live alone.

"Also," he says, "I want you to recognize that when you were here you did a lot of good stuff. Remember the work you did at Uphams Corner, and at the Blackstone."

"How about that," says Tracy, with studied nonchalance. "You fire me when I was already thinkin' about quittin'." Then she asks Tony for a letter of recommendation.

"I can't recommend you," says Tony. "I'm firing you for not doing your job."

Tony reports Tracy's dismissal at the next team meeting. She does not return to say goodbye to the team.

June loves her internship. She is doing well, her supervisor reports. She is thrilled not to have to wear a uniform to work each day, and she has a crush on one of the workers in the store. ("He's so nice!" she tells me. "And he's Chinese!") Tony is pleased to see her so happy. Her parents are pleased, as well.

One day June comes by the headquarters and asks Tony for a job recommendation. She wants to apply for a full-time job at Tello's as soon as the internship is over. Tony is crushed. The strides June made during her time at the Blackstone School and the internship have led him to hope that she is beginning to like being in City Year. Now she wants to quit.

Tony reminds June that she will lose the five-thousand-dollar public service award if she quits, but June doesn't seem to care. The award is still four months away, and she wants to work at Tello's now.

Tony speaks with the manager at Tello's by phone, and describes June's situation. He tells him that he thinks June stands to benefit by remaining in City Year. The manager is surprised: he explains to Tony that there is no paid position for June available at the moment, in any event. "She really needs a reality check," Tony tells him. "She seems to respect you. Perhaps you could talk with her."

The next day, the manager tells June in person that he does not have a job for her, and urges her to remain in City Year. But June does not want to continue. She doesn't miss working with the team, she says. Even without the prospect of a job, she wants to quit. She knows that our next project will probably involve physical work, perhaps even working outside in the cold.

"It's hard," she tells me. "I come from other country. People don't understand me. Five more months seems like a long time to do things I don't want to do. And for what? I don't want to waste my time."

We have a little party for June on the last Friday of January. A cake, a little laughter, some hugs, and she, too, is gone.

Three corps members from other teams also leave City Year during the internship period. One is reportedly pregnant; another is dismissed for poor attendance; and the third one, a good friend of Richie's, drops out on account of his drinking. The staff is especially disappointed by his departure; he sought their help and the support of his teammates in fighting his dependence, and was given time off in the fall to go to a detoxification program. But in December he began drinking again, and during the internship period, suddenly free of the daily support and admonishments of his team, he stopped coming to work.

Perhaps because they come at a time when the team is not working together each day, Tracy's and June's departures do not seem to affect people greatly. They were both quite isolated on the team. What concerns people most is the rapidly diminishing size of the team. Amy dreams one night that the Reebok Team gets so small that the staff decides to dismantle it. That old sense of the Reebok Team as the underdogs of City Year is beginning to return.

It is boosted by another incident that takes place one day midway through January.

It is a Wednesday afternoon at the after-school program in a little Roxbury storefront where Richie and Earl are working, and the session is in full swing. The children are playing and doing homework in small groups. Richie is taking a break and talking on the telephone when someone taps him on the shoulder and gestures toward the window. There on the sidewalk looking in is Charles, accompanied by two other young men, much bigger and more muscular than he. Charles is speaking to his companions, and pointing at Richie.

Before Richie has time to think what to do, all three are inside the room, surrounding him. Charles stands back while the other two attack. One holds Richie against the wall while the other pummels him and, as Richie falls to the floor, Charles steps in and begins to kick him. One of the others has a chair raised high and is poised to bring it crashing down on Richie's head when Maura, a City Year staff member, grabs the chair from behind. Frightened of being caught, Charles and his associates run off.

Richie is taken to a nearby hospital, where he is swabbed and bandaged and released. He files a complaint against Charles with the police. He is released from his assignment at the after-school program and spends the last week of his internship in the City Year headquarters, answering phones.

Thereafter, the door at the after-school program is kept locked. Some are worried that the incident will be damaging to the program. But while many parents of the children enrolled hear about the fight, and some express concern, they do not withdraw their children. The program is immensely popular, and working parents in this distressed neighborhood have few alternatives.

Richie has little to say about the incident. He is surly and withdrawn. He is afraid to go out on the street. "He might come after me again," he says. "And if he does, I know that this time it'll be with a gun."

A week or two after the incident, Charles shows up near the City Year headquarters. A staff member spots him and notifies Jon, who telephones for the police. Charles is standing on the street talking with a couple of friends from the corps when the police arrive and take him away in handcuffs. He has violated the conditions of his probation by failing to check in and by incurring the new assault charge, and must return to jail to serve a jail sentence that was formerly suspended. He is sent to Norfolk County Prison and a date is set in March for trial on the assault charge, for the attack on Richie.

A few weeks later Tony receives this letter, written on prison stationery:

> What up
>
> Tony Dara said you had asked abought me well Im doing fine you no.
>
> Wow i kinda messed up agine i got back in to the gang and the Drug selling the hole 9 yards. But it's not that bad i could've got more time than i did. A Do me one thing tell Jhon i said thanks ok for real i needed to be stop because i was out of my mind word tell Him Im sorry for the Dissrespect And thanks for careing abought me not that many people do thanks for being a freind Tony i respect that a hole lot Tony man. Word . . . (turn over)
>
> All right Tony I'll guess this will be the end of this letter. see you later Tony good bye.
>
> PS Tell my homeboy Dave i said hi and tell all the staff member's who believed in me I'm sorry for letting them down and tell Jhon Im reall am sorry peace.
> Charles Jones
> X Fuck up
> belive
> that

Tony is touched by the letter, and surprised that Charles has the insight to thank Jon for having him arrested, but he also views it with some skepticism. "He could be angling for a recommendation from us for early release," he says.

But even if that is true, it is a remarkable letter. The Charles we all saw at work each day would never have had the humility to write those words, no matter what his motivation. Perhaps he was on drugs from the start, I think, remembering his sleepiness and his abrupt mood changes, and only in jail, where he presumably does not have access to drugs, can his human side emerge.

I am startled, as well, by Charles's terrible spelling and syntax. Charles has always appeared to me extraordinarily intelligent, and the contrast between his bright and witty speech and this nearly illiterate document is stark.

How Charles must have hated it in the Blackstone, with the constant fear that the children would uncover his inadequacy. Perhaps he envied Richie his facility with the written word. It must have infuriated him to see Richie lionized while he was becoming a pariah. By contrast, Charles likely felt powerful and appreciated within the structure of a gang. Little wonder he returned to that life.

All empathy aside, however, I and everyone else feel a tremendous sense of relief at the knowledge that Charles is behind bars. We are afraid of him.

Twenty

The Reebok Team needs new blood. That, at least, is what Tony decides, along with the rest of the staff. With only eight of us left on the team, the amount of work we will be able to accomplish in the second half of the year is severely diminished. Besides, there seems to be a critical mass of at least ten people required for a team to generate a high level of energy and enthusiasm. We need more personalities.

Initially, the team rejects the idea of adding new members; anyone who joins now will not have been through any of the learning and bonding and proving experiences we have. They will not have earned the right to be there, say some.

But eventually, with Tracy and June gone and team morale at a new low, the consensus shifts. New people will be good for the team, say some. They will bring new energy and ideas. Besides, each person secretly hopes that he or she will find a friend in one of the additions. Late in January, City Year admits four new corps members. Tony announces that one will be placed on the New England Telephone Team, which has lost two members; the remaining three will come to us.

On January 31, the last day of internships, Tony arranges for us to meet our new teammates for the first time and eat dinner together. We choose the Shanghai Restaurant, the same place we ate the night after Tyrone was killed.

Chris seems at home with us right from the start. When I arrive to meet the team at the headquarters, before we head out to dinner, Chris is already sitting at a table playing chess with Richie. He greets me with a wide, friendly smile that crinkles up his nose and exposes not only his large white teeth but a healthy expanse of gum as well. Twenty years old, he is a sophomore at the University of Michigan. He is taking a semester off to save money. Chris is black and he lives with his grandmother in "The Berry," he says, meaning Roxbury. He has also lived in Detroit, where his mother moved when he was a teenager. His younger brother, Joe, is already in City Year and loves it—it was Joe who convinced Chris to come back to Boston and join City Year when he decided to leave school for a while. Unlike Joe, who is known in the corps as "Buddha" for his rotund physique and shaved head, Chris is an athlete, lean, muscular, and handsome. He played football at school until a knee injury ended his play.

We chat for a bit and discover that we share some history: through a voluntary program—called METCO—that brings minority youths from the inner city to attend public schools in Boston's more affluent white suburbs, Chris attended and graduated from Concord-Carlisle High School, my own alma mater. We even had some of the same teachers. Unlike many of the METCO students of my era, who graduated embittered by the persistent barriers that prevented them from being fully integrated into the life of the Concord schools, Chris says he loved it at Concord. His eyes sparkle when he talks about it.

Chris exudes a sense of innocent delight. Chess game finished, he wanders around the office, checking things out. "Hey!" he says, standing before a world map tacked to the wall. "You guys got a Mercator projection! I got one of those, too!" He turns and smiles, pleased at the coincidence.

Rosa is quieter and more shy—at least she seems that way at first. She is seated next to Chris when I arrive. While Chris and I talk, she keeps her eyes lowered and fidgets, turning a book over and over in her hands. She is pretty and feminine, with thick, carefully styled black hair, tight stretch jeans, and plenty of lipstick and black eyeliner. Nineteen years old, she came to Boston from her native Puerto Rico a year ago to live with her brother. The two of them share a Dorchester apartment with her aunt and uncle and a friend. She doesn't like the neighborhood where she lives; it isn't safe, she says. She misses Puerto Rico.

Since coming to Boston, Rosa has been going to beauty school; she wants to be a model. But at the moment, she needs to earn some money, and she is interested in helping people. Her brother, who works as a youth counselor in a Hispanic social service agency, directed her to City Year.

On this first night, Rosa is not too talkative, but she makes an impression. Richie watches her closely, and I am not surprised to learn that by the end of the night he has asked her out. She declined.

The third new team member, Will, misses the first dinner. We meet him a few days later, just before heading off to Camp Grotonwood (in Groton) for a five-day "midyear retreat."

Will is twenty-two years old, and white; he is tall and handsome with an open face, a strong chin, and wavy brown hair. He recently graduated from Skidmore, a small, private New England college. After graduation, he spent much of the summer touring Kenya—the trip was a graduation gift from his stepfather. Will grew up in Westport, Connecticut, where his mother still lives, but since returning from Africa he has been living in Boston in an apartment he shares with a friend on Beacon Hill, waiting tables and painting houses.

"My stepfather told me about City Year. He read about it in the newspaper. I had been feeling guilty about not doing anything for society, and he suggested that I turn that guilt into something positive by doing something. I decided to apply to City Year."

Will is older than most of the corps members and one of only two college graduates in the program, but his good humor and congeniality make him immediately popular. On the second day of the retreat, he is asked to choose a "word of the day," and the word he selects is *camaraderie*.

At this moment—the January internships have ended and a new "semester" of service is about to begin—a number of issues are troubling the City Year organization. Staff and members alike are concerned about the loss of five corps members in January, and worried that the time spent apart in internships has brought about some disintegration in the corps-wide sense of community built up over the previous few months. They are concerned, as well, about who is dropping out of City Year: many of those who have quit or been fired are minority group members, or from disadvantaged homes, and many are high school dropouts. Their departure suggests that City Year is not entirely succeeding at reaching young people who come from groups traditionally, and euphemistically, labeled "at risk." Their loss is also beginning to threaten the overall multicultural balance of the corps.

In addition, there is a sense of restlessness—even rebelliousness— within the corps. Some of it can be attributed to a midwinter dip in energy and morale, and some of the tension is simply the product of clashing personalities within this intimate group. It is also true, however, that some corps members who were enthusiastic and cooperative in the early months of the year are now beginning to challenge the staff on a variety of issues from disciplinary policy to hiring practices.

Their new assertiveness is, in part, applauded as a measure of the empowerment City Year has encouraged, but it is also a little threatening to the staff. "They are very sensitive to hypocrisy of any kind," says Tony, "and they are pushing in areas where they feel we may not be 'walking our talk.'" One complaint often heard is that the staff is not as racially and culturally diverse as the corps, and that many black and disadvantaged corps members feel there are few people on staff they can relate to. Tony reports a sense of nervousness among the field staff in response to more and more frequent challenges to their authority.

During the internships, the entire staff participates in five full days of discussions—a "plenary session"—in which they revisit events of the first four months, share reactions, and set out goals for the second half of the year. Much of the discussion focuses on streamlining systems to help transform City Year from a sometimes improvisational start-up to a smooth-running institution. Other important goals are set as well: excellence, or "kicking service butt," will be an important theme of the second semester, and great emphasis will be placed on fostering corps members' leadership skills. People hope, it seems, to defuse the unrest some corps members are feeling, not by making substantive changes in the organization, but by refocusing the corps members' attention and energy on the demands of providing quality service.

Many of these goals and themes are introduced in workshops and discussions during the midyear retreat at Camp Grotonwood. On the second day of the retreat we gather in the dining hall to discuss the corps members' written evaluations of the first semester. We sit in rows facing the hall's huge stone fireplace, and Alan and Michael sit together facing the corps. Each corps member has filled out a questionnaire asking open-ended questions such as, "What are City Year's top three accomplishments this year?" "What three things are you proud of personally?" "What have you learned?" and "What are City Year's weaknesses, and do you have any suggestions for addressing them?" Members were allowed to respond anonymously, if they wished.

Now Alan and Michael read the responses aloud. They take turns, earnestly reading every single response. It is an hour before they are through, but nobody appears to grow bored. It is striking to hear how proud the corps members are of City Year and of their accomplishments so far; it is also instructive to hear the criticisms that come out again and again.

People are proud of what they have learned: "that I can be anyone's friend if I want to"; "to care more about people"; "to walk away from a fight"; "to speak up in groups"; and that "you must fight to find common ground, but it is worth it." City Year's strengths and greatest accomplishments are "opening the eyes of the public"; "diversity" (this is mentioned again and again); its "talented staff"; "commitment"; "hope"; "love"; and its ability to help children and young people. Weaknesses include a "gap between the staff and the corps"; a "contrived family atmosphere"; "too much lateness and lying" by corps members; a "lack of minorities on staff" ("corps members need like staff members to look up to"); and a need to involve the Spanish-speaking corps members better. Among the suggestions members make are increasing the stipends, providing housing, and more academic opportunities. People say they were surprised by "how slowly democracy works"; "the staff's dedication"; and by "how people can change."

"Just being around City Year," one person writes, "makes me more relaxed and proud of my generation."

When, finally, they have finished reading all the evaluations, Alan and Michael choose to respond to one of the most common and controversial complaints: the lack of minority staff members at City Year. The full-time staff of twenty-seven includes just three blacks, two Asians, and two Hispanics.

"Michael and I did not have the benefit of a City Year experience when we were your age," says Alan. "And when we went to start City Year, we went to people that we knew. But because of the way we grew up, we did not have friends from the same wide range of backgrounds as you now have. And because of that, the program is not always as good as it can be because the staff do not always understand the life experiences of corps members. Sometimes that creates gaps in communication. We believe that this program will not reach its full potential until a majority of the staff are graduates of the program."

Alan goes on to mention other themes in the evaluations as a way of introducing some of his and Michael's goals for the retreat and the second half of the year. "We have spent a lot of the first semester building the community and dealing with people's personal problems and stuff," he says. "Now it's time to move forward with Project Excellence. We're not going to stop projects in the middle to deal with personal crises or conflicts. You don't have to like everybody on your team, but you have to respect them and you have to work with them, because we have a lot to accomplish. We must put our focus on service."

For the Reebok Team, the retreat is also a chance to get to know our new team members. On the next-to-last day, there is an opportunity to put the "new" Reebok Team to the test: we are to repeat the ropes course with the spider web challenge that so frustrated us in September. Though the place is different, the spider web is more or less the same. The team goes through it smoothly and easily, this time in less than ten minutes.

Building

We begin the second semester on February 11 with high spirits. P.T., which in December was becoming a tedious ritual, returns to life with an explosion of energy and enthusiasm. We line up in sharp rows and bark out the count as we hustle through the routine: running in place, high stepping, stretches, windmills, chainbreakers, cherrypickers, elbows-to-knees, four-count jumping jacks, and so on. We count off each exercise in a joyous crescendo, making the plaza ring with our voices. I sight down the Reebok line. David is so wired with energy, he looks about to spin out of control. Tony, who has shaved off his goatee in honor of the new semester, struts along the line checking us out, his chest thrust forward and his fists clenched at his sides. "I've missed this," he says, grinning.

After P.T. we have our customary team huddle, and Tony leads us in a moment of silence that is just a little longer than usual. Perhaps it is for the benefit of our new team members. Chris, Rosa, and Will look around quizzically, then bow their heads and solemnly join in.

We take the subway to Central Square in Cambridge and walk along Massachusetts Avenue to Pearl Street and the local branch of the Cambridge Public Library, where we have reserved a room for our project orientation.

"This project will be called Cambridge Homeless Services," says Tony, standing to address us once we have seated ourselves in a circle in the bright, carpeted room. He leans earnestly forward as he speaks. "I've put a lot of work into planning this project, and your project sponsors have as well. They are going to tell you what we have planned. This project will last seven weeks."

City Year has a staff member responsible for planning service projects, but keeping six teams busy is an enormous amount of work for one person, and so during the month of January, Tony and the other team coordinators have all tried their hands at planning projects for their own teams. Until now, Tony has shared few details with us other than to proudly refer to his plan as a "work of art."

Now he introduces Linsey Lee, who works for St. Paul's African Methodist Episcopal Church, one of four agencies sponsoring our project. "I've worked with a number of City Year teams," she says. "I'm always amazed not only at the work that gets done but the spirit."

Linsey speaks for a while about the problem of homelessness. There are between three and six million homeless people nationwide, she says, and the majority are families. Children under five are the fastest-growing segment of the homeless population. One expert projects that the homeless population will rise to nineteen million within three years, and yet the federal housing budget has been cut 82 percent in the past nine years.

David, Alison, Richie, Amy, and Will are taking notes in their journals, scribbling fiercely as they try to keep up.

"In Cambridge," Linsey continues, "the Housing Authority has 3,500 families on the waiting list for public housing and just 200 shelter beds for a homeless population that is increasing by twenty percent each year. People are living doubled up and tripled up in small apartments."

Our work over the next two months will be aimed at increasing the number of shelter beds in Cambridge and improving existing shelter space. We will be divided into small groups to work simultaneously at four different work sites. Tony explains that he will change the groups from day to day, to give everyone a chance to work with different people and at different jobs. On one site we are to help rehabilitate a building St. Paul's A.M.E. Church has recently acquired to create an emergency lodging house for families. Tasks will include scraping, puttying, painting, and perhaps installing Sheetrock. A second project will also involve rehabilitation work—more heavy construction. Second Home, a nonprofit shelter provider, is planning to convert a former roominghouse to semipermanent housing for homeless people. Tenants there will pay a portion of their income, if any, for rent, and will have their own rooms but will take part in communal meals and other activities. The idea is to build a stable community for people who have become detached from family, friends, and other support systems.

Dan Dixon, a homeless man, will supervise some of our work there. Dan joins us for part of the orientation at the library. He is neatly dressed in a clean pair of jeans and a plaid shirt, and he has a handsome, bony face, thinning red hair, and sharp blue eyes. He speaks with desperate intensity.

"I'm a Vietnam veteran," he says. "I used to have my own business doing carpentry and painting. I came to Cambridge in 1986 and things were easy then. I got a job and an apartment within two days. I was earning $45,000 a year. But I didn't save any of it."

Dan goes on to explain that six weeks earlier he and his wife split up, and since that time he has been staying in a shelter. He struggles not to weep as he tells us this, and we all listen keenly to his unsettling tale. How does a man like him become totally cut off from his own world?

Besides St. Paul's A.M.E. and Second Home, two other nonprofit agencies will be sponsoring our work: the Salvation Army and the YWCA. At the Y we will be helping to spruce up single rooms that are available by the month at low rates for women, many of whom are in crisis or in transition, and at the Salvation Army we will help supervise a day care program for children of homeless families.

After lunch we tour the sites, starting with the Second Home project, which is called Cornerstone. It is an attractive brick row-house, built in 1875. Pat Reinhart, the project manager, explains that although there are a lot of new walls in the building, we will be tearing them down and starting over, because they are not up to code. Much of the Sheetrock is only half an inch thick instead of the $\frac{5}{8}$-inch board the city requires.

"Why is that necessary?" asks Will.

"It's for fire safety," says Pat. "It takes fire two hours to burn through that thickness."

Will smiles. "I love knowing stuff like that."

The St. Paul's A.M.E. site, called the Hildebrand House, looks to be in pretty bad shape, but Linsey Lee assures us that it won't take as much work as we might think to get it into shape. We will make few structural changes; much of the work that is needed is cosmetic. At the Y we get a brief, comprehensive tour—our work will be auxiliary to a larger renovation project already going on. At the Salvation Army, we stop in and watch a group of small children drawing pictures at low tables. "Will we be able to paint?" asks Chris. "I mean with the kids," he laughs, in response to our puzzled looks.

Tony assigns me to work first at the Y, where we apply a coat of fresh paint to dingy hallways, then at the Hildebrand House, where I spend

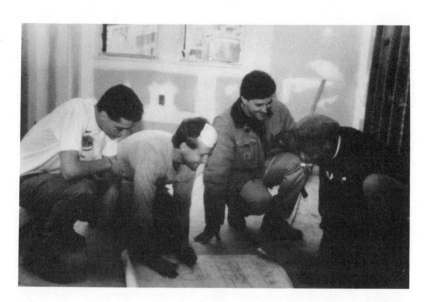

a couple of days helping to clear debris from the basement. Both jobs are demanding, but they do not prepare me for the tasks at the Cornerstone House, into which I rotate two weeks later.

The team has already knocked out all the old Sheetrock and removed some of the studs in places where walls are going to be relocated. They have removed a truckload of debris from a dingy, cavernous basement that is to be converted into a kitchen and an informal sitting room. Already, the gutted house looks entirely different.

I start out working with Earl, Will, and David, dismantling the stairs from the first to the second floor, which are not the proper dimensions to meet the housing code. We pry them apart with crowbars and hammer claws, careful not to harm the antique mahogany railing, which Pat wants to offer to neighbors. Neighborhood acceptance of a shelter is grudging, and she is eager to build goodwill.

Rhythmic crashes are ringing up from the basement, and after a while I venture down to investigate. I find Jackie, Chris, and David clustered around an old cast-iron stove lying on its side on the concrete basement floor. They are taking turns banging at it with a sledgehammer.

"They want us to get it out of here," Jackie explains, pulling down her dust mask to talk, "but it weighs a thousand pounds and it's too big for the doorways. So we have to break it up into pieces."

The task looks impossible. The stove is enormous, and it is not hollow but honeycombed and reinforced with iron struts. It is a hundred years old, Jackie informs me. Once it provided the heat for the entire house, burning coal. Chris is pounding away at it, lifting the ten-pound hammer high overhead and then bringing it down straight and clean, his face set in deep concentration. With each blow, the beams overhead tremble and we are showered with sawdust from between the floorboards upstairs. Sparks fly; but nothing seems to happen to the stove. When Chris finally sits down, however, sweating and shaking, I can see a small hole in the side.

"That's the hardest part," he says. "Getting it started. It'll start to go faster soon."

Jackie raises her mask and takes the hammer. She doesn't have Chris's power, but she throws herself into the task with a doggedness I have not seen in her before. She brings each hammer blow down hard, some landing squarely, others a little wobbly, throwing her off balance. "My arms are going to be so beautiful," she assures herself between blows. Finally a small piece of iron crumbles away.

David yodels and chants as he takes the longest turn, spinning around between blows, fully absorbed in the rhythm of this destructive ritual. He breaks off some more of the stove, and then it is my turn.

The sledgehammer is heavier than it looks. Just lifting it overhead is a challenge, and it comes down with surprising speed. My first shot is poorly aimed and the wooden handle, not the head, strikes the ragged edge of the hole the others have made. My next blow wobbles a little, but at least metal strikes metal. Tremors from the impact go up my arms and into my head and torso, rattling my teeth. I try again—and again, and again. There is no change in the stove. I am determined not to stop until I have broken off a piece. Finally, after ten or fifteen blows, a small chunk of iron comes loose. I put the hammer down carefully and flop onto a pile of lumber, relieved.

The four of us keep up our assault on the stove for the rest of the day. By quitting time my arms are twitching, my hands are trembling, and my thighs and back are cramped and tight. I have not been wearing a mask—neither has David or Chris—and it is an oversight we later regret, as we find ourselves coughing up black grit and blowing black mucus from our noses for days afterward. But we are elated. Such unrestrained labor brings a tremendous sense of release. Besides, we have succeeded. No trace of the stove remains in the basement except a heap of soot in the corner where it once stood.

At the outset, some on the team object to Tony's plan to divide us up at scattered sites. "We've been apart for a month and a half," Amy complains. "Now we need to spend some time working together." But in some ways the small groups seem to promote team bonding. During long mornings and afternoons spent painting at the Y or puttying at the Hildebrand House or cleaning the basement at Cornerstone, we have the opportunity in groups of two and three and four to talk privately, to tell stories, to complain good-naturedly and to get to know each other in ways we could not when we were all working together at Virginia-Monadnock and Taunton, or when we worked individually at the Blackstone School.

During those long hours of absorbing, mindless labor, we learn the little details about one another that give texture and a degree of intimacy to even thorny relationships. Our sense of intimacy increases with our increasing knowledge of each other's working rhythm, eating habits, and moods. And we share information. One day while I work with Amy at the YWCA scrubbing walls, she tells me about the eating disorders, addictions, and other unhappinesses that plagued her teenage years. Another day, when I am working with Will, moving furniture into freshly painted rooms at the Y, he tells me about his chubby teen years, and about his parents' divorce and how he tried as a boy to be perfect, thinking it would help him win back his mother's love. David tells me how hard it has been to give up his veneration of Charles ("He was my connection to the drug world. And I don't *need* a connection to the drug world")—but also that they are still exchanging letters. He shows me a poem that Charles wrote and mailed to him. Earl talks about his new girlfriend, whom he says he really loves, even if he does cheat on her occasionally.

Because we are divided during the day, we establish informal rituals that bring the team together. We all stop at Dunkin' Donuts for coffee each morning, and for lunch we gather at a restaurant in Central Square that offers big sandwiches for little money. More often than not we share, and Earl, who never seems to have any money, ends up eating a little of everyone else's lunch.

Each day we work in different groups, and each day's work results in a strengthening of the bonds that make up the cross-weave of our team family.

As we turn this new corner and begin a phase of greater frankness and intimacy, I begin to see that my own role on the team and my place in the corps is evolving, as well.

I joined City Year with the intention of carving out a place for myself as a dispassionate observer, one who participates in activities in order to get as close to events as possible but who does not play an active role in the human chain of events. I have been listening, watching, and taking notes, keeping my opinions to myself and trying to avoid actions that might alter the course of events. I have especially avoided aligning myself with any person or group. And I have moved freely between the worlds of the staff and the corps, acting during the day in the capacity of a Reebok Team member, but attending evening staff meetings and social events that are off-limits to the corps.

Lately, however, I have come to feel more comfortable in team meetings than in staff meetings, and I am beginning to feel more like a corps member and less like an outsider. My teammates tell me they

feel that way, too, and they frequently urge me to get more involved, to say what I think, to stop being so annoyingly neutral. I begin, hesitantly at first and then with increasing enthusiasm, to reveal some of my personal thoughts. My teammates notice the change and express their relief to me. They feel much more comfortable with someone who is not so guarded.

As I reveal more of myself, I grow closer to my teammates. They are opening up their lives to me in ways that they had not before. Because of my own reticence, they have been holding back—in ways I was not even aware of. I begin spending time with my teammates outside of work. These new experiences are sometimes compelling, sometimes troubling. I am beginning to tap one of the opportunities membership in such a diverse group offers: a chance not only to learn about others different from myself but to enter their lives and share their everyday experiences.

Twenty-Two

When Rosa invites me to a party at her house, I accept with pleasure. But I can't help being disappointed when, a few days after telling me about the party, she hands me an invitation printed on a glossy card:

YOU ARE INVITED TO EXPERIENCE THE MIRACLE OF BEAUTY STRAIGHT FROM NATURE. JOIN ME FOR A FREE DEMONSTRATION OF OUR WORLD FAMOUS LINE OF SKIN CARE AND BEAUTY PRODUCTS. LEARN THE SECRETS KNOWN TO THE WORLD'S MOST BEAUTIFUL AND YOUTHFUL WOMEN THROUGHOUT THE AGES. COME AND RECEIVE VALUABLE DISCOUNTS AND A FREE GIFT.

This is not a party, this is a promotion. The cosmetic equivalent of a Tupperware party.

Still, it might be fun. Rosa assures me that Amy and Jackie are coming, too. Her aunt will make the presentation, but Rosa will help, and will receive a part of the profits. Since coming here from Puerto Rico a year earlier, leaving behind poverty, a mother she says she hates, and a grandfather who abused her, Rosa has been living with her aunt and uncle and her brother. Now her aunt is encouraging her to earn some money by selling cosmetics from the home, as she does. It isn't exactly a career-track job, but perhaps it is a start for Rosa, who is interested in modeling and is not planning to go to college.

I accept the invitation but when I arrive at Rosa's house at the appointed time, nobody is at home. When I call Rosa the next day she sounds stricken. She forgot to tell me that she changed the date. She is so sorry; she hopes I will come on the new date.

A little hurt, I tell her that I might be busy. When the rescheduled date arrives, a Saturday, Rosa telephones me at home in the morning.

"Soo-*sanne!*" she yells—Rosa always yells on the phone. "I'm still having the party tonight. Are you *coming?*"

"I'll try," I say, touched that she has called. She calls again a half-hour before the party is scheduled to begin, and I'm already halfway out the door.

Rosa's house stands all alone on a desolate block in Dorchester, bracketed on either side by lots filled with bushes and thick brush. The street is a neglected, barren place. The trees are spindly-weak and twisted. Even the road is dying: chunks of broken asphalt lie like dry crumbs in the gutter. Nearby, another solo house stands abandoned and boarded up. Looming heavily across the street is a graffiti-crusted brick apartment building, seen from the rear, rising sharply from a weedy slope, its black and grimy windows looking out on Rosa's little home. It's called "The Courtyard," Rosa has told me, and it is notorious for the troublemakers who live there.

A chain-link fence encircles Rosa's house, holding back the ghetto overgrowth and maybe offering some measure of protection from nighttime marauders. Inside the fence, however, things are not much better. The three-floor yellow house is peeling everywhere and in the side yard and in back sits a fleet of ailing cars, rusted and dismantled, up on blocks with open hoods.

In the front bay window on the second floor there is a bullet hole, neat, round, and surgical, lashed with tiny cracks, a single blind unblinking eye.

The Courtyard boys, Rosa has told me, sometimes like to shoot at cars that drive along her street. Apparently, they need the practice; some of them have lousy aim.

Rosa clatters down the stairs to greet me and stands smiling on the landing, toweling her hair. "I'm going out later," she explains. "I still gotta get dressed." She is wearing a T-shirt and tight, torn jeans. Her big eyes, usually ringed with kohl, are unpainted and she looks startlingly young. In this arid place she is a flash of sudden color, like a stray petal in the dirt.

She ushers me up a narrow flight of stairs and into a comfortable room, furnished with a soft sofa and two matching chairs, an air conditioner, and an array of shiny knickknacks. Children are running back and forth, playing hide-and-seek around the chairs, yelling to each other in Spanish. Jackie and Amy are not there but three young women I don't know look up at me with curious expressions from seats around the room. A fourth woman stands beside a table

arranged with rows of colored bottles, jars, and tubes. She has one hand planted jauntily on her hip.

She looks like a carefully wrapped gift: her trim form packed into a Lycra minidress, black stockings and white, high-heeled shoes. Her hair is dyed reddish-blond and secured with a bow. Rosa tells me her aunt Ti-Ti is thirty-eight years old.

"People can't believe my age," says Ti-Ti, smiling coyly. "Somebody today thought I was twenty-six." In contrast with her expert grooming and trim figure, however, her teeth are yellowed and crooked, and her eyes are shadowed by deep, tired pouches.

Rosa introduces me around, then passes out brochures and order forms, which we balance on our knees and peruse thoughtfully. She continues rushing about the room, fanning herself, fluffing her wet hair, and dusting powder on her face with a long brush.

"I suppose I have to do it in bilingual," says Ti-Ti, looking at me with a hint of irritation. She begins in Spanish, then translates into English. "This is the leaf of the aloe plant. It has the power to heal." She brandishes an enormous, fleshy leaf. She squeezes the cut end and a clear liquid oozes out. Ti-Ti rubs the liquid on her hand. Then she produces a small slice of leaf and passes it around the circle, encouraging us to squeeze it and rub the plant juice into our skin. "All of our products are made with aloe," she informs us as we rub.

Now she steps aside to show the tempting array of products on her table. A dozen lipsticks stand open in a rack, fingers of color all protruding, rich and glistening, from their gleaming cylinders. Beauty implements—brushes, pencils, tweezers—stretch fanlike from a flowered jar. Rows of bottles in ascending order, by size. In front, a neat row of little cardboard squares, each bearing a shiny dollop of some cream or other, and each hand-labeled: CLEANSING CREME; EYE BEAUTY CREME; TENDER TOUCH.

"I need a volunteer," says Ti-Ti. Rosa looks over from where she is seated on a stool at the front, examining her face in a hand mirror. "Soo-*sanne!* You be the model!"

"Sí! Suzanne!" says someone else, and two small girls come running up to stare at me expectantly.

I do not want to be the model. I didn't come for a makeover—I am only here to watch.

"Okay," I say.

Ti-Ti's presentation is long and well rehearsed. As she describes each product, she passes around a sample and each woman takes a daub, fingers it, sniffs it, makes a comment. I am instructed to rub it on my face. Cleanser, toner, four different kinds of moisturizer.

"You know how you have thirty-five layers of skin?" says Ti-Ti. "This one penetrates twenty of them." She leans forward, conspiratorial. "It can get rid of stretch marks! It's my most popular product."

Rosa brings in a tray of paper cups filled with pink tropical punch. She has changed into party clothes: a black bustier with rhinestone trim and swinging fringes, a broad-shouldered satin jacket, and a white stretch micro-mini skirt over bare legs. The women make admiring noises. Rosa smiles and passes the tray, bending low so the skirt slips up to her behind, revealing her panties. We all laugh, except for Ti-Ti, who says something sharp in Spanish. Rosa exits quickly.

"Did you tell her it was too short?" I ask.

"I told her I didn't want any competition," Ti-Ti replies. "We're going to the same party."

Rosa returns, wearing knee-length white culottes and white stockings. Ti-Ti nods. She leans over me, stroking on foundation, over and over. She wants to cover up my freckles. Rosa stands behind me, playing with my hair.

Finally, I am done. "Looks good!" says Rosa. The ladies nod approval. Rosa drags me to the mirror. "See?"

I look and do not recognize myself. My skin is smooth and beige, my blue eyes ringed in black, my cheeks war-painted with diagonal purple stripes from ear to mouth. My lips are thick with pink about to drip.

Behind my shoulder, Rosa is triumphant.

I smile weakly. "Wow. What a change."

We fill out our order forms and, of course, I buy things I don't need. Night cream; cleanser; and then if I get the suntan lotion, I'll get a free lipstick. The total is disturbingly high.

Before letting me go, Rosa wants to do my hair. "Please, Soosanne! I love your hair!" Touched, I seat myself and allow her to complete the transformation. She brushes my hair straight back, so tight my eyebrows arch, and fastens it into a ponytail high on the crown of my head. She looks at me proudly. "There," she says, and sends me off into the night.

Twenty-Three

I catch a whiff of stale alcohol while talking to Earl on the MBTA platform with the team, waiting for a Cambridge-bound train. It is a Monday morning. "Yeah, I know," he says when I discreetly mention that he smells like booze. "Tony already said something. I gotta get a cough drop. Hide the smell."

Once we are on the train, Earl crowds up to where Tony, Richie, and I are standing. "Yo, Tony! I can't decide what I should wear tomorrow! Should I wear my white Adidas suit?"

"What's your goal?" asks Tony.

"Not to get locked up."

"Slacks and a shirt," says Richie.

"Maybe I should wear my Carhart..." Earl muses. "I got a hearing tomorrow," he says, flopping down in a seat next to mine. "I got arrested at Downtown Crossing. Trespassing. Back in February. I was drinking in the station, cops told me to leave. One of my friends was writing graffiti on the wall, but I was the only one who got arrested! My moms bailed me out—I think it was fifty dollars. I gotta get that money back."

The next morning Earl arrives at Boston Municipal Court accompanied by Jon, City Year's field coordinator, who is also a lawyer. Earl is wearing his Carhart: a matching, plain brown canvas jacket and pants of the kind construction workers often wear. Earl's case is listed on the docket outside the room as number nineteen of the thirty-one scheduled for that morning. The courtroom is packed, but we watch in silence as case after case is called and set aside because not everyone is ready to begin. A warrant from the governor hasn't arrived; or a prisoner has not been brought up from the penitentiary in Concord; a witness is missing. I am surprised to see how much goes on in the big, gloomy courtroom without any trials actually taking place. Earl waits patiently, his elbows on his knees.

"These benches are hard," I remark.

"That's how they're supposed to be," he says. "They're for criminals."

Finally the bailiff calls Earl's name. Earl stands slowly and hulks to the front, swinging his arms in a show of confidence. The prosecutor stands and asks the judge for a little time to confer with the defense. The judge sends Earl back to his seat.

During a recess, Jon speaks with Earl's court-appointed lawyer in the smoky lobby outside the courtroom. Earl stands with the two men, looking back and forth at their faces as they talk; he says nothing.

"The case is going to be dismissed," Jon explains to me afterward. "It's a tiny little garbage case and the judge will be impressed that Earl showed up for both the arraignment and the hearing, and that he's doing good work. What I'm trying to do now is to get his lawyer to ask the court to waive the fees."

Jon interprets the morning's proceedings. "It's a system of triage, heavily weighted toward the prosecution. Usually the first time a case is called the prosecution is not prepared or the prosecution's witness doesn't show. They're assuming the defendant won't show up. If he doesn't show, he defaults. If he does, the prosecution asks for a continuance and the defendant has to take another day off work to come back to court. They wear him down."

After the recess, the judge begins recalling cases for trial. At twelve-twenty Earl is called. Again, he swaggers to the front. The prosecutor calls a police officer to testify: a young man, white, with a crewcut.

"On the night of February 2, I observed the defendant and others in the Downtown Crossing station. They were yelling and screaming and urinating on the wall. When I told them to leave the station, they gave me some lip but finally they left. I came back fifteen minutes later and observed the defendant back in the station, still behaving in a disorderly fashion. At that time, I arrested him."

Earl's attorney stands. "Your Honor, the defendant is currently working in a program where he helps homeless people and does other good work in the community. A representative of the program was here this morning and spoke highly of the defendant's performance."

"I'm still here!" mutters Jon, waving his hand. "I also wrote a letter of recommendation for Earl," he says under his breath.

The judge asks the prosecutor for his recommendation. "I recommend dismissal, with a requirement that the defendant pay $100 in court fees and a $25 witness fee," says the assistant district attorney. The judge looks at Earl, who is still standing stonily.

"I'm going to dismiss the case," the judge says, looking sternly down at Earl, "on one condition. You must behave in an orderly fashion when you are using the T. Can you agree to that condition? Will you behave in an orderly fashion in the future when you are using the T?" Earl makes an almost imperceptible nod.

"All right. I dismiss the case on that condition, and on the condition that you will pay a $25 court fee."

Earl returns to his seat, looking pleased, if a little sheepish. The fine is $100 less than the prosecution asked.

Outside the courtroom, Jon catches Earl's arm and points to Earl's lawyer, who is hurrying by us. "You should go thank that guy before he's gone." Earl stands still and watches the man leave. "I don't know his name," he says.

The next morning, Earl wears his sunglasses to work to hide his eyes. He has spent the evening drinking to celebrate his victory.

In the weeks that follow, it is obvious that Earl's drinking is getting worse. He is rarely late or absent, but he is groggy and sullen in the mornings. He always wears sunglasses, even indoors. He works slowly and is always tired; he takes a lot of breaks.

Within the staff there is some debate about how to deal with Earl. One team coordinator, a former alcoholic himself, is incensed that Tony does not send Earl home when he comes to work with alcohol on his breath. Tony sees little benefit in sending Earl home, perhaps to spend the day drinking. He has another strategy in mind.

"I talked to Earl's mom, and she said she's worried he might develop a drinking problem. I think I can work this out better with her help." Tony does not say what I believe he is thinking. Earl is not "developing" a drinking problem; he already has one.

Twenty-Four

Alison shares an apartment with two other corps members on the ground floor of a wooden house on an alley in Somerville, a small city adjoining Cambridge that is heavily populated by students, second-generation Irish and Italian immigrants, and recent arrivals from Haiti, Puerto Rico, and Brazil. Alison's neighborhood has some of the lowest rents in the Boston area.

I arrive at Alison's apartment at about nine-forty-five one Friday night. "People say this place eats you up," she jokes as she shows me around the cluttered flat. It is a two-bedroom apartment with the living room converted into a third bedroom to accomodate another person and keep the rent down. It is an agreeably messy place, filled with interesting junk. The walls are decorated with funky posters advertising obscure bands. There is a crossword-puzzle book lying open on the couch. Alison and I have made a habit of doing crosswords together at odd moments—lunchtime, riding the bus. I've been addicted for years, and now I've gotten her hooked, too.

Alison has plans this evening to see a local band called Maelstrom play at the Channel, a nightclub in Boston, and she has invited me to come along. She plays a couple of cuts for me from their record; the music is fast and loud and cacophonous. Alison knows some of the band members, and it is an "18 Plus" show, meaning that anyone over eighteen can be admitted, although to drink you've still got to be twenty-one. I've been to the Channel before: a cavernous place with black floors and walls and a beer slick on the floor. The clientele wear denim and leather, and the music is so loud it can make your ears ring for days.

Alison is wearing black jeans, her usual clunky but fashionable Doctor Marten army boots, a black T-shirt with the collar cut off, dangly earrings, a wide, black velvet hairband, and strokes of liquid eyeliner. I check my own attire: I'll pass.

The crowd at the Channel is scruffy and very young. They wear high, laced-up combat boots, and some of the boys are shirtless. Many have shaved heads. We wander for a bit; Alison sees many people she knows. Their greetings are warm and nonchalant; they all seem at home here.

When Maelstrom comes on we crowd the stage, getting close enough to catch flying drops of sweat as they begin to play. The dancing is fierce and violent; it could easily be mistaken for a brawl. People are pushing and shoving and bouncing off one another, flailing their arms and legs and whirling about. Some are laughing; others pursue the dance with intent, angry frowns.

After a bit, one of the dancers jumps up on the stage and stands a moment in front of the band looking out at the audience with a delirious grin. Then he dives forward into the mob and the dancers begin passing him around overhead, his heavy combat boots poking up into the air. I take a few steps back.

"Stage diving is okay, guys," the lead singer announces, "but please watch out for the equipment. We're too poor to buy new stuff if you break it!"

By now, a steady flow of dancers is mounting the stage and leaping into the crowd. Those who balk at the stage's edge or who approach the band members are quickly removed by brawny bouncers who are lurking in the wings.

I ask Alison if she likes to dance this way and, gesturing to make herself understood over the loud music, she indicates that she gave it up after breaking a rib. She smiles and shrugs.

I muse a bit as we stand there in the sweaty crowd. Alison is the only person on the team who has invited me to join her on a purely social outing, and despite my unfamiliarity with the musical scene at the Channel—even my distaste for it—I feel comfortable there with her. We are beginning to be friends, and I find that I both welcome and resist such a friendship.

City Year is set up to make it easier for people of different backgrounds and ethnicities to become friends. So it is a little disappointing to find that even in this safe environment, the person I find easiest to be with is the one who is the least different from me. Like me, Alison is white, the child of college-educated, professional, middle-class parents.

It seems to me that there is a social ease derived from common experiences that is difficult to replicate. Alison and I converse with a certain confidence that the other will share our perspectives, whereas conversation with others on the team is sometimes more tentative and uncertain.

I worry about what this may imply about my own racial or class attitudes.

And yet I'm not the only one. Across the team, and across the corps, I have noticed that while many people work hard to make friends with those different from themselves, and derive pleasure from those friendships, the closest friendships rarely cross race or class lines.

Alison has noted this, too. "It's all socioeconomic," she says one day after taking a visual survey of the corps at lunch and noting that the little clusters in which people arrange themselves are often racially segregated and even more often segregated by other factors, like social class or education. Preppies at one table, dropouts at another.

I find this troubling, but Alison is philosophical. She looks at the corps and sees progress. She has been to schools with diverse student bodies, and she knows how hard real integration can be. Just learning to respect each other and cooperate, she says, is a tremendous accomplishment.

Here at the Channel, what impresses me most about Alison is her aura of security and calm. In the midst of this frenzied scene, she is a small oasis of serenity. I admire her, all the more because I know her life is not as easy as it looks. To be financially independent at eighteen, especially while doing full-time service at $100 a week, is in itself impressive. She never complains, nor does she talk about the family difficulties that drove her from her parents' home. She is solid and sane, and she seems to negotiate her way through life like a steady ship, moving easily between days of service and nights of shock-treatment music.

Around midnight we leave, and I drop her off at her boyfriend's apartment. She thanks me for coming, and disappears inside.

Twenty-Five

Toward the end of March we have a one-day "recruitment blitz." Each team is to go to three or four different schools and make a presentation designed to entice graduating seniors to think about joining City Year. The day before the blitz the Reebok Team meets in a big room in the basement of St. Paul's A.M.E. Church to rehearse.

The presentation has been created by the team. We start with music and a round of high-energy jumping jacks to represent morning P.T. and draw in the audience. Then we proceed to a skit that has us all trying to think how best to explain City Year in half an hour. Each person plays an exaggerated version of himself. Next, there is a skit about our work at Cornerstone. "Heeey! City Year!" Will bellows, hamming it up in the role of supervisor Bob Reinhart. "Glad you're here! There's sledgehammers in the corner! Start banging down those walls!"

Everyone knows the skits are corny, but it doesn't seem to matter as long as the energy is high.

Brendan and David do a skit based on David's experience at the Blackstone School with Harry, the boy with cerebral palsy. Their skit is not humorous but rather focuses on Harry's frustration and the pain that sometimes comes with helping people who are in need.

Earl, Jackie, and Alison each offer personal "testimonials"— accounts of something they have learned in City Year.

Last on the program is the City Year rap. "City Year '91! A little work and a lotta fun! . . ." Richie wrote the words, and all of the teams are using his rap in their presentations. Richie and a friend have made a tape, working late one night in a borrowed recording studio, where they mixed their own voices over a hip-hop background track sampled from professional recordings.

For our presentation, of course, Richie doesn't just want to play a tape—he wants to perform the rap. The difficulty is that everyone knows Richie is a somewhat clumsy rapper, given to stage fright.

Several team members favor using the tape, rather than risk our presentation to Richie's jitters. But Richie wants badly to perform.

"I've put months of effort into preparing for this and I'd like to do it, not use the tape," he says.

"But with the tape, it's foolproof," says Alison.

"It's more gripping to see him do it, though," says Will.

"Okay, I guess," says Alison reluctantly. "As long as you feel confident that you're not going to screw up."

Tony has mixed feelings about even allowing Richie to take part in the recruitment blitz. Richie is present today for the first time all week—he was out Monday through Wednesday and never even called in to offer an excuse. He still won't explain himself to Tony. "It's personal and I can't say anything about it," he says.

Tony could fire Richie now. With three unexcused absences, he has come to the end of the lengthy rope the contract allows. Instead, however, Tony chooses to accept Richie's assertion that he thought (mistakenly) that he was suspended for other absences on Monday and hence was illegitimately absent only twice this week. With just two unexcused absences, the contract prescribes at this point a three-day suspension rather than dismissal. Tony gives him the suspension and allows him to perform in the recruitment blitz.

The entire corps spends a day rehearsing recruitment presentations. There is some griping among both staff and corps members about this; what with one day devoted to rehearsals, another day to the blitz, and a fair amount of time in the past few weeks spent planning, the entire corps is missing nearly three days of service for this recruitment effort. Is this really how corps members should be spending their time? ask some. Alan and Michael remind us that spreading the City Year message is part of the corps' mission.

After all the rehearsing, we feel exceedingly prepared by the time we gather Friday morning for the blitz. We did three full run-throughs of our presentation the day before; we had agreed that anything that did not go well—including Richie's rap—would be dropped from the routine. But everything went smoothly, even the rap. The head of recruitment, sitting in on our rehearsal, has told us that if any of the TV stations she has contacted decide to cover the blitz, she will send them to film the Reebok Team. Everyone on the team is proud and excited.

The first school we visit is a Catholic school, a new target for City Year. In the past, the school has not allowed City Year to recruit there. After all, students who choose to enter a youth service corps after graduation bring down the percentage of those who go directly on to college, a crucial statistic for a lot of schools. But a graduate of the school who found his way to City Year on his own has brought glowing reports back to his teachers, and so we have been invited in.

We find a disappointingly small audience when we arrive. Rather than call an assembly, school officials have sent us to a single class: the business class. This, apparently, is a class for non-college-bound students in a school known for high achievers, and they are a tough-looking lot, straddling their chairs, lying across the desks, making loud cracking noises with their chewing gum. They are also almost all black, even though blacks are a minority in the school. This is a good thing for City Year, which, perhaps because so many of the top staff people are white, has more difficulty recruiting blacks than whites (just the opposite of the situation at CVC and many other urban youth corps). In this small classroom we have only a narrow space between the twenty desks and the blackboard to perform in, but the tight quarters contribute to a sense of immediacy and excitement. The audience of students snaps to attention quickly as soon as the team runs into the room and begins their jumping jacks.

When we get to the testimonials, Earl goes first. Hands thrust into his pockets, head drooping and bobbing, he talks about his relationship with Daquan. "I took him aside one day and I told him how I was in school and how it didn't get me nowhere. I think he listened. He's not a angel now, but I go back there sometimes and he's doing his work, he's not trying to leave the classroom. I felt I had a little somethin' to do with that. It really made me feel good."

Jackie is glowing: "After my father died, I was grasping for straws. I heard about City Year and I decided to go to Boston. It was the best, quote unquote, mistake I ever made. It helped me to get focused and to do a lot of jobs they wouldn't usually let a nineteen-year-old do. Next year I plan to go to either Harvard or Howard."

Alison looks humble as she speaks. "I went to a diverse high school, so I thought I knew about diversity, but I didn't. I don't think you've really experienced diversity until you've worked with people. We are forced to accept each other's differences and not push them away. When an issue comes up, we have to deal with it."

Even at the end, the students are still attending closely. Every one of them fills out a City Year application form.

We make two other stops, both at public high schools, and in each school we have an audience of over a hundred. Each time the team's performance gets better. Richie loosens up, and Will hams it up a little more each time. At Hyde Park High School, our last stop, we perform in dim light in a cavernous auditorium. Nobody knows how to work the stage lights, and the sound system the school had promised doesn't work. Earl almost refuses to go on; he is nervous because this is the school he attended and dropped out of. Nevertheless, each part of the presentation gets huge applause. Earl gives his testimonial without a hitch, and when he is through, he grins with unabashed pride. And when Richie strides onto the stage to do his rap, the girls in the audience scream and lean toward him as if he were a pop idol. Feeding on the audience's energy, Richie swings into his rap with a jaunty swagger and a confidence we have not seen before— at least not on stage. Toward the end, he jumps down and prowls the aisles. Between verses, I look over and see he is trying to hide a smile.

At the end of the day, we have collected the names of more than a hundred interested students.

Twenty-Six

David, Jackie, and I are painting a hallway on the third floor of the YWCA women's residence. David is reproaching Jackie for snubbing Amy. A growing tension between the two, once fast friends, is beginning to be felt throughout the team.

"Why don't you talk to her?"

"She barely even says hi to me!" says Jackie. "She'll say a few words to me, then just walk away!"

"Why do you think she's mad?" David asks.

"I have no idea," she answers.

"Really?" David asks, with an edge of sarcasm. "Come on."

For months, a battle has been brewing within the corps over an idea widely referred to as "corps governance." After the first blush of enthusiasm about City Year wore off, corps members began to think more critically about the program. The most common complaint was that they did not have enough of a voice in policymaking. The program emphasized egalitarianism and participatory democracy, but corps members felt they were too rarely consulted about anything, from project assignments, to planning of enrichment-day activities.

It was Amy who, working with a friend on another team, came up with the idea of addressing this issue by establishing a mechanism for corps members to participate more directly in the planning and discussion of program goals.

But when word got around that Amy and her friend were putting together a proposal, there was an immediate backlash of resentment within the corps. Reebok Team members were particularly offended that Amy had never even discussed the idea with them before taking it to Alan for comment. Others simply dismissed the idea as sounding too much like student government, which many remembered as little more than a way for the most popular kids in school to ingratiate themselves with teachers.

Initially, Jackie was an outspoken critic of the corps governance idea, and accused Amy of being on a "power trip." When weeks later a standing "program committee" was formed that would meet frequently with staff and focus on policy questions, Amy herself—by then angry and embittered—did not volunteer. Many others in the corps boycotted the committee because they felt no ownership of the idea; the final proposal had been put together by Alan and the staff rather than by corps members. Most people on the Reebok Team had mixed feelings about the committee and did not want to join. The only two who volunteered were Chris and—interestingly—Jackie, and so by default, they won the two Reebok Team slots on the committee. The committee has appointed them both to positions of leadership, and since everyone knows that Jackie and Chris are seeing one another romantically—in fact, Jackie is practically living with

Chris and his brother Joe—the apparent hegemony of a couple breeds further resentment of the program committee in the team and in the corps, as well as considerable envy of Jackie and Chris.

Amy is now hurt and resentful, and generally closed off to the rest of the team. Tony discusses the issue with Amy. "She's making a passive protest," he observes later. "In the best of all possible worlds, she would like to be on the program committee. But Jackie slammed her, and then got on board with the program."

David thinks it is up to Jackie to make the first move in patching things up with Amy, and he is pushing her to make such an effort.

"For the sake of the team!" he pleads. "You've gotta do something! Ask her to have lunch! Prove to her that you care enough to spend an hour talking about it!"

"*Lunch?*" says Jackie. "That's *my* time!"

"Then ask to paint with her one day!"

"No way! We'd fight all day! I never saw anybody so negative as she is. I even like Earl better than her. At least he's not so negative!"

The tension between Jackie and Amy continues to fester. But because Jackie blithely ignores it while Amy nurses it, its most visible result is to isolate Amy from the rest of the team.

There are other tensions festering within the team, such as resentment over Richie's poor attendance and concerns that Jackie and Chris's romance is negatively affecting the team's equilibrium. Tony takes us one day for a group "feedback" session aimed at helping people learn to communicate about such issues. The session is led by Stanley Pollack, a consultant to City Year who runs the organization called Teen Empowerment, Inc.

Stanley reviews what he calls "feedback principles"—things like being balanced, specific, and caring in telling people what you think, and being selective rather than letting pent-up anger out all at once. In receiving feedback from others, he recommends listening carefully and avoiding defensiveness.

"If you can stay in touch with a part of you that cares about the person, even if you're angry, the feedback will be much more productive and effective," he says.

We break into pairs for individual feedback sessions, and the experience is surprisingly cleansing. Everyone is required to say both positive and negative things to everyone else, and people return from the private sessions smiling and relaxed—even Amy and Jackie.

Then Stanley instructs us to apply the feedback skills to the team, beginning with a positive.

"I love this team," says Brendan. "It's the best. We really get things done. Just look at Cornerstone."

"This is a cool team," says Chris. "You all welcomed me with open arms and I am glad for that."

"We're much more unified than ever before," says Alison.

"Everybody we work with, it's amazing how we respect them," says David.

We move on to the negatives.

"Some people here are quick-tempered. Not me, of course," says Earl.

"Disagreements on the team sometimes become personal attacks," says Alison.

"And then they become team problems," says Brendan.

"All of us have problems we're not strong enough to deal with, and we have to admit them," David says. "Use the resource of twelve caring individuals. We need to create an environment where we can ask for help from the team."

"Order up a pizza," says Chris. "Spend time together."

"We need to change from being so service-oriented," says Brendan. "The attitude that no matter what happens, work comes first. Maybe we should just set aside a day every so often to do this."

"Every two weeks," says Jackie.

Tony promises to build some feedback and recreation time into our next project.

The homeless-services project in Cambridge ends somewhat abruptly. Another team will rotate into the project and pick up where we left off. To create a sense of closure, our sponsors treat us to lunch at a local restaurant. Jean Mahoney of Reebok and Michael Brown attend. Linsey and Pat and Bob, the contractor who has been supervising at Cornerstone, speak effusively about the team's accomplishments.

"They told me I was going to do a major reconstruction and for a crew I was going to get a bunch of teenagers," says Bob. "I said, 'you've gotta be crazy.' But I was wrong. I was very impressed."

Cleanup

The second-semester flagship project is to have a new twist: the team will plan it themselves. As early as January we begin discussing what populations we would like to serve, and the two groups that arouse the most interest among team members are veterans and immigrants. Tony suggests we do some research before choosing between the two. We begin the process while still working in Cambridge, setting aside Thursday afternoons for research and planning. Tony arranges for the team to begin by meeting with representatives of two agencies that serve immigrants and two agencies that serve veterans so that we can interview them about the needs of each group and explore the kind of service opportunities we might find in each field.

Before we begin our research, Lisa, City Year's director of project planning, warns us that we will not have carte blanche permission to select any project we want. "I want to be up-front with you about this," she says. "The staff is here to guide you through this process and to make the final decisions about your project."

But few people really listen to her warning.

We meet first with Regina Lee, director of the state's Office for Refugees and Immigrants. She tells us that Massachusetts has the fifth-highest immigration rate in the country and that while services are provided for those officially classified as refugees, many people escaping from war-torn countries deserve but cannot get refugee status and so are eligible for no government assistance when they arrive, if they are lucky enough to get here at all.

One Boston homeless shelter estimates that a quarter of its clients are newcomers, many of them undocumented, she says. Asian immigrants are the fastest-growing group among the victims of hate crimes in Boston. In a bad economy, when jobs are hard to find, newcomers find themselves particularly unwelcome. And with the war in the Persian Gulf, Arab-Americans have become convenient targets of harassment and discrimination.

Tony has given everyone on the team a fresh new pad and pen for taking notes. Chris writes copiously in a flowing script. Richie prints carefully. Rosa writes her notes in Spanish.

"Where do you think a group of people like us can help the most with the immigrant and refugee situation?" asks Brendan.

Lee suggests we might tutor English or help people learn job skills and find work.

We go on to the private agency Catholic Charities, where we meet with Mary Diaz, the director of their office of immigrant and refugee services. Catholic Charities often contracts with the state to provide resettlement services to refugees, among other things. Mary Diaz introduces us to a Vietnamese nun who escaped the country in 1979 in a small boat after being imprisoned by the Communists for continuing her Catholic teachings after the war.

The sister works with the Amerasian children who are the unwanted offspring of Vietnamese women and American servicemen. They face great challenges in Boston schools because, outcasts in their own country, they come here with almost no schooling. They need tutoring, recreational opportunities, and role models.

Mary Diaz also suggests that the team might develop an anti-discrimination educational package—a video, a play, or a book—to take around to schools. Or perhaps we can fix up an apartment for a refugee family, she says.

After our meeting at Catholic Charities, we adjourn to Will's nearby Beacon Hill apartment to talk things over. It's a fifth-floor walk-up, but pleasant and well furnished. We seat ourselves somewhat gingerly on the antique chairs and on the floor.

Everyone is excited and eager to speak. Making a video sounds fun, but to Jackie it does not seem like rigorous service. Richie sees a possible compromise: working with Vietnam veterans, or with the Amerasian children of veterans. Chris suggests that our time is too limited to take on the responsibility of acting as big brothers and sisters. Someone suggests we might split up the team and do more than one thing. Ideas are flying.

"The questions we should ask ourselves," says Tony, "are these. Is there a need? Can we learn something? Can the agency accommodate us? And is it something that we uniquely can do?"

"Oh, there's a lot of needs," says Will.

"But we haven't seen something we uniquely can do," says Jackie.

"How effective can we be, anyway, in just seven weeks?" asks Brendan.

"Look at the Blackstone. We were very effective in seven weeks," answers David.

"It's a chance," says Richie. "It's a gamble. Whether we can make a difference."

The following week we go to see the commissioner and deputy commissioner of Veterans' Services for the City of Boston. Deputy commissioner Tom Lyons tells us about his own experiences as a Marine serving in Vietnam. His agency, he says, is currently setting up programs for soldiers returning from the Persian Gulf who suffer from posttraumatic stress disorder. That is one place we might help. Another thing the agency needs is people to help decorate the 63,000 veterans' graves in Boston for Memorial Day. It is the agency's mandate to do this every year, but it is getting harder and harder to find volunteers to help.

We meet next with the Veterans' Benefits Clearinghouse, a private agency focusing on the needs of minority veterans, which has some more compelling proposals for the team. They are renovating an old building to create a supportive living environment not unlike the one we were working on in Cambridge, but for homeless and disabled veterans. They are starting a program that will match veterans with elementary school classes for educational field trips and oral history projects. They need help with outreach for a support group they are starting for families of soldiers stationed in the Persian Gulf.

"The kind of work I'm thinking about is not necessarily labor-intensive," says director Ron Armstead, shaking his long dreadlocks. "It is mentally taxing."

The three men who run the agency—Armstead, Ralph Cooper, and Ernest Branch—are engaging and enthusiastic speakers. They speak angrily about the way American historians have neglected the contributions of black soldiers as far back as the Civil War.

Several people on the team are clearly excited about the prospect of working with these impressive black activists.

"Let's do veterans!" say Jackie and Chris in unison as soon as Armstead and Cooper leave the room. Some of the others are not so enthusiastic.

"The construction work is the same as what we're doing now," says Alison.

"The school project isn't organized enough for us to jump into it," says Brendan.

"I think the immigrants need help more," says Rosa.

"I feel like I don't belong here," says Brendan. "I'm totally up in the air, and I feel like other people have already decided."

"Only two people in this room have made up their minds," says Alison, staring at Jackie, then at Chris. "Not pointing any fingers. Just a rough estimate."

"This could be a battleground," David says anxiously. "I know some of you are like, 'Wow, this is great! I wanna do this!' But, like, don't decide yet. Keep listening. Because people are saying things. Important things."

A week later, we sit around the dining room table at Alison's parents' house in Cambridge. We have boiled a big batch of spaghetti and defrosted some of her mother's homemade sauce, and now we are busy digging in.

"As you are all aware," says Tony, "we have a dual purpose for this meeting, the first being lunch and the second being to decide on our flagship project."

Earl starts the voting. "I'm a go for veterans, because it's gonna be hard to communicate with the immigrants."

We go around the table. Will chooses veterans because he sees more tangible service opportunities there. Alison chooses immigrants; she thinks that the public's enthusiasm for the war in the Persian Gulf will bring out other volunteers to help veterans. Amy selects immigrants, saying her own background and career plans give her a personal interest in immigrants' issues. Richie, who has been bucking for veterans all along, now agrees with Alison and goes for immigrants. Rosa chooses immigrants because, she says, she knows what it's like. Jackie chooses veterans. Her father was a veteran, she notes. Chris, who is absent, has cast a proxy vote for veterans. Brendan chooses immigrants and David veterans, "because war and peace is the big issue I am trying to confront in my life right now," he says.

Five to five—a tie. Tony announces that he will take a week to think it over and discuss our options with other staff members and then will cast the tie-breaking vote.

Later in the week the corps is visited by a representative from a group called Children of War. He shows a videotaped documentary in which young Palestinians, Salvadorans, Cambodians, and others talk about what life is like in their warring countries. The interviews are interspersed with footage of shootings, fields of skulls and bones, and other horrifying sights. The film is extremely upsetting to some corps members who are themselves "children of war." A young man from Guatemala stands to tell us his reaction in Spanish while another boy translates.

"You have an opportunity," he says, his voice hoarse with emotion. "An opportunity that you don't know you have. To be born in a country where fathers do not kill their children and children do not kill their fathers." He begins to weep, but keeps speaking. "You do not know what it is like in Guatemala. I feel sick when I see what happens here in the streets. The gangs, the stealing. You are so lucky to be born here."

A few days later, when Tony announces his decision to work with immigrants, no one takes exception to his choice.

The next Thursday we all take the number 111 bus to Chelsea, a tiny city just north of Boston. Tony has selected Chelsea as a good place for us to investigate service possibilities with immigrants because of its large immigrant population. He has divided the team into pairs, and has scheduled interviews with the directors of five different social service agencies in Chelsea. The pairs fan out across the city and convene at three-thirty in the conference room of a centrally located teen agency called ROCA (Reaching Out to Chelsea Adolescents).

"Here's the idea," says Tony. "For the duration of this project we could split into pairs, with each pair working at a different agency. The project could culminate, I thought, with a cultural festival for the community that we all plan together. You see? Let's hear what you found out today."

Earl and David have been to the rectory of St. Rose's Church, where plans are being made for an after-school recreation program for junior high school boys. Fifty children have already signed up, but there is only one staff person to organize and run the program. He needs assistance, both to supervise the boys and to plan field trips and other events.

Amy and Will met with the director of Chelsea Main Street, Inc., an agency dedicated to revitalizing the city's commercial district. Director Ned Keefe wants help organizing residents for a community cleanup day.

"I was intrigued by this part of the program," says Amy, "because our team has done absolutely nothing in the area of organizing people."

Alison and Brendan have been to Chelsea Neighborhood Housing Services (CNHS).

"This agency helps people buy houses with low-interest loans," says Alison. "They had some good ideas of things we could do. We were surprised."

Another agency, the Chelsea Commission on Hispanic Affairs, has canceled an appointment with Rosa and Chris. The reason for the cancellation is unclear, and with nothing to report, they feel a little left out.

Jackie and Richie have met with Molly Baldwin, director of ROCA and Tony's main Chelsea contact. ROCA started as a teen pregnancy prevention and "parenting" program but now also houses a number of other programs for teenage, primarily Hispanic, youth. Team members working with ROCA might supervise field trips, recruit members for a Central American youth group, give AIDS education seminars, or help immigrant kids who are looking for summer jobs.

"Chelsea is small," Molly explains. "You can have an impact here. You will be recognized and respected."

We must come to a decision about the project within two weeks, Tony tells us.

"I'm feeling set up," says David. "All of a sudden, I'm feeling like this is the only option."

On April 3, Tony announces that we will be doing our flagship project in Chelsea, at the five agencies we investigated.

"Wait a minute," says David. "How did that get decided?" Others begin chiming in. "We're going to work with *them*?" "I thought we were going to decide!"

Why was Chelsea chosen? How were the agencies selected? How did we make the leap from our decision to work with immigrants to this big, decentralized project plan?

In some ways, it does seem as if the team project planning mandate has been pushed aside and that Tony has developed an idea of his own. The team resists ceding the final decision to Tony, but their sense of indignation is tempered by the realistic knowledge that planning is a difficult job and that to do it by committee would require far more time than is available to us. Besides, the script for the project is far from written. Each pair of team members is to work with the staff of their sponsoring agency to outline specific goals for their seven-week tenure there. A good deal of planning still lies ahead.

Twenty-Eight

There is nothing stylish about Chelsea. At first glance, Broadway, the city's main thoroughfare, looks as if it hasn't changed in twenty or thirty years. The most modern-looking store in the downtown area is a Dunkin' Donuts, the presence of which is reassuring; a morning "dunk" has become a team tradition. The other stores look as if one might walk in and find clothing that was fashionable in the 1950s or sixties, and in some cases, one can.

Many of the buildings along Broadway are three-story, turn-of-the-century brick buildings with apartments above the stores. Other kinds of architecture are haphazardly thrown in: an enormous, boxy, cinder-block Moose Lodge; a 1960s-era brick-and-cement unemployment office. Apart from the Dunkin' Donuts and a Store 24, there are no national chains represented on Broadway: the shops are small, locally owned laundries, hairdressers, coffee shops, insurance and travel agencies, and ethnic restaurants.

For all its dusty, small-town feeling, however, a closer look will show that Chelsea has long been on the cutting edge of change in America. The signs along Broadway are written in many languages—Spanish, English, Khmer, Vietnamese, Arabic—and the shops and other institutions in and around the center reflect the successive waves of immigrants that have come to America, and to Chelsea. Italian restaurants and Irish pubs. An old Hebrew school, converted into apartments. Dillon's Russian Steam Bath. Tito's Bakery. A Cambodian restaurant. Likewise, the people who bustle and saunter along the sidewalks of Broadway are of many colors and nationalities. According to the 1990 census, the decade between 1980 and 1990 has brought 7,396 new Hispanic residents to Chelsea, raising their numbers to 9,018—nearly a third of this tiny city's population. Southeast Asians have increased in number from 174 in 1980 to 1,435 in 1990. Immigrants and members of ethnic minority groups make up almost 42 percent of the population of the city.

We begin our project in Chelsea in mid-April, on election day. The residents are voting on a proposal to override a statewide legal cap on property tax increases so that the city can continue to meet its payroll obligations. Chelsea, never affluent, has seen a dramatic decline in property tax revenues in recent years and now faces a $2.4 million budget deficit as the end of the fiscal year grows near. City services have been reduced to a bare minimum and the city is preparing to lay off thirty-five police and firefighters. The state has threatened to take over city government in Chelsea if the proposition does not pass. But residents are fed up with taxes and disaffected with local government. The override is defeated by a margin of three to one and the situation in Chelsea seems fated to get worse before it gets better.

We begin with a team meeting in the conference room at ROCA. This agency has more room than any of the others we will be working at, and so its conference room becomes home base for the team. It is a comfortable room, with a big conference table and a couch, as well as a folding crib and a baby swing. The walls are decorated with posters about responsible and safe sex.

Tony starts the meeting. "You're going to be on your own a lot during this project, and I want you to document your work by putting down on paper whatever you do as much as is physically possible." He passes around a pile of manila folders.

"Richie and I are going to need a lot," says Jackie.

"Don't you think we should start with just one?" says Richie crankily. Earl shuffles a pile of folders and smiles. Tony continues.

"If somebody comes to you and asks you, 'What are you doing in your project right now?' you should be able to pull out your folder and quickly run down a list: this is what we're up to right now, these are the things we are trying to get started, et cetera.

"This project involves some real white-collar work. Administrative work, pushing paper. You're going to have to get used to all the paperwork. It's a different routine."

Alison and Brendan head off to Neighborhood Housing Services, and Amy and Will go to meet with their supervisor at Chelsea Main Street. Rosa is in the next room using the phone to set up a meeting with a graphic artist; the Hispanic Commission is putting her and Chris in charge of the posters for the cleanup day. Jackie has a meeting with a ROCA staff person. "You can make a list while I'm gone,

Richie," she says on her way out, oblivious to his somewhat resentful look. "Stuff we need to know. We need to ask about money for the dance; other resources; whether we can get a van."

Two primary goals have emerged for the Chelsea project: first, to organize a community cleanup day and recruit as many citizens as possible to participate; and second, to bring an infusion of energy and manpower to local nonprofit agencies at a time when many are financially strapped and demoralized. It looks like a lot of work. Richie and Jackie are very busy, planning programs and presentations and field trips. Amy and Will are assigned to be the main organizers of the community cleanup day, and there is a lot of planning to do. They have long lists of community groups to call to recruit volunteers. They need to round up tools and supplies. They contact the local newspaper, which runs pictures of the team on the front page for three weeks in a row, with articles about the cleanup and about City Year.

David and Earl are supervising an after-school program for middle school boys, and they spend the mornings planning activities. They also, on David's initiative, visit local stores to gather donations for the program: a trophy, a fish dinner, and some garbage bags for the cleanup. Alison and Brendan are planning a summer program for children that CNHS will administer, and are also making plans for a specific aspect of the cleanup day: an attempt to restore an overgrown and forgotten historic cemetery that is currently being used, even by the parks department, as a dumping ground.

Rosa and Chris are not so engaged. Their supervisor, the head of the Hispanic Commission, seems never to be able to meet with them, and when he does, they say, he looks at them as if they are taking up too much space. Without supervision, they do not know how to make a role for themselves within the agency and instead help out doing odd jobs at ROCA.

On a visit to David and Earl at the office of the Chelsea Youth Education and Recreation Program (CHYERP), which is in the basement of a local Catholic church rectory, I find them working on a letter.

"All right," says David. "This is what we gotta do. We gotta write to the parents about the cleanup." He hands a pad and pencil to Earl.

"This letter is to inform you that your child has been dismissed," says Earl.

"C'mon, Earl, stop fooling around." David turns to me. "You know, he calls me Tony. He thinks I'm pretending I'm his boss. But if I didn't say anything, Earl would sit around and pick his nose all day." Earl smirks.

"You write the letter in English," he says to Earl. "I'll write the Spanish version." Both young men bend over their pads.

After a few minutes, Earl looks up. "Okay, how does this sound?" David puts down his pencil. "TO THE PARENTS OF THE CHYERP MEMBERS: This letter is to inform you . . ." Earl stops. "All right, all right." He starts writing again.

"Tell me when you're ready, man," says David.

Ten minutes pass.

"How does this sound?" Earl asks. "There will be a cleanup of Chelsea on May 11. We hope to see you and yours there. It will be great, and then some."

Where are we meeting?" asks David.

"A park," Earl tells him.

"Yes, a park. What park?"

"I don't know what park."

"Quigley Park. Q-U-I-G-L-E-Y. What time are we meeting? You gotta put that in. Plus, you can't say 'you and yours.' It's too casual."

After they finish the letter, I accompany Earl on an errand. Out in the street, he begins talking about David. He doesn't mind David telling him what to do at all, he says. He likes David.

"You know, D is cool. He can relate to me. And you know, I needed that, since Charles was gone. D is cool. He don't be getting on my nerves."

Amy and Will's supervisor, Ned Keefe, arranges for them to meet with the mayor, John Brennan. When the time for their meeting arrives, they go—along with Ned, Molly Baldwin, Daniel Vigianni (the staff director of the Commission on Hispanic Affairs), and me—to City Hall and are ushered into Brennan's spacious, oak-paneled office and seated around a large conference table. We are joined by the mayor's assistant, a spry little man named Arthur Angelo. Brennan is friendly and seems relaxed, despite the dire financial straits the city is in and a vicious campaign that his opponent in the upcoming election is waging against him.

"You're helping me out," says Brennan. "The city streets are dirty. There used to be thirty-eight guys cleaning the streets. Now there's seven. It doesn't make me look good when the people are saying the streets are dirty. So what can I do to help?"

"Any place that you're connected where you can help out with donations of food would be good," says Will.

"We'll call McDonald's for some pop and things. We'll also see if we can get a cop up there on detail that day. Arthur, make a note. Arthur will coordinate with Atlantic Waste. We'll have a truck up there all day. Tell Faye to waive the fee. It's gratis. After all, it's a Chelsea cleanup day. How many people are you expecting? With the citywide cleanup last year, they were expecting a hundred people. I don't think they got twelve. The aldermen weren't even there."

Amy and Will are not sure what to say. The mayor goes on.

"People basically are stupid," he says. "With the citywide cleanup, we said if you want to clean in front of your house, a truck'll come by to pick up the stuff. And we had people clean out their cellars. They were leaving sofas on the street. You've got to put it in big black print. *This has nothing to do with cellars.* Plus, in some of the Hispanic areas, there's gotta be a flyer in Spanish. Keep indoctrinating them."

Amy and Will nod politely.

"You got any more needs, you call Arthur Angelo. He'll be the point man. Maybe you kids can come on my cable TV show next week and make an announcement, okay?"

Amy and Will nod.

"It's nice to see young people doing this out of a sincere desire to help the community," says the mayor. "Remember, come to the cable station next Thursday, one o'clock."

Brendan and Alison's sponsor, Chelsea Neighborhood Housing Services, is on Shawmut Street, in a poorer section of town. Shawmut Street is the kind of place where many of the apartments have no doorbell; where those that do have a doorbell often have no name beside the bell; and where if anything at all is written by the bell, it is likely to be a column of four or five names, not just one. It is a neighborhood of recent immigrants—people who have come to seek haven and a chance at comfort—from places like Guatemala, the Dominican Republic, El Salvador, Cambodia, and Vietnam. Part of Brendan and Alison's assignment at CNHS is to do "outreach"— going door-to-door, recruiting people to help with the cleanup day and letting them know about the services CNHS provides, like low-interest home-improvement loans. I go with them on an out-reach mission one rainy afternoon.

We have a stack of fliers in envelopes marked with names and addresses from a list that Brendan and Alison have painstakingly compiled from voter registration rolls and the slender Chelsea phone book. Despite their hard work, however, the list seems to bear little relation to reality. In a building with three apartments, chances are there is only one envelope for the address; and likely as not, the person named on the envelope has moved.

José Santiago, CNHS's outreach coordinator, leads the way, which is helpful because he speaks Spanish. We visit about thirty apartments. We planned to take turns talking, but because of the language barrier Brendan and Alison and I generally stand in the hall while José chats with the women who come to the door with infants in their arms and children clutching their legs. Blasts of warm air pass through the open doors, often surrounding us with spicy cooking smells. We steal little glimpses of the lives of those who live inside. We glean a sense of careful economy: a clothesline in a kitchen, a refrigerator in a living room. An altar or shrine with pictures and incense is visible inside one apartment. We hand out our letters and brochures. The residents are unfailingly polite, listening with interest as we pitch the cleanup day, and taking all the literature we offer. Will they come out and help with the cleanup? They would like to, but they work on Saturday. Will they volunteer their name and address for the mailing list? Certainly. Alison takes down the names carefully, although the rain has wet her pad and the ink is beginning to run across the page.

By the end of the afternoon, we have gathered twenty names and addresses, but we have not recruited a single person for the cleanup.

Twenty-Nine

On April 23 we take a break from Chelsea to attend Reebok International's annual shareholders' meeting at the World Trade Center in Boston. It's a chance for team members to meet corporate executives and people with financial clout, and a chance for Reebok to show its investors and board of directors where some of the money they give to charitable causes each year is going. We are invited to come early to chat with shareholders and then to act as ushers at the meeting. Tony urges the team to try and make a good impression on the people who have pledged half a million dollars to City Year over the next three years. We are to wear our cleanest uniforms and everyone is to try hard to be friendly and polite.

The team at first resists. Over the course of the year they have frequently been asked to talk up City Year with politicians, foundation representatives, and reporters. At first it was a thrill; now it is growing tiresome. Sometimes they feel like they are being turned into walking advertisements for City Year. "I hate this," says Richie as we head toward the World Trade Center on the morning of the meeting. "I ain't doin' it. I can't stand kissin' ass."

"There's only so far you can go in coming on to these people," says Jackie. "They know it's a come-on. Enough is enough."

But their cynicism is mixed with excitement. The rooms at the World Trade Center are plush and fancy, and the shareholders who filter in slowly in the hour before the meeting begins have a strong aura of wealth and power. Despite the griping, most of the team members socialize skilfully. Jackie and Chris seem right at home chatting with the suited shareholders. Will is invited by the public relations woman in charge of the event to act as escort for a special guest. Only Richie slinks off into a corner.

Alan has arranged for the team to meet privately with Reebok CEO Paul Fireman before the start of the shareholders' meeting. When the time comes, we file into a small conference room and sit in leather chairs arranged around a table with an exotic flower arrangement at its center. We glance at the food laid out at one side of the room—cakes, scones, croissants, strawberries, blackberries, grapes, melons—but restraint wins out and nobody takes any. Presently Paul Fireman strides into the room, looking tall and robust and just like his picture in the newspapers and the annual reports.

There are no chairs left, so Fireman stands. He introduces himself and board director Bertram Lee, then asks for everyone's name. "We're very proud of you and the work that you're doing out in the world," he says.

He begins to tell us about the company he built from an $800,000-a-year custom sneaker maker into a $2 billion sporting goods empire. "If you ever wondered about starting a big company, I'm living proof that it can be done," he says. "In 1980 we started with almost nothing. It was a cottage industry kind of a company. I decided right at the beginning that we would only do products that made a difference. You may think that's strange, talking about making a difference with running shoes, but in 1980 just improving comfort was a big contribution. Shoes back then took two months to break in, and you got a lot of blisters during those two months."

Several people nod. Fireman is charming the group, which until a few moments ago was torn between resisting the mandate to schmooze with these corporate bigwigs and being seduced by their friendly attention.

I was expecting Fireman to talk about the company's work to promote human rights. In December we attended the Reebok Human Rights Award ceremony, which brought together a crowd of music and movie stars to honor such people as a Tibetan monk, a leader of the student democracy movement in China, and a Palestinian peace advocate. Some on the team were impressed, while others viewed the whole event as a publicity stunt. Everyone seems to have grown both more appreciative of and more cynical about the symbiosis that exists between philanthropy and advertising.

But all skepticism dissolves in the face of Fireman's simple comments. It seems a little thing, almost frivolous—running shoes as a "contribution." But it is appropriate that Fireman should speak proudly of the source of Reebok's largess: a growing market, a well-made product, a small innovation.

Alan suggests that the team members take turns describing what they have learned from their time in City Year. We solemnly go around the circle, each person reaching to find something meaningful to say to the corporate executive in just a few seconds. Fireman listens intently.

"When you work with this diverse a group of people," Jackie says, "you just have to learn to listen."

"I grew up in Boston and tried to be aware of what was going on in the world," says Alison, "but now there are things I can no longer push away."

Richie says, "Before City Year, I never even heard of nonprofit. I just wanted to be a lawyer and be rich. Now I want to fill the people's needs before trying to be rich."

"It's given me an unbelievable feeling of hope and optimism about the power of youth," says David, his eyes shining.

"I've learned a lot of techniques for starting my own nonprofit," says Chris.

"I've learned about self-empowerment," says Amy. "I think that's the greatest thing you can give a person."

Tony goes last. "I consider it a privilege to work with a team like this. It's part of a new consensus in our country that helping other people is as important as helping ourselves."

Later, team members tease one another about laying it on so thick. "It's like, 'I was blind but now I see,'" says Alison. Everyone is a little embarrassed at his or her own earnestness, and dispels the feeling by taking a poke at somebody else.

Throughout the year there have been many such testimonials: the project presentations, interviews with reporters and other City Year visitors (those visiting the program are generally invited to a round-table discussion with corps members who talk about their service experiences), and recruitment presentations. With practice, people have learned to narrate their own experience, and while such story-telling often involves some simplification—and occasionally a kind of "airbrushing"—it also teaches people how to cull a concrete lesson from a range of memories. It gives a chance to focus, to force oneself to find what is good in an experience, and to learn from it.

After our audience with Fireman, we attend the shareholders' meeting. In a presentation about the company's charitable activities, Fireman describes City Year and then introduces the team. He asks us to stand up for the shareholders and they applaud loudly as we all bask in the crowd's approval.

Thirty

It isn't long before the initial rush of tasks in Chelsea slows to a trickle. Amy and Will have called everyone on their lists and are waiting for people to phone them back. Brendan and Alison have done all they can to plan the cemetery cleanup and are uncertain what else is expected of them. David and Earl keep busy, but Rosa, Chris, Richie, and Jackie are running out of things to do at ROCA. Chris and Rosa are particularly demoralized.

Each day we gather at a different Broadway lunch spot. People share their anxiety about the amount of "downtime" they are experiencing.

"We have almost nothing to do," says Will, with a plaintive note in his voice. "There are people we're supposed to call, but Ned says we should wait till next week. So we just sit around. Sometimes I think I should say something to Tony, but I don't really want to burden him. Plus, I think he knows, but he can't do anything about it."

Amy has a different reaction. She has always wanted to learn how to organize communities and she loves the work in Chelsea. I've rarely seen her so energized. "You're totally wrong," she says. "I can think of six people we could call this afternoon. We could write up an action plan. This is great experience."

Others on the team share Will's anxiety, however. They tell me guiltily about an afternoon when Rosa, Amy, and Will lay down on the carpet at Chelsea Main Street and dozed while Chris read aloud to them from the book he was reading at the time, *The Blackman's Guide to the Blackwoman.* "I was snoring!" confesses Will.

With so much downtime, there are lots of long, lazy lunches at Al Zack's, or at the Pizza Factory, or at Dotty's Lunch—we all agree that Dottie's serves great homemade soup. The team goes shopping up and down Broadway and explores the Chelsea Mall. Tony tools around in his beat-up Honda, accumulating parking tickets as he goes from sponsor to sponsor, checking in on team members, coordinating efforts, talking with their supervisors. He knows that everyone is not busy all the time, but he takes it in stride, simply encouraging people to be creative and to document their efforts as carefully as they can. Community organizing is like that, he points out; it is not conducive to a steady work flow.

Over time it becomes clear that the team is, in fact, accomplishing a good deal. Amy and Will have garnered support for the cleanup from schools, churches, and other agencies throughout the city. David and Earl have taken the boys in their after-school program to the Aquarium and the Science Museum, and have even brought in Tony for an afternoon of *capoeira* instruction, which the children loved. At ROCA, Jackie and Richie are helping to make a video about safe sex and are putting together a presentation on health to take to the schools. Brendan and Alison have done considerable research on the Garden Cemetery and are making a day-by-day educational plan for a kids' summer program at CNHS. Rosa and Chris are working on posters and flyers to publicize the cleanup, and Rosa is doing some translation work at ROCA.

There is a benefit to the downtime: it gives us a chance to relax together and to get used to one another as friends rather than just teammates. Thursday afternoons have been set aside for social activities—the team calls it "Team Bonding Day." We go bowling. We go boating on Jamaica Pond. One Thursday we go together at lunchtime to Faneuil Hall, a popular open-air market, and the women on the team spend an hour browsing together in a lingerie store. Rosa and Jackie try on a variety of matched sets and model them for the rest of us. When we finally emerge, the men are waiting, tapping their feet like annoyed husbands and smirking. "Why didn't you just stay all day?" asks Richie. "I'm glad you guys did some female bonding," says Tony, then asks, lowering his voice to a whisper, "Were you guys really trying stuff on?"

Team members are rarely absent on team bonding days. Even Richie is pretty consistent about showing up. We enjoy spending time together, and nobody wants to be left out. When someone is absent, everyone else feels the difference. The team as a unit seems to have taken on a life of its own, and each person has a special role to play within the team. Will is the analyst. David is the truth-teller. Chris is the cheerful optimist. Jackie is the prima donna. Amy is the activist.

Alison is the cynic. Richie is the renegade. Rosa is the child. Earl is the comic. Brendan is the critic. I am the big sister. And Tony is the parent, sometimes resented and sometimes revered. In these roles, we are exaggerated versions of ourselves, but the element of playacting adds enjoyment, and the sense of belonging is strong and welcome. For once, our group feels complete.

Thirty-One

Charles enters the glass-walled prisoner's box from a door at the rear. He looks thicker and more muscular than I remember him, and his hair, once close-cropped, is longer and combed upward in a flattop style. He glances around the courtrooom and glares at Richie, who looks away.

Richie is to testify against Charles today on the charge he brought for the assault at the day care center back in January. Charles has been brought by a prison bus from the Norfolk County Jail for the trial.

Richie is nervous, the more so because he feels abandoned. Jon was with us earlier for a little while, coaching Richie and offering support, but he left before Charles entered the courtroom, reminding Richie on the way out to ask for a court order banning Charles from City Year activities. Jon had been instructed by Alan not to let Charles see him, in part for fear of the retaliatory violence Charles might bring against City Year. Tony has been asked to stay away, although he wanted to come.

"I think Jon felt he had to leave because he really wanted to stay," Richie whispers to me, a little forlornly.

"Charles Jones," the judge announces, and I feel Richie's thigh tighten next to mine on the wooden bench.

Charles faces three charges this morning, arising from three separate complaints. The first is a charge of disorderly conduct. Charles is found guilty of that charge. The second, a charge of disorderly conduct and carrying a dangerous weapon, is dismissed because the police report is missing. The third is Richie's charge: assault and battery with a dangerous weapon—the chair that Charles's friends used to beat Richie.

Charles smiles as Richie is sworn in at the witness's podium across the room and identifies himself. Richie speaks carefully, but his sharp nasal accent seems to intensify with nerves. "I'm a corps member, we do nine months of community service in exchange for a scholarship, we help the homeless, the elderly," he says. The assistant district attorney stands up to question him.

"What were you doing the day of January 12, 1991?"

"We were planning activities at the day care center where I was working."

"At 4:45 P.M., what were you doing?"

"Talking on the phone."

"What happened?"

"I looked outside and saw Charles Jones. He pointed at me and said something I couldn't hear." At the prosecutor's request, Richie points to Charles, who is leaning forward and glaring at him. "I turned around again. He was out of the window. I looked again, and he was back with two other guys. They were pointing at me and talking. Then they came inside."

"Did Charles Jones say anything?"

"He asked me why I got him fired. He said he should steel on me now."

"What does that mean?"

"Steel on me. Hit me."

"What did you say?"

"I said, 'I didn't get you fired, Charles, you got yourself fired.' Then he hit me."

"Where?"

"In the face. Then somebody pushed me. Then I was down on the ground and the three of them were kickin' me and hittin' me."

Charles is laughing silently, his head thrown back as if the hilarity is too great for him to keep his composure.

The prosecutor returns to his seat, and the defense counsel cross-examines Richie.

"What's the name of the program?" he asks.

"It's called City Year."

"And are there benefits that come to you as a result of your being in this program?"

"A hundred dollars a week and a $5,000 scholarship at the end."

"And who is in this program?"

"It's a very diverse group. All walks of life."

"It's an opportunity?"

"An opportunity to serve others."

"You had an argument with Mr. Jones before, yes?"

"Yes."

"And he got fired?"

"Yes."

"And you did not?"

"No."

"That's all," says the defense counsel.

Maura, the staff member who broke up the fight in the day care center, has been subpoenaed as a witness. She testifies that she saw Charles punch Richie repeatedly in the face and the shoulders, then kick him when he was down on the floor. She notes, however, that it was not Charles but his two unnamed associates who tried to beat Richie with the chair. In fact, by the time they picked up the chair, Charles had already fled from the room.

The charge of assault with a dangerous weapon carries more serious penalties than simple assault. Charles's defense attorney asks the judge to strike the dangerous weapon from the charge. The judge is not sympathetic to his request.

"What about a joint enterprise?" asks the judge, looking toward the table where the prosecuting attorney is sitting. He gestures toward Charles. "This is the only person who said anything to him. This is the only person who threatened him. And we had evidence that he was kicked with a shod foot."

"But Your Honor, my client had already left the premises when the chair was used," says Charles's lawyer.

"Would you say he was abandoning the enterprise at that time?" asks the judge.

"Yes," says the attorney.

"Well, then, it sounds like a joint enterprise to me," says the judge. The lawyer looks dejected.

The judge asks for a report on Charles from the probation department and a man brings him a computer printout. "Steve Williams," he reads. "James Smith." These are aliases Charles has used in the past. The judge holds the report up and lets it open out, accordion-style; it is three pages long. He looks at the prosecutor. "And this isn't all, is it?" says the judge. "Because he's serving nine months out of Brookline now and that's not even on here."

The assistant D.A. asks for a one-year sentence, six months to be served in jail, and another six to be suspended for two years. The judge turns to Richie. "Do you have anything you want to say?"

Richie stands up. "Your Honor, I think Charles Jones could do it again and would do it again, and I don't want him around me ever again. And my employers have said they don't want him around the program."

The judge nods. "I find the defendant guilty," he says. "I sentence him to one year in the House of Corrections, to be served after he completes the sentence he is now serving."

Charles is still in the defendant's box as we leave the courtroom, and our path goes right past him. Richie walks by stiffly, facing front to avoid Charles's glance. Charles turns his head slowly to watch him leave.

Richie has gambled a lot in bringing this case to trial. Experience has shown that Charles is bitterly vengeful. But even though he has won, Richie does not feel triumphant. We stand a moment in the bright sun outside the courthouse, watching the court workers stream out onto the concrete for lunch. Richie has a pained look on his face.

Back at the headquarters, a couple of people congratulate Richie on his victory. "I don't know why they're congratulatin' me," he says. "It's not like I won a contest." Richie doesn't mention the trial to anyone else on the team; most do not even seem to be aware that it happened.

Thirty-Two

"I thought I couldn't have a baby," Rosa says softly. "I never used no contraceptive. I just thought I couldn't."

I am visiting with Rosa in the late afternoon, having driven her and two of the others home from work. Rosa got out last and invited me in; now we are sitting on her back porch. Rosa is perched on the railing, looking out over the broken cars and trash to where, a little farther out, the elevated tracks of a commuter train line rise up, rusting and huge. The tracks run from the wealthy suburbs south of Boston to the downtown financial district.

When she learned she was pregnant, Rosa telephoned the boy who was the father. They had already stopped seeing one another. She asked him for some money for an abortion. He refused.

"He wants me to have it!" she says, incredulous. "'Are you going to be there?' I asked him. 'No, of course you're not.'"

"My brother, my aunt—they both say abortion is wrong. I think so, too. But I'm not ready for a baby!" She looks at me, hard, then again across the yard, to where the sun is glinting dully off the tracks.

"I know what it's like. I raised my three little brothers. I fed them, I changed them. But how I'm going to know how to love a baby?"

When Rosa learned she was pregnant, she gulped down a handful of Tylenol—eight pills, maybe more—all that were left in the bottle. Afterward, she felt sick.

"You could die," her brother told her.

"I don't even want to live," she said.

Now she looks at me with a grimace. "I just didn't want to feel it no more. Sometimes I feel so bad, I just hit myself." She pounds her stomach fiercely with her fist. "There's something growing in me and I just want it out."

Rosa has made an appointment for a sonogram to determine the fetal age. It is a routine test, and without it a doctor will not perform an abortion. She thinks she is four weeks pregnant.

"If it's more than a month, I won't do it," she says. "Then it's really something there."

The light is fading. In the distance, there is a cracking noise, a brittle *pop pop pop.*

"Shooting," Rosa says.

"How much is eleven millimeters?" Rosa asks.

She is standing in the doorway of the tiny office at Chelsea Main Street. The rest of us are lounging around the edges of the room, waiting for something to happen. It has been a lazy morning—the big cleanup is just a few days away and all the preparations are just about complete.

Will holds out a finger and points to the fingernail with the other hand. "I think it's like that."

Jacquelyn pulls a ruler out of a drawer. "There's two point two centimeters in an inch," she says, cocking her head and looking at the ruler. Rosa and Will huddle around her.

"Why do you want to know?" asks Will.

"That's how big it is," says Rosa.

Will straightens. "That's nothing!" he scoffs. Jackie chimes in. "Just tissue and blood." Rosa nods, as if waiting for someone to say something more. She throws herself down on the floor next to me and drops in my lap an envelope stamped "ULTRASOUND REPORT." I open it and pull out a computer printout.

The fetus is 7.8 weeks old, according to the report, with a projected due date of December 1991. Eleven millimeters long. Status: alive.

"Alive," she whispers. "I gotta give them that paper when I go for the abortion."

On the morning of the abortion, Alison and I sit waiting in my car, looking out over the channel of water that divides Boston's financial district from the industrial neighborhoods of South Boston. A slight breeze brings the smell of salt water and petroleum products in through the car's open windows. It is nearly eight-thirty and Rosa is late. She asked us to meet her at eight. We both wonder if she has changed her mind. We watch for Rosa and Jackie in the rearview mirror. Rosa has asked us all to come and provide some moral support. Jackie has spent the night at Rosa's house, I know, so as to be with Rosa first thing in the morning.

The two appear together, running, slightly out of breath. "It's her fault we're late!" Rosa yells, pointing at Jackie.

Rosa is wearing a pink-and-white-striped shirt and white cotton pants. She is carrying a knapsack packed with all the things she has been told to bring. Towels. Kotex. A pair of white socks.

"I don't know why you gotta wear white socks for a abortion," says Rosa as they clamber into the car.

Twenty minutes later we are striding quickly across Beacon Street in Brookline. Already the day is getting steamy. The clinic is located in a genteel, residential-looking brownstone; it looks like any of the other buildings on the block, except for the discreet Planned Parenthood sign in the window. There are two men loitering on the sidewalk. Jackie is walking in front as we head for the building. As she crosses the wide sidewalk one of the men steps into her path, holding out a pamphlet.

"Don't go in," he says. "Skip your appointment. You don't want to do this. You'll be operated on by a doctor whose name you don't even know."

Jackie stares at him, incredulous, as Alison, Rosa, and I sweep by. Alison already has her arm around Rosa, shielding her. We rush up the steps and through the double glass door into an entrance hallway where another woman is standing, fumbling nervously with the inner door. "It's locked!" she whines.

Confused, we look around. A man has followed us in and is standing just inside the outer doors. Jackie pushes in behind him.

"Your baby loves you!" yells the man. His loud, plaintive voice quavers as it echoes around the hall. Alison is fumbling with the door. "Shut up!" I hiss at the man.

"Don't do this! Your baby loves you!"

"Mind your business!" Jackie screams.

Rosa is huddled in the corner, her face to the wall, sobbing passionately. Alison is hugging her, stroking her, trying to soothe her.

"Here! This is what your baby looks like!" The man holds out a tiny, flesh-colored rubber doll in the shape of a perfectly formed baby, curled, fetal-style. He is moving toward Rosa but Jackie and I block his path. He reaches into a pocket and the sound of a baby wailing fills the hall.

Rosa whips around, wailing herself. "Are you going to be there?" she demands, her eyes flashing. "Are you going to take care of it?"

"We want to help," he chants. "Your baby loves you! Your baby wants to love you!"

Jackie and Alison are pushing him toward the door. He backs up slowly, continuing his chant. "Your baby wants to love you!"

They maneuver him out the door and Alison pushes it shut and leans against it. The man is standing behind the glass, still holding out his doll, his mouth still moving. In that moment, we can see how small and old and withered he is. He no longer seems dangerous. Someone finds the doorbell, and a receptionist buzzes us in.

Rosa's face is wet and her hand skitters out of control across the page as she tries to fill out the registration form. But gradually her breathing slows. She heaves a shaky sigh.

The abortion is already paid for, Rosa tells us. City Year permitted her to take a $320 draw on the $2,500 public service award she will be owed at the end of her half-year of service. City Year sometimes allows corps members who are in good standing to borrow from their P.S.A. if they have a compelling need. Rosa received the advance and brought it over to the clinic last week.

We sit down and peep through the venetian blinds at the two men.

"I thought he was a priest," says Rosa.

After a while, the receptionist calls Rosa's name. She goes inside but soon comes back out; a nurse has taken some blood. The next time she is called it is to talk with a counselor; she returns looking calmer than before. Then there is a long wait. We chat quietly. Jacquelyn tells us how she and Rosa spent the prior evening.

"We got all dressed up and went down to Ruggles to see how many phone numbers we could get," she says, casting an impish glance at Rosa, who looks embarrassed. "I wore my polka-dot halter dress—you know the one?"

"You could see her boob at the side," says Rosa.

"Well, you should have seen what Rosie was wearing! She had this little low-necked push-up dress. We paraded around and watched the cars slow down when they went by. I'd flash them a brilliant smile. You should have seen their heads go around. We talked to a lot of guys."

"Did you take their numbers?" I ask.

"I didn't. But Jackie got a number," says Rosa.

Rosa's name is called again. "This is it," she says. "Wish me luck." She disappears through a door behind the receptionist.

An hour and a half later she emerges, looking pale and groggy, pressing her hands against her stomach. Our plan was to take her out to lunch, but she has no interest in eating. "Let's go," she says quickly, heading for the door. Outside, the sidewalk is empty—the men have apparently gone to lunch.

Inside my car, Rosa gingerly pulls the seatbelt halfway around her and holds it there. It hurts too much to fasten it, she says. "I have cramps," she says. "I didn't feel nothing when they were doing it." She sounds wistful. "But now it hurts. I want to lie down."

I can't tell if she wants to talk or just to be quiet. We are all a little awkward. Should we say something comforting? Pretend everything is all right?

Rosa leans her head back and closes her eyes. We drive in silence to her house, where her brother, Albert, is in the kitchen cooking vegetables and chicken. Rosa brushes past him to her room and throws herself on the bed.

We stay with Rosa a short while, and then leave her to be watched by her brother. We go out for lunch and talk about everything but Rosa and the abortion. On our way out of the restaurant, however, we stop to call Rosa from a pay phone. She says she is all right and not to worry.

I drive Alison home, and there Jackie makes a sudden change of plans. She wants to go back to Rosa's house. "I think I should stay with her," she says. It is with a certain relief that I drive her back to Dorchester.

Rosa lets us in and returns to where she has been lying on the couch, dozing and watching television. Jackie fetches a blanket and curls up in a chair; she falls asleep immediately.

I sit in the other chair and watch TV. Fred Flintstone has gotten mixed up with his evil twin and his entire life is falling apart. Rosa falls asleep and soon I do, too.

I awaken to find the room growing dark. The winking beam of the TV sends colored shadows moving across Rosa's face. Her eyes are closed. I try to tiptoe out quietly, without waking her and Jackie. But Rosa's eyes flutter open and she looks at me, concerned.

"You'd better get home and rest," she says. I nod, feeling useless: *she* is worrying about me. She closes her eyes again and I tiptoe out.

Rosa takes the next day off and returns to work the following day.

Thirty-Three

Everyone can see that Earl is drinking more than before. On Saturdays, he often shows up at Chris's house in the early afternoon with a half-finished forty-ounce bottle of malt liquor in one hand. Chris, Jackie, and Alison all try to tell him it is time to think about slowing down, but their words have no effect. He is sluggish and irritable and his eyes in the morning are often swollen and bloodshot. It is rumored on the team that Earl is also smoking a lot of marijuana, perhaps even coming to work high.

"I think Earl is an alcoholic," Tony tells me in private. "And he has a drug problem, too. I want to refer him to a thirty-day detox program immediately after graduation. I keep thinking if I say something to him about treatment, he'll skip out on us—that he'll quit. And I think it's important that he get that sense of completion first by finishing the year, so I'm just going to have to drag him through. But after that, I want him to get treatment."

Tony hasn't discussed the matter with Earl yet, but he has spoken with Earl's mother, who has pledged her support for the plan.

But Earl's situation is getting more desperate. He is very close to earning a G.E.D., but on the day he is scheduled to take the last portion of the test, he doesn't show up. And one Sunday night early in May, he is again arrested while hanging out with his friends and drinking. The arrest doesn't result in any charges, but he spends the night in jail and misses half a day of work.

Richie's performance is also slipping as the end of the year draws near. Everyone is aware that Richie has long ago run out the clock on absences and latenesses, but Tony is somehow letting him slide by. Richie's conduct and Tony's leniency are both beginning to affect the team's morale.

I ask Tony why Richie is still in the corps. "If Richie doesn't make it here," he answers, "I think he'll just go back to the life he was living before. He wants to do well, but he needs encouragement. And what has he got outside City Year? There are no adults in his life."

Richie now seems entirely changed from the person he was early in the year. On the days when he comes in to work at all he is groggy, dirty, and ill-tempered. He has been staying at Amy's apartment most nights, but she reports that she has not known him to use the shower yet. He smells of stale sweat, stale cigarettes, and stale chewing tobacco. He does not wash his clothes, either; his City Year T-shirt looks as if he has been sleeping in it and his once bright-red uniform jacket is dull with ground-in dirt.

He is tired all the time. Sometimes he catches a nap on a bench or on the couch at ROCA at lunchtime. Many on the team suspect that he is high most of the time, and Alison sees him take a bag of marijuana out of his pocket on the street in broad daylight. She is disdainful of his lack of discretion.

Richie still has his moments, however. He is popular with the kids who come to ROCA in the afternoons, and he enjoys organizing and supervising activities. "LET'S CHILL WITH THE CHIMPS," reads the poster he makes to advertise a field trip to the zoo. ROCA has a health awareness class for teenage girls, which Jackie is helping to teach. Richie, concerned that there is no analogous class for boys, starts one.

But Richie's descent continues. A corps member on another team reports that Richie has been trying to sell a new pair of City Year boots, raising suspicion that he may have stolen them from the headquarters. His attendance is growing even worse, and he makes no attempt to explain his absences, or else he lies about them. Finally, after a particularly egregious string of absences, Tony has to admit that it is time to fire Richie.

Tony speaks individually with each member of the team, explaining why Richie must be dismissed and lining up their support. "Isn't there anything we can do?" Jackie asks. But she knows there is nothing. The others simply nod assent. It has been months since Richie has shown any interest in the team or recognition of their concern for him. Even Amy, who has sheltered Richie off and on throughout the year, has lost her desire to help him.

Tony tries to telephone Richie with the news, but he can't be found at his grandparents' and Amy hasn't seen him for days. Nobody seems to know where he is.

Richie does not return to work to learn of his dismissal, but he does clandestinely remove his clothes from Amy's apartment one day while she and her roommate are working. He has his own key. Two days later, Amy and her roommate come home to find that their television, VCR, CD player and CDs, and a camera have been stolen. A Walkman that Richie knew to be broken is still lying on a bureau. There is no sign of forced entry. Amy accepts what has happened with apparent calm, but she feels deeply betrayed. She packs her clothes and goes to stay with her mother for a while.

Richie's abrupt departure comes just five weeks before he would have graduated from City Year. A couple of days after his disappearance I am going through some papers and I come across a copy of an essay Richie showed me just weeks earlier.

> The biggest lesson I have learned this year is a personal one. I have learned how to complete something. Before this year I had never completed anything in my life. I always found a way out and that doesn't get you anywhere.

Thirty-Four

During our final two weeks in Chelsea, we are quite busy preparing for the cleanup day. We walk the streets and the halls of a nearby shopping mall, handing out promotional flyers written in English, Spanish, and Khmer. Neighbors in Action is the name of the Saturday event. We put up posters, designed and drawn by Tony, all over the city: at bus stops, on lampposts, in the windows of most of the businesses along Broadway, even under the glass table tops in a Spanish restaurant. Amy and Will appear on the mayor's cable TV talk show and become celebrities of sorts. The newspaper keeps running pictures of the team and announcements about the cleanup.

By Thursday, two days before the event, 225 volunteers have signed up to help, and we are all hoping that even more people will show up. We will have seventy-five brooms and hundreds of heavy-duty garbage bags. City Year will also provide work gloves. Tony spends the day working the phone at the Main Street office, taking care of last-minute details: looking for hot dog buns; getting a friend to bring his ice cream truck for the day; making last-minute logistical plans. Amy and Will are writing yet another press release to send over to the newspaper; others are assembling folders with instructions for the "team leaders" who will be taking groups of volunteers to work in designated neighborhoods.

On Friday we go to the City Year headquarters for a presentation by another team about their project, which involved delivering drug awareness presentations in the schools. At the end of the day, Tony gathers the team together.

"Tomorrow may be a challenge," he says. "You may run out of bags. You may get lost. You may get to a block and find another group already swept it. You may have to improvise. Use your imagination. Keep your cool.

"This is a big event. But the planning is done. Let's work hard, but also enjoy it. This is the climax. Also remember, this is our event.

If there's anybody that's going to be the last to leave, it's going to be us."

The cleanup day is clear and hot. We gather at the Chelsea Main Street office at 8:00 A.M., two hours before the volunteers are to arrive, and then move to Quigley Park. Tony takes some tools over in a van borrowed from a local church, and we find that many more have already been dropped off. There are still tables to be fetched, as well as refreshments, but everything is going as planned. "Everything's coming together!" Tony keeps saying, as if he can't quite believe it himself.

At ten, the volunteers begin to arrive. Many of them are young children who have been recruited through the school (David and Earl have been visiting classrooms to talk up the event), some are teenagers affiliated with ROCA, and some church groups are represented as well. All in all, about a hundred volunteers come out. The number is half what we have anticipated, and we are forced to reduce the area we were planning to cover. But we manage to field three brigades, with at least two team members leading each brigade. The organizers from Chelsea say they have never seen so many people come out for a cleanup day, and the event generates a momentum of its own. As the day progresses, residents who see us working come out to help on their own streets and in front of their houses.

It is dirty work: picking up decomposing garbage that has blown into vacant lots, rolling away old, abandoned tires that are filled with stagnant water, and sweeping around the wheels of parked cars. But the children are energetic and don't care about the dirt, and their enthusiasm ignites the rest of us. "It's so important to keep the world clean," a sixth-grade girl tells me. "If we don't do it, who will?" She and her friend latch onto Alison and follow her around all morning, their eyes big with admiration. I wonder if those little girls will end up joining City Year, or something like it, six or seven years down the line.

There are other gratifying moments: for every person who stares dumbly at us from his stoop as we go by with our brooms and garbage bags, there is someone else who shouts encouragement or stops to help for a bit. A little boy drops his mother's hand and runs over to pick up a candy wrapper from the gutter and carefully place it in my bag. Brendan's group concentrates on a single vacant lot for a while, and their efforts bring out many of the residents along the street;

together, they assemble a veritable mountain of trash, ready for pickup. Tony is proud as a peacock: he cruises around in the van all day, troubleshooting and running errands, with an enormous grin on his face.

At the end, there is a celebration. We planned a festival of live music and dancing, but Richie was the one assigned to organize the entertainment. Nevertheless, Molly at ROCA has arranged for a deejay with a sound truck, so there is music, as well as plenty of refreshments, many of them homemade by members of the Hispanic Commission and distributed to the excited children by Alison, Amy, Rosa, and Will. There is also, of course, a long thank-you ceremony, and each Reebok Team member is awarded a framed certificate of appreciation. We stand proudly together for group photos and pro-nounce the day a success.

Later, when we evaluate the project, team members reveal mixed feelings. Will still worries that our time was underutilized. Jackie wishes we could have worked together more as a team. Amy would have liked more time for planning, so that the team could have really made the project their own. Rosa complains that we departed from our mission of helping immigrants by focusing on a cleanup day. Chris is angry with the residents who did not help with the cleanup. Earl is concerned at the fleeting nature of what we have accomplished; on a visit to Chelsea the following week he noticed that the streets we cleaned are already getting dirty again.

But people are also proud of their contribution to the fight against apathy in Chelsea. "On the cleanup day I had an overwhelming sense that City Year did something terrific there, and I hadn't even really been aware of what we'd been doing," says Will. For weeks afterward, Tony gets letters from our project sponsors in Chelsea, praising the team's efforts. Some claim their own energy and optimism have been renewed by the success of the volunteer cleanup day. Tony shares the letters with the team, and what bad memories people have are replaced with a growing sense of accomplishment.

Ending

On May 21 we return to the Virginia-Monadnock Garden to spend our last three weeks completing the work we began in the fall. Monadnock Street is quiet and bright with morning sun. There have been a few changes in the garden in our absence; the jungle gym has been transplanted to a new location near the street, and someone has repaired the chain-link fence. A backhoe and two operators are there when we arrive, getting ready to start work spreading sand in the new play area at the front of the lot. We stroll about the little park, checking out the place we once knew so well and telling Rosa, Will, and Chris what we have done so far. Bob Haas's house still looks the same; so does the empty house next door. And, of course, we all look up to see that the black Adidas sneakers are still dangling from the telephone wire high overhead.

"You still want to get them down?" asks Chris with a smile.

"Of course we do!" says David.

"Yes!" says Tony.

We go over and stand beneath the sneakers, wondering how on earth to reach them. They are almost twenty feet overhead.

One of the backhoe operators has been listening to our conversation, a big man with an admirable gut and a friendly face. He saunters over, carrying a twelve- or fifteen-foot board. While we were talking, he was deftly nailing a saw blade to one end. He now gives his creation to Tony and David.

Together they hoist the contraption, trying to catch a shoelace in the teeth of the saw, but they have no success. The sneakers dance and twirl, eluding them like agile fighters taunting a clumsy opponent. They try slapping the sneakers with the saw, and one shoe flies up and over the wire, but remains hanging—it's wrapped around several times. After a while they give it up and join the rest of us to begin laying out a work plan for the week.

Fifteen minutes later we stand and stretch, ready to start work. I cast one regretful look at the sneakers, and am surprised to see that one is gone.

"Hey, you guys!" I point at the remaining shoe, hanging alone from a single lace. The other, big and stiff as a dead crow, is lying on the ground below.

"We can get the other one!" cries Tony. "Somebody come help!" He and David have already raised the long saw again. I join them, and soon Chris comes over to relieve Tony. We poke and stagger. It isn't easy to sight up the board as well as keep one's balance. We miss. We miss again.

Suddenly the second shoe comes dropping down. It hurtles past my head and splatters on the ground, a leathery old thing, swollen with rain and snow. Surprised, we stare, then look at one another, still balancing the board with the saw aimed skyward. We begin to laugh.

It is a long, shared belly laugh, deep with pleasure and shot with irony. We laugh for our sweet victory, a silly thing: removal of two stinking sneakers from a telephone wire over a patchy garden. Our aspiration: dubious war against symbolic foe. Our tool: a rusty saw nailed to a stick.

It is one of those moments one doesn't soon forget, and it stays with me, a snapshot of our year that seemed to capture everything we have accomplished, as well as all that we have not. The team that has returned to finish the project in the garden is a different team from the one that began the job eight months before. A stronger, more successful team. A gamer team, more prone to spend a morning fumbling to cut some sneakers off a wire. A less rebellious team, more willing to acknowledge wisdom in the rules of others and to take a leap of faith. A sadder team, because our victory includes the losses of the ones we've left behind. Here in the garden, I feel as if the others are still near. Tyrone and Lisa, giggling on this very spot; Tracy, trundling off to take a break or buy a snack; June, delicately pulling weeds, one strand at a time; Charles, shoveling feverishly until he can no longer breathe; Richie, tenderly transplanting a forsaken, gangly bush.

Their failure to complete the year does not diminish what they did when they were here. And as for all the rest of us, well, here we are—still doing what we had set out to do.

Thirty-Six

We work hard in the garden for three more weeks. We put in new garden beds, reinstall the playground equipment, and build paths throughout. We all focus diligently on the details of each task. Perhaps it is a way to avoid focusing on each other—and on the fact that we will soon be separating.

Although they rarely speak about their plans within the team, most people know where they are going next. Alison and David are both going to attend Earlham College in Indiana in September. Chris is going back to the University of Michigan to finish up his degree, and Jackie is going to Harvard, where she will enter as a sophomore—they say they knew all along their romance would end with graduation from City Year. Amy is going to transfer to the University of Massachusetts at Amherst, and Brendan, while he has not yet enrolled in a degree program, plans to begin taking courses at UMass in Boston over the summer. He received his high school equivalency degree in April.

Rosa will return to City Year in the fall to serve for another semester, and Will, eager to continue in public service, will join the City Year staff as a junior member. Earl, without prompting from Tony, has decided to enter a residential treatment program for alcoholics and drug addicts after graduation.

We have a final retreat at Tabor Academy, a private school by the sea near Cape Cod. Paul Fireman is a big contributor to the school and has arranged for City Year to borrow the campus now that school is out. Our city year is ending as it began, in an idyll far from the city that brought us together. We spend two languorous days in this beautiful, sun-washed spot, swimming and sunning, listening to music and talking. Some of the team members begin the work of taking leave of one another. Most of us do not; it is easier to pretend that things can go on this way forever.

Just before we are to get on the buses and head back to Boston, Alan calls the corps together on the grass overlooking the water. We stand, as we are now so accustomed to doing, in a huge cluster as he faces us. His look conveys a mix of pride and sadness.

"Back in the beginning," he says, "at Camp Becket, we talked about family and about creating an environment where we all cared about each other. In retrospect, I can see that that was a little premature. But I look at you all now, and I can honestly say that those hopes have come true.

"We fight like a family, that's for sure. But we make up like a family, too, and we all care about each other. The staff here at City Year will come and go but you will always have each other. Stay connected to each other.

"You're entering a world that is different from City Year. City Year is an alternative community, one that I am incredibly proud of. But the world isn't always like it is here. The first time you come across somebody in need and the group you are in ignores it, it will be hard for you. Don't get frustrated.

"Stay involved with public service in some way. It's in your blood now, whether you believe it or not. You signed up for this, and you spent a year living out your values. The challenge now is to continue, because it will get harder as you get older. There's a new battle being fought in the world today, one you've been fighting all year. It's the battle between idealism and cynicism. Idealism is looking at the world and saying, 'We can do better. I'm going to make it better. I'm going to start an after-school program. I'm going to organize a community cleanup. I'm not going to accept things the way they are.' Idealists say, 'Let's go.' Cynics say, 'Why try?' But once we lose the idea that positive change is possible, we've lost the battle. Practice idealism."

Alan stops, his face radiant in the waning light, and at that moment, the school's dinner bell begins to toll in the distance—our signal to depart. When it stops, the corps breaks into applause. Then we grab our bags and pile onto the buses.

The entire corps spends the next two days preparing for graduation—making decorations, preparing skits and presentations, rehearsing speeches. The ceremony is held on a Friday night at the Cyclorama, a large hall in Boston's South End that often hosts public events. We decorate the walls with displays that illustrate our year. Each team creates its own mural. The Reebok Team's contribution includes six panels devoted to "Reebok Moments"—important events in the life of our team. The spider web. Tyrone's death. Cleaning out the basement at the Cornerstone House. Cutting down the sneakers.

My favorite panel is the one commemorating the addition of three new members to the team. Rosa made this panel. "WELCOME," it says. "*Welcome* means that you are loved, since the first time they saw you. *Welcome* means that you can stop looking for a safe place, because you have found one. *Welcome* is a beautiful word that the Reebok Team told to Chris, Rosa, and Will when they joined City Year in January."

Nearly 300 people attend the graduation, including parents and siblings and children of corps members, politicians, project sponsors and supervisors, reporters, funders, and even some of the teachers and children from the Blackstone School. Bob Haas from Monadnock Street is there, as are all of our friends from Cambridge and Chelsea.

The auditorium is round, and the corps and staff are seated beside the stage, facing the rest of the audience. Just as the lights are about to dim, I hear a rustle and turn to see Tracy standing near the wall, just behind the section of the audience where the corps is seated. "Can I sit here?" she asks, then answers herself. "Oh, no! These seats are for corps members!" She remains standing to watch the presentation.

Jackie and Will have been chosen to emcee the graduation ceremony, and they are radiant in their roles. "Ladies and gentlemen," they begin, "we're here to tell you how together we can change the world!"

The ceremony lasts almost three hours. There are music and dance numbers, and presentations of plaques and awards for project sponsors and funders. G.E.D. dipolomas are awarded. There is a tribute to Tyrone, and his mother, Tiajuana, is honored on stage. A group of corps members read their own "State of the City" address, a testament to the needs we have all encountered in our year and the promise of improvement we have seen through service.

The Reebok Team has decided to have each member bring a souvenir of the year and recount its meaning for the audience. I sit with the corps during their presentation and watch with rising emotion. They look proud and confident, their faces shining in the hot stage lights.

Will has brought a miniature bench, representing a park bench he and Rosa spent days installing at the Virginia-Monadnock Garden. Rosa has brought a team photo—"to represent all the things we have shared."

Jackie holds up a drawing of an airline ticket: the one she contemplated buying to go home to Florida when she wanted to quit City Year, back in the fall. She is glad she did not quit, she explains. If she had, she would have missed an important chance to learn and grow.

Alison has brought the sneakers we cut down from the wires over the Virginia-Monadnock Garden; she explains their value as a symbol of accomplishment for the team.

Brendan holds up the picture his student Matt drew for him at Christmastime: "City Year—Reebok—I love you—Matt."

Amy has the disposable lighter that she retrieved from Linda, the lost and drunken woman who passed out in the Dorchester House of Pizza and was aided by the team. She reads her journal entry from that day.

Chris has a menu from the Shanghai Restaurant, a memento of a gesture he appreciates: the team's choice to include him, on the day he joined us, in a team ritual that dated from the night of Tyrone's death.

David shows off a potholder that he made with the boys in the Chelsea after-school program.

Earl has brought his uniform pants—the ones with the green stripe of paint across the legs. "I done crazy work in these pants," he explains.

When the ceremony is over, many on the team are in a rush to join their friends and families, some of whom have come a long way to attend. We have a last, hurried team meeting in the darkened wings behind the stage.

"Congratulations," says Tony. "It's a huge accomplishment, not just to finish City Year but to finish City Year on my team. I have tried very hard to make this year challenging for you. I wanted you to know that if you stayed true to your values, you would win out and get the things you set out to get. You guys have been true to your values."

We all stand motionless in the darkness as Tony continues.

"At the beginning of the year I said to you all that I didn't like any of you and I wasn't here to be your friend. Tonight, I am proud. I don't just like all of you, I love you—and I want you to think of me as your friend, and as someone who will support you for the rest of your lives."

"Also—" Tony's voice gets thick. "Also, remember Tyrone. I know that he would have loved to have been here tonight with us."

"Whatever you do, remember this experience. The children you taught, the work that you did, the friends that you made. The work and the people—that's what counts."

Finished, Tony puts out his hand and David takes it. And then, solemnly, we shake hands all around.

Epilogue

In 1991, one year after my team completed the program, City Year received a $7 million federal grant from the Commission on National and Community Service to expand and develop over two years as a model for a system of national service. The corps grew to 220 members the following year and made plans to enroll 500 by the fall of 1993 as well as to launch replication efforts in Rhode Island and South Carolina. Governor Bill Clinton visited City Year during his campaign for president, and later announced that national service would be a "defining idea" of his presidency. He identified City Year as a promising model.

In the spring of 1993, nearly two years after the end of my City Year, I sought out my teammates—those who had completed the year and those who hadn't—to learn what they were doing and to find out about the impact of the experience on their lives.

ALISON

Alison spent the summer after City Year working at the library where she had done her internship, and in the fall she went to Earlham, a Quaker college in Indiana. David attended Earlham as well, and they saw each other at school often. Alison took courses in sociology and agriculture and did community service through the campus volunteer center, helping out with chores and babysitting for a poor family in a nearby trailer park and organizing a recreational program at a housing project in Richmond. After a year and a half, she was forced to transfer to the University of Massachusetts, in Amherst, for financial reasons.

When I went to visit her at UMass, she had been there only two months but seemed to be adapting well. She was majoring in sociology and had signed up to work at a local jail, teaching a class for prisoners that was intended to help them learn to set goals and make responsible decisions. We talked in the cafeteria at the UMass student center.

"It seems weird, but before City Year no one had ever asked me to do anything. My Sunday School fasted for Oxfam; I read books for multiple sclerosis. I walked for hunger. But volunteering wasn't in my high schools, it just wasn't accessible in general. City Year struck me as an opportunity. Someone was asking me to give back to the city that I had been in a parasitic relationship with. I wasn't your prime citizen—I was a little brat doing bratty things. I wanted to give something back.

"I always had a diverse set of friends. But this was different. When Tyrone died, it was hard to explain to people how things really were. 'Well, no, we weren't really close friends. Yes, we worked together, but it wasn't, like, stand at the water fountain and chitchat, or wait in line at the fax machine. We really did things together and we had to cooperate, and it's just a whole different relationship.' It's a relationship I don't think many people encounter in their lifetime. Especially working with people who really are from different places and have had such different experiences.

"Our team was not happy-go-lucky. We had a real identity problem: kind of a bunch of hooligans. I felt kind of detached a lot of the time. I don't think anyone alienated me or anything. It's just me. It was a kind of coping mechanism. Every time a new situation arose, a problematic situation, I coped the same way. I just refused to make myself vulnerable, because I knew that I really was vulnerable. I knew it was a really risky situation. You can't escape from your team; you're stuck with them.

"I felt really good about the work. I *really* enjoyed our projects, especially the physical work. Who knows what impact I had on those kindergartners? Probably the most important thing is that I showed them that somewhere out there someone cares. A little bit. I don't think they'll remember it, but they'll carry it with them.

"In terms of the physical service, you can really calibrate the work that you've done. Physical service is concrete. And that's very, very satisfying and it's something our team needed. Sometimes we got sick of it, but there wasn't a sense of futility. *We've done work.* If all else fails, we've gotten this done.

"I think it's really ridiculous to think a year's going to have that much impact on years and years of whatever has happened to a person. It's not going to save people, and expecting that is really damaging.

"But I'm sure everyone has changed to some degree. And I think that we did a pretty good job of working together. Some of us were polar opposites. But we functioned and worked together. People learned how to communicate. I'm sure some stereotypes were broken down. And I think that's *plenty!* I went to a diverse high school, but you don't talk about morals and values when you're sitting in a math class. It just doesn't happen. You can go to the University of Massachusetts and supposedly experience diversity, but it's not in your face. There's a very big difference. City Year forces you to do that. If you're going to do your job, it's an obstacle you're going to encounter.

"I can't imagine anything else that helps so many people so much. It makes me disgusted that for so long service has been something for the elite: volunteerism. And there are so many people out there who aren't doing anything—who need to be asked to help. Who need to be called to service. If everyone took a year off before college—because in my plan, everyone gets to go to college—if everyone could take some time and do City Year, what a different place this would be.

"I always felt like I didn't have any skills. I was never really artistic or athletic, and all my friends had something. And I'm not religious, but this is the closest I could ever come to a calling. I can't imagine ever doing something where I didn't feel like I was helping people. This is really what I need to be doing. So that's my goal."

AMY

After City Year, Amy transferred from Boston University to the University of Massachusetts, and in March of 1993 she was preparing to graduate with a degree in sociology. I visited her the same day I visited Alison. She had just taken a midterm exam and she looked a little weary, but she was cheerful. She showed me her attic apartment off campus and then we drove to a coffee shop to talk. She said she was beginning to look for a job after graduation, perhaps in Washington, working for an advocacy group that deals with women's health issues. She had spent a summer working to organize a clinic for women in West Virginia and was volunteering on campus at the Everywoman Center as a counselor for women who had been raped and battered.

Amy had once told me in confidence that she had been raped by a former boyfriend during her second year of college, and that the confusion and depression she felt after that were a primary reason she had taken a year off and joined City Year. At the time, she asked me to leave that fact out of the book. But a few days after this interview, and after she had read the manuscript of this book, she telephoned me and asked me to include the rape in her story. She felt it helped to explain both her moodiness during the year and the choices she had made subsequently. Through her work counseling women in crisis she had grown more comfortable talking about her experience, and allowing it to be included in this book was for her another step in healing.

"The day of the orientation, with all the new corps members, I went to my mother's and said, 'I don't want to do this program. This is not for me. I don't want to deal with all these people, I don't know who they are, and what they are.' I was scared. I hadn't been briefed in the type of people that would be in it, and, you know, I grew up in suburban Massachusetts, and I went to Boston University, and I knew my token inner-city friend, but not like this. I didn't know anyone who had ever gone to jail.

"And when I got my name called for Tony's team, I went, 'Oh, my God.' I got along with Brendan at the time; I didn't know Jackie or Alison; and Charles, Tyrone, Richie, and Earl scared the living shit out of me.

"Right away, we had problems. We were arguing and arguing. It was pretty pathetic. The ropes course was a low point for the team. At that moment I hated Tyrone and Charles. And I couldn't stand having them tell me what to do when I knew damn well it wouldn't work. I was really frustrated those first couple of weeks in the garden. Fear was no longer an issue. It was just, 'Why aren't they working? Why are they expecting me to do their work?'

"At that point I had already dropped out of school. And I knew that if I didn't finish this program I would never finish anything else again in my life.

"The day we were in Charlestown cleaning apartments, I was pissed off at Tyrone and I'm sure he felt the same about me. He considered me a rich, spoiled brat. Which I probably was. But something happened. We got done early and Tony said we could take a long lunch. So Tyrone and I went to lunch together at this pizza parlor and he and I just sat and talked. We were laughing, and joking. And the things he said to me, I gained so much respect for him that afternoon. I thought, maybe we can be friends. And the next day I came to work to hear that he'd been shot.

"We all lost it after that. I think we had to pull back from each other. The fear of losing yet another member. And then we lost Lisa. And then we lost Charles, and then Tracy, and then June. One right after another and well, hell! Why get close to anybody? Who's going to be around until the end? I couldn't deal with getting close to anybody else on the team and having them take off. Those are issues I've been dealing with all my life, about people leaving me.

"Most of the people on my team that City Year was supposed to help, it didn't help. People like Charles and Richie need more than City Year, and they need more than somebody saying, 'Oh, you poor thing, come here and let me help you.' I think what they needed to do was offer some sort of support system that City Year did not have. The teams were supposed to be a support but it was a very superficial support system.

"With Richie, there's a part of me that really wants to believe he didn't rob my apartment. Factually I know he did. But it's easier for me to think that he didn't do it. And when I think about him, I feel sorry. He almost made it, and I thought he was going to make it.

"I would have liked to have had half the year spent at the Blackstone and half the year spent at Chelsea. The project in Cambridge had so much potential, but it went nowhere. We could have done anything—why didn't we? Interviewing homeless people and what it was like for homeless children. We could have organized them to help us paint—paint *with* us. Teaching them skills. With us.

"City Year began to help me formulate what I wanted to do. I am now doing organizing work on campus around the issue of violence against women. I had to do community service to find out that organizing is what I want to do. I want to work to empower women in the area of health care, and especially in the area of birth. If you can deliver a baby into the world with a happy environment, the child is going to do wonderfully. And it all begins with teaching the mother.

"City Year was a very interesting year. And I will say, it totally changed the course of my life. No matter how painful it was, and you know I went through periods of great depression and sadness and anger—but the greatest lesson I learned from City Year was, I learned how to feel something. You couldn't go through the year without feeling something. Up until that point, I had gone numb. So much of my life the only thing I could feel at any point was depression. I didn't know what it was like to feel happy, or sad, or angry. I couldn't deal with my parents, and my parents' divorce—or anything else in my life. And during City Year I learned how to feel angry. It took me a while to figure out how to express it properly, but at least I could feel it, you know? And I learned how to get frustrated and it'd be okay. And I learned it was okay to be irritated. I learned it was okay to cry and it was okay to feel sad and to mourn. All those things I needed to learn. And City Year taught me that. It taught me how to be a human being. Instead of a machine. Just living. That's what I'll always credit City Year for."

BRENDAN

Brendan, who had earned his G.E.D. about a month before City Year graduation, waited tables and took some courses at the University of Massachusetts in Boston over the summer, and in the fall he began taking a full course load. He moved out of his mother's home into an apartment that he shared with friends. He also worked out at a local gym and got a part-time job there as a trainer. He decided to major in exercise physiology and within a year had begun entering local "all-natural" (no steroids allowed) bodybuilding contests. He retained his interest in acting—he continued to take acting courses at school and still dreamed about getting into the movies—but bodybuilding had become an overriding interest. He might like to own his own gym one day, he said. I met him outside Gold's Gym in downtown Boston, and he gave me a quick tour before we headed off to a pizzeria for lunch. He was no Arnold Schwarzenegger, but his arms were enormous. He seemed more confident and spirited than I had seen him in a long time.

"Our first project—at the Virginia-Monadnock Garden—was really good. For me that was fun. I like hard physical work. It felt good that I was doing something and that when I went home I was tired. I felt like Superman when I had that uniform on.

"But it was definitely very trying to have to be willing to let go of my own personal wanting to be the leader. I wanted everything to be perfect, I wanted people to see us in the perfect light, and when I thought that we weren't being perfect, I was pissed. Very angry. I wanted everyone to know that, hey, these kids are doing something, not just goofing off and wearing these stupid jackets everywhere.

"For a long time, Tyrone and I hated each other and just that day—the day he was killed—we started to make ground in starting a friendship. We discovered that we weren't that different; we just both wanted things to be perfect. And I felt so betrayed by him and by everyone that this could happen to him.

"After that, I kind of closed up and shut off and kind of went into my corner. Closed the door, locked it, zip. Just now I'm kind of coming out of it, but very slowly, you know? I just started feeling things like the way I used to. Just in the last two months or so.

"For the rest of the year I was by myself. I was too scared. Afraid to lose another person. By the end of the year I realized that was stupid and tried to make an effort, but it was too late.

"I learned a good lesson: that you have to appreciate the people around you more. Their feelings are just as important, maybe even more important than your own. I'm working to be a little more open, a little more friendly. Not so pushy or so me, me, me.

"Before City Year, I had always quit things: I quit football, I quit the Boy Scouts, I quit school, and sometimes I had good reasons and others it was just me wimping out. This time I was like, 'There's no way in hell I'm quitting.' It was very important to me that I finally accomplish something.

"I felt the people who quit City Year let themselves and us down. Tracy and Richie irked me the most. Richie especially, because he came so damn close. And Tracy just gave up. I get really angry about that, because I used to give up. And when I stopped giving up I felt so much better about myself. I tried to tell them that, but you can't tell somebody how to live their life. They have to figure it out on their own. That's another thing I learned through City Year.

"There were times when I thought we were just doing slave labor. There were also times, like when we were at the Blackstone school, that I thought if we weren't there, the job wouldn't have gotten done.

"Since City Year, I've done some stuff around my community, organizing, but I haven't actually done any service work—I'm a little embarrassed about that. It's more lack of time than lack of interest. But I also think that at some point in time you have to put yourself first so later you can make a contribution.

"I think everyone should do service at some point. If nothing else, for the experience of working with nine or ten other people. It's different than working in an office situation. I've heard a lot of people say that City Year as a national thing would cost too much. But what it gives to the individuals who do it, and what society gets back for it, far outweighs the cost.

"City Year has definitely changed how I'd like to look at myself and how I look at other people. It's a group that you can fit into, no matter if you're black, white, poor, rich—you all wear the same uniform, you all do the same stupid work. The uniform's important. It's time to stop emphasizing all our differences so much.

"People are not all that different. We go through the same hardships, we see people die, see people live, we all have problems with our parents, we all have money problems at some time, we all have problems defining ourselves—we all have these problems. The only difference, in my mind, is how we deal with them."

CHARLES

Charles appealed his conviction for assaulting Richie, and when the case came to trial it was dismissed because Richie did not show up to testify. Charles was released sometime during the summer of 1991, but at the time of these interviews, he was back in jail, serving time in the Norfolk County House of Corrections, just outside of Boston. I went to see him during his visiting hour one Thursday night.

Charles was not expecting me, and I was a little afraid he wouldn't want to see me, but he laughed and greeted me as a friend, and we spent an hour conversing across a wooden table in a room with the other prisoners and their guests.

He looked well; he was wearing new wire-rim glasses and he had grown a goatee. He answered my questions sincerely, without the reluctance and hostility he had so often shown in earlier conversations. One thing in particular struck me about his demeanor: he was constantly distracted by whatever else was happening in the room. In mid-sentence he would turn around to look behind him. Once I had seen this same behavior as disrespectful; now it appeared to me involuntary. It impeded conversation, and it made me wonder how the course of Charles's life might have been different had his treatment for hyperactivity not been discontinued when he was little.

"I'm doing fine, I'm straight, there's no drugs here. I'm doing six months. Probation violation. I didn't go to my probation officer. Didn't feel obligated. I just stopped going. I said, let them find me!

"When I joined City Year, I had just gotten out of jail. Thirty months I'd been in. Thirty months. I was so glad to be out of there, I felt invincible. I felt like I ruled the world. They couldn't do nothing to me. I was crazy. I was wild.

"My family sent me to City Year. 'That's the program for you,' they said. But it wasn't the right time. I thought working and going to school would clear my mind and keep me out of trouble, but I was wrong. Every day I was just waiting for those eight hours to end, and *psssshhh*! I was outta there.

"I had fun, though. I liked the Blackstone School. I got a lot out of that, and what I could give to those kids. That felt good.

"I liked Richie at the beginning. I had fun drinking and getting high with him and Earl. But we had some words. It was just childish words, and Richie took it wrong.

"I can't believe I got convicted for that. I never touched him! 'Joint enterprise.' I appealed it and they dismissed it.

"I look back and I say, it's good what happened, happened. When I went into jail, I was saved. I was sniffing heroin, selling cocaine. Carrying a gun everywhere. If I'd stayed out, I'd have been dead. I'd have been in the paper. All my enemies are in jail now for murder. Jail saved me.

"After I got out of jail last summer I tried to find work but there were no jobs. I worked for about a minute at Au Bon Pain. I quit as soon as I got enough money to go solo. I was all fucked up. I was all fucked up.

"Jail doesn't have nothing for me now. I'm not taking any classes, I'm not motivated to get a G.E.D. We got seven hours a day free time. Nothing to do but watch TV and play ball. I read a lot. Everything I can get my hands on."

I asked him if he thought he'd go back to drugs when he got out of jail in two months.

"I hated that stuff. I wasn't addicted, because I didn't want it. My body needed it, but I didn't want it.

"Maybe I'll go down to Atlanta, stay with my aunt. She has a chicken farm there. I went there when I was little. Massachusetts doesn't hold much for me.

"I still got the picture of the team—you know, the one we took down Dudley? I take it out and look at it sometimes."

I recently came across a copy of a poem that Charles wrote in jail and sent to David, who shared it with me. The title is "The Man on the Street."

I see this man sitting in a cage
Running threw his mind is a raw kind of rage.

He nows his days are numberd.
But before he's put to rest he said it will be like a champ.

Not if he keep's messing around with all those cheep tramps.

He's say's to him-self that when he gets much older that his life will
     be set
but only if he new but soon he will regreat.

But while he's still young he's going to have all his fun.

So he goes down the street to find some-body to beat for a buck or
     two instead of dropeing back into school.

I invision this old man sleeping
In a storm drain
I wish I could help
But that's all I felt.

His life just went bye at a blink of an eye.
No more money no more girls.
Was it really worth him killing his own world.

Some-times socity is a curse if you really
understood my peom you'll here it in ever verse.

Now this kid grew up to fast to only be the biggest nobody should
     this thing we call socity laugh.

I invision this old man with a bottle of Night-Train in one hand.
When I look to my windo just to only see the Rain.

CHRIS

I couldn't find Chris to interview him for this epilogue. His phone in Detroit had been disconnected. Jackie reported that he had not gone back to school as planned but had been living in Detroit, working and trying to save money. They had fallen out of touch, she said. When she last heard from him, he had been planning to enlist in the military. His aunt in Boston said she had heard the same thing but had no telephone number or address for Chris, his brother, or his mother. I wrote to the Armed Services Locator Service and was informed that Chris was not on active duty.

Many of the others spoke affectionately of Chris, but they also told me something surprising: that he had been selling marijuana to other corps members, and had occasionally smoked pot at work with Earl and Richie. I would have liked to ask him about this.

DAVID

David drove a truck in Tony's ice cream business on Cape Cod the summer after graduating from City Year, then went to Earlham College, in Richmond, Indiana, where he became interested in Marxism and the history of revolutionary movements. He went with a group to Nicaragua and met some of the Sandinista leaders, and on his return he became involved with a campus group called the Committee in Solidarity with Latin America. He grew disaffected with Marxism, however, and began studying yoga. In his sophomore year he took a semester abroad to study at the Yoga Institute in India.

When I talked with him by phone from his dorm room at Earlham, he had been back in the United States a couple of months.

"When I joined City Year, I wanted to work through some of my own problems by serving the community. I wanted to work with people of different races, really explore parts of myself that I couldn't explore when I was in school. I wasn't that thrilled with who I was, who I'd been in high school. I didn't really like that person. That year was almost like an exploration of who I really wanted to be.

"I also had this fascination with the city; it seemed so glamorous, such a high lifestyle. I wanted to see if it was for me.

"City Year gave me a framework to interact with people I normally wouldn't come across in my everyday life. At the beginning I thought they were beyond me. Too cool for me. But City Year gave me the ability to interact with them and find out that was not really what I wanted. I really gained an understanding of what the inner city was like through Charles, hanging out with him. Talking to Charles about what dealing was, I got another view of what drugs can do to people.

I had used pot and alcohol, and I had a complex that they were the right thing to do. I was brought up that way. But when I saw what it did to other people—my friends at City Year, the shit they went through—I realized that wasn't completely true. Now I've eliminated drugs and alcohol from my life.

"I felt that with Charles I was so interested in the beginning to go and explore and to experience what his drug culture was, that I totally left myself. I just tried to experience Charles, and I kind of lost touch with who I was. I lost any kind of power that I had to bring in my own beliefs. I didn't think that I had the right, being white, to talk about his lifestyle. But if I'm gonna spend a lot of time with him, then I do have that right—the right to share my views.

"Charles can do what he wants, but I decided I wouldn't do it with him. In my heart, I feel that it's wrong. By knowing that wasn't me, that whatever I experienced with Charles wasn't what I wanted to be, that gave me hope and understanding of who I wanted to be.

"Tony played an important role for me. He pushed me to explore my options with T'ai Chi, and that moment of silence at the beginning of the day, those were very important parts of my spiritual searching.

"I remember two-thirds of the way through the year saying that this was great but there's something more; I needed something more. I think that my City Year experience helped me to begin to have some fundamental understanding of love and giving. That was an important part of spirituality and of my growth as a person.

"Being a teacher's aide was part of it. It was a lot of fun feeling that I was helping, and feeling the love that the kids gave me, it made me want to be a better person, so they would have better people around for their world. I wanted to grow, to be of some use to the people.

"City Year gave me a lot, opened my eyes to a lot of the problems of the world, in a more realistic fashion, and just a much deeper sense of who I am. And I think it can do that for other people, as well. It was definitely a turning point in my life.

"The goals that I got out of it were that I had to become love. And now that means just trying to be a creature of love and bless whatever comes my way. Now when I try to go out and do something, I feel it's like taking my limited views and imposing them on someone else. For me, that's not as effective as just kind of living my life, and whoever comes my way just being with them for their problems. I have to bring love into the place where I am by being a better person and being available to people.

"Alison tells me that's wrong—to go out and do some community service. But I really feel that my greatest good is just trying to be there.

"Next year I'll be a yoga teacher here, which affects ten percent of the school population each term. That's a hundred people that I'm gonna be able to talk to about life and philosophy. And I don't feel as much of a need to go out and serve—it's better for me to accept whatever God sends my way."

EARL

I ran into Earl often after the year was over; he spent a lot of time hanging out in public places. He had left the detox program just a few days after entering, complaining that they wouldn't let him use the phone often enough, and although he claimed to be trying to stop drinking, when I saw him he often had a beer in his hand and appeared drunk or high. He called me from time to time to chat—as he did Alison and Tony and some of the others—and he often bragged about this or that recent arrest.

In the summer of 1992, I stopped hearing from him and later learned that he had served a few months in jail for assault. He had picked a fight with a man who looked at his girlfriend the "wrong way." When he got out his mother would not let him return to her house, and he got an apartment. He took a job working at McDonald's and a second job washing dishes in a Cambridge restaurant. He was working fifty hours a week, he told me, and selling marijuana on the side.

He was arrested again in January 1993 on charges of armed robbery and attempted murder. He had been involved in a mugging in which a friend of his clubbed the victim with a handgun. He called me a couple of times from jail but did not let on where he was until later. He was convicted of a reduced charge of assault and given a twenty-four-month suspended sentence. After his release, he managed to get both jobs back and he continued to call for a while. He had no phone of his own, so I could not call him. During our last conversation he sounded frightened and confused. He said he feared he was "going crazy" and that he had lost all of his friends. We made an appointment to get together but he didn't show up. He missed a second appointment as well. The following is compiled from notes I took (with his permission) during three earlier telephone conversations in February 1993.

"I was a real roughneck kid. I appeared to have it all, the nice clothes, the nice house, but I was kind of disturbed. Always getting in trouble. And I joined City Year so I could contribute to the community in a positive way, not street violence. I wanted to achieve goals I otherwise wouldn't achieve: the boardroom job, stay out of trouble, go to school.

"I liked the Reebok Team. The first two months after Tyrone was dead, the people that I knew in the program was gone and I felt alone. Charles, then Tracy. I could relate to these people because they was like me or they had those, like, street smarts. When they were gone, I felt alone. The upper-class people in City Year, the people born with a silver spoon in their mouth, they thought they knew it all. Like they were on top. Like they thought they were better than everybody.

"But Alison was always there, she was always down to talk to me and give me advice and shit. Not that I took it. But she didn't get tired of me.

"What was good about City Year was I got to meet a piece of everybody. We got a chance to eliminate some stereotypes that people had in their puny little minds. Before, I couldn't stand white people.

"The Blackstone School project made me feel good inside. Because I haven't done that kind of work before. I felt like a big brother. I felt like, you know, that sentimental feeling. It gave me that role-model feeling.

"Finishing City Year is an accomplishment. There was times when I wanted to call it quits. But graduation was good. Two hundred bills in my pocket, more money coming to me.

"You hear about drugs, what they can do to you. But for me, I always have to see things firsthand. Sometimes I make good decisions, sometimes bad decisions. Things I regret in the long run. I live it up for a long time, but then something always happens. I seldom cry but there's times when I feel sorry for myself and I want to burst into tears.

"City Year might have helped me a little bit—I might find something that came out of it but I'd have to look hard. It was just nine to five. And afterward I'd just go and get fucked up. And I'm still getting in trouble.

"But I can use a power tool now. And I can work an eight-hour day without dying.

"I got this feeling of accomplishment, like I done something for the community, even though they never did nothin' for me. Before when there was a bum on the street askin' for change I would kick him or play with him and pretend like I was gonna give him a quarter and take it back. Now I'll kick him a quarter. I gave one dude ten bills.

"I'm glad I did City Year. Because if I didn't, I'd probably be dead right now. The time I was in there, eight to five, that was the time I would've been getting into some shit."

JACKIE

Because she had already earned an associate's degree, Jackie entered Harvard as a sophomore and declared a major in African-American studies. She maintained a close connection to City Year: her older sister moved to Boston and went to work for City Year, and Jackie continued to volunteer her time there often. She was named to the Massachusetts Commission on National and Community Service, and helped put together the application that eventually garnered City Year $7 million in federal funds through the National and Community Service Act.

After her sophomore year, Jackie spent the summer living in Mission Hill, a section of Roxbury, and worked as a counselor in an academic and recreational program for inner-city children. During the following school year, she worked part-time for YouthBuild, a program for disadvantaged inner-city youths, most of them black and Hispanic, that teaches construction skills while providing remedial education and leadership training classes. We met at her dormitory in the Radcliffe quadrangle, then headed off to a Cambridge café for lunch.

"I was looking for something educationally and economically diverse. Because that's what I hadn't been exposed to. I was one of the few African-Americans from a predominantly white environment. That was my norm.

"It's so hard being African-American middle class. White people don't want you. African-Americans from lower economic strata don't want you. You're caught in between.

"So in City Year I made a conscious effort to hang out with black people. Living with Chris and Joe in Roxbury was definitely an experience. I'd never lived in a black neighborhood. I lived in a lot of places that year—I had the full flavor.

"Now I can understand things better with different people. Like inner-city people that I'm supposed to relate with anyway, because I'm African-American, but before I never could.

"I learned about appreciating each other's differences. Instead of having just a tolerance of differences. And realizing that everyone contributes something.

"I think that whole melting pot thing is a mess. It shouldn't be a melting pot. It should be a salad—where everyone keeps their own identity and keeps their culture and we appreciate it and accept it. I think in City Year we all appreciated each other and accepted each other.

"But after City Year I went through this whole resentful thing. I felt exploited. I felt they manipulated me in ways. The way I was always chosen for roundtables, to speak to funders or reporters. And they really didn't seem to care too much about people from lower incomes or people of color. It was almost like a numbers game.

"That's something that I really started looking at. Why did so many African-American men drop out or not graduate? When we started off with so many? And why is it that I was the only African-American woman and I stayed the whole time?

"That made me start thinking: What type of person is City Year best for? And do they have any support mechanisms for those it was not geared toward or not best for? And they don't.

"It's like they're almost fostering or proving true all the stereotypes that white suburbans hear: that black people aren't reliable, that they slack off, play the system. City Year was catering to that. 'Oh, you need more chances? We'll give you more chances. Because we can't hold you accountable to the same standards that we hold white corps members accountable to.' I think they probably even believe that. That people of color from the inner city can't be held to the same standards.

"I think there's a lot of guilt involved. A lot of white guilt. All that stuff plays into it.

"I'd be really interested to know what Earl learned out of this. He just played the system. *I* played the system. You know, with latenesses. Charles came in on a very positive note. I just don't think City Year was the program for him. He could see that he could play the system. He could see that they needed him, that they needed that statistic. They needed to graduate a certain percentage.

"They need to draw a line and realize there's some people they can work with and some people they can't.

"It also bothered me that they didn't have more people of color on staff. Their excuse was, 'We can't find them.' And I wondered, maybe you're looking in the wrong places. Maybe you're using the wrong credentials.

"City Year is not *the* model. It's *a* model. And people need to recognize there's not one model for everything. Once again it's the majority cultural group saying, 'We know what's best for you.'

"They're not looking at, 'what are the needs of the participants?' They're just looking at creating this model. Saying that it can work. But what does 'work' mean?

"I'm very into youth development. And I don't think that's happening at City Year. Getting your G.E.D. and being able to speak in front of people, that's very important, but after you take off that City Year uniform, are those people still going to listen?

"I don't think youth development can happen for people of color in a program like City Year. Self-love and realizing that they can do it independently of the white powers that be. That they alone can run a program, that they alone can perform a service in their own community. There's nothing more empowering than saying, 'We did it.'

"I think we have to be separate before we can be this whole multicultural thing. Because we've been denied a culture for such a long time and now we've got to go and find it.

"African-Americans have no culture. It's completely lost. We've been going through assimilation for such a long time. Or maybe it isn't lost but we're just discovering it. At least, my generation.

"My field of concentration, African-American studies, has been a journey of self-discovery: being in a group of African-Americans like me, who've always been singled out, who've always been middle-class. Always being with people who've been ostracized by the masses of the black community.

"I'm more comfortable with myself now. I see so many things that I have to offer. And I don't know if it's City Year that did all that, or my major. They both had a profound effect.

"I'm still into service, but I'm more focused on service in my community, which is the inner city, or people of color. That's my moral responsibility. There's a whole trend of African-Americans at Harvard whose parents left the community to do the integration thing. And we're the products of integration, and we realize what didn't work. So now we're going back into the community to invest."

JUNE

When I asked June on the phone what she was doing these days, she quickly answered, "Nothing." She was still living at home with her parents and several of her siblings, and in more than two years she had not found a job or gone back to school. With some prodding, she acknowledged that she spent her days caring for her two nephews and was paid by her brother for her help, but she was still somewhat sheepish in describing her situation. She told me she had worked for three days in a dry cleaner's but had been fired for working too slowly. Meanwhile, she still felt needed at home but she worried about her future.

As always, she declined my offer to come and get her at her house, preferring to meet me in Boston's Chinatown. She surprised me with a dozen roses for my birthday. We talked over dinner in a Chinese restaurant.

"I joined to learn, to make more friends, to help and to meet other people from other backgrounds. I wanted to know more things about the country. Other places besides my home. I used to hang out with only Chinese. That's why I wanted to try to hang out with different people and see how it works.

"First training, I liked it. But I miss the second training, because I already out of City Year. I feel sorry about that. I wanted to see how it go for second training. And for the rest of the year.

"Our team was great. I really liked the team a lot. At first I don't know them. Sometimes I'm shy. I don't know what to say. I might say something that hurt their feelings. Something mean. I have a bad attitude. I don't want to give people the wrong impression. I better keep my mouth shut.

"My parents, they say, 'It's nice to meet all these people from different backgrounds. But if your attitude is not changed, it's hard for you to make friends with them.'

"To me it seem like I not helpful, I not help enough. The team are nice. But to me it's like maybe I don't help them enough. I don't work hard enough. I try very hard but I can't. I just have a lot of things in my mind about my family.

"And my dad, he sick, and he don't have any life insurance. I tried my best, but I want to help my family. At City Year they don't pay enough money. One hundred a week is not enough. I want to buy my family stuff, help them more. Now I stay home, help my mother. I take care of my nephews. They live with us. My mother can't handle them because she's old. Five year old, three year old, they are worst. They don't listen. They make a lot of trouble, especially for old people. I don't want my sisters to stay home from school just for that. And my brothers are working, so this is the only thing I can do to help my family. So I decided to help.

"At the time, a lot of things go in my mind. I don't know what I really want. And then after I got out, I go, 'Oh, my God.'

"I'm looking for a job, but I cannot find the right one yet. 'Make money, training program, no experience necessary.' I look through the newspaper; I look for these jobs.

"In City Year, I only worked for four months. They don't hire people that work for four months. So I don't tell them about City Year.

"I don't know what I want to do. As long as there is no experience necessary. I want to go to training school. Maybe for computers, or professional designer, for modeling, lot of things. I'd like to work for the immigrants. But they need more experience. I like to work in a job that have I.D. card. The I.D. have my name and my picture. But I don't know where to find those kind of jobs.

"In City Year, I learned things that I never did, like painting, playground, teaching kids, clean the yard. I don't do that but when I go to City Year I have to do it and I get used to it. Now I can help my mother in the yard, the house. Ever since I join City Year I like that kind of work.

"I also learned responsibility. Help people. Learn how to be a professional. Learn how to be like staff. Answering the phone, take a message. I just see people do that, I learn it. City Year help other kids learn more about life. How life is hard. Not just life; how to help people; respect; have good manners; all that. So it's good.

"I hope my life go on like . . . I don't know. I just hope I can meet a lot of people, make a lot of friends. Like in City Year."

LISA

Lisa left no forwarding address when she quit City Year, and she never contacted anyone from the team again. Charles said he'd heard she never left town at all but moved in with a boyfriend in Dorchester. Nobody that I spoke with knew where to reach her.

RICHIE

A few weeks after graduation, Earl told me that Richie had been in a car wreck and was in the hospital. I went to see him. Richie had a broken clavicle, a collapsed lung, and several broken ribs. Police had tried to pull him over one night, he said, and since he was drunk and did not have a driver's license he took flight instead. He reached a hundred miles an hour on the highway and then tried to exit without slowing. The car jumped the rails and rolled over three times before landing on its roof. Rescue workers were surprised Richie and his passenger were alive.

Our conversation that day was awkward. Richie was surly and in pain. He told me that he had been carrying a gun in his knapsack to work each day when he was fired, and had been selling marijuana to other corps members. He said he hated everyone on the team, except Tony.

Later, Richie disappeared again. His grandparents moved and were not listed in Massachusetts, and so I was uncertain whether I would be able to find him for an interview a year and a half later. I tracked down his grandfather, who told me Richie was working in a McDonald's off Highway 89 near the Vermont–New Hampshire border.

Richie met me in the McDonald's parking lot. He was driving a station wagon that belonged to the mother of his new girlfriend, who was away at college but whose family was putting him up. He took me to see the newspaper press room where he worked at night, putting in color inserts, and afterward we had breakfast at a nearby Friendly's.

"I thought we were the best team there. I liked Tony a lot. Tony was cool. At the time I guess I didn't show it at all. But now I respect him. He's a better man than me. He's got his act together. He stands by what he thinks. Plus, he's tough—physically and mentally. I thought he was a drill sergeant back then, but he's got a lot of leniency to him, too.

"At times I thought I was getting something out of City Year. Felt good about myself at times. But then again, I don't know. It was all fucked up. I sit here and say that, but then again, I quit.

"I loved the Blackstone. I loved the kids. I still have the picture sitting in my house, on my dresser—of me and all my kids. I can't explain it. The kids. Someone looked up to me. Actually, twelve kids looked up to me. They all liked me. I think that every kid in the school liked me.

"I thought about going into teaching while I was there, but it ain't realistic for me. No money for schooling. They don't want people with my criminal record teaching young children. I'd love to go to work in a school. I've seen day care things in the papers and stuff, but they'd never hire a nineteen-year-old kid. Especially a nineteen-year-old guy. Who really wants their kid taken care of by a nineteen-year-old guy?

"What I didn't like in City Year was all the people like Amy and Jackie and Will. I felt like they had no right whatsoever to tell me what to do. Everybody was always coming down on me.

"I did just as much work, if not more, than anybody else on that team. I was irresponsible, I didn't show up a lot of times, but that was my own life. They just needed something to gripe at, and I was it. *Condescending* is the word I would use.

"I was drinking a lot. Drinking too much, playin' around with girls too much. I have no idea what happened.

"I found out I could make a lot of money selling weed. More than I was making at City Year. Anybody who wanted it, I'd get it. That's another reason I was out a lot. Business would be good in Newburyport and I would get partyin' for four or five days. I suppose I was making in a good week probably three to six hundred dollars over City Year.

"Money was good; I was high. It was social. And like, if you had weed, you could do anything socially.

"It also made me feel big. Big man. You know, he's the man to go to. Like every other kid in Boston that does it. There's two main factors in it. One, you're the man. Two, you got money. Which equals: you're the man."

I asked Richie if he had robbed Amy's apartment, and he said no. Nor did he give or sell the key to someone else, he said.

"That year I quit City Year, left Diane, got into drinking, drugs—well, marijuana—burnt a couple bridges. That whole year right there is where I made every mistake I've made in my life. Still haven't finished a thing to this day. I have no fucking idea why. The only thing I've finished is a jail term.

"After City Year, I started going to Hampton Beach every night, cruisin' the beach, pickin' up girls every night. I hooked up with this one girl who was fifteen, and her parents caught us havin' sex. They called the cops, there was a statutory rape charge. Scared the shit out of me. That carries up to a life sentence, maximum. I said, 'I'm outta here.'"

He described how finally he was arrested in a raid on an apartment from which he and friends had been selling drugs. The drug charges didn't stick, nor did the statutory rape charge, but he pled guilty on a drunk driving charge that resulted from his accident. He served thirty days in jail.

"Then I met Jenny and we hit it off. I came up here to visit her a few times, got offered a job up here at the *Valley News* and ended up stayin' up here. Got a second job at McDonald's, now I'm working both jobs and I'm settled. Straight. Still drink a little, but basically I'm straight. Legally. I have no desire to do anything like that again whatsoever.

"I feel good about myself and I feel like I'm straightenin' out. It's safe, and it's more respectable. I'm the man for workin' two jobs. Her parents like it. Everybody does. I'm respected for working my ass off. If I was selling drugs, they wouldn't even let me near their house. At the end of the summer, we'll get a place, which we probably could afford now, but we'll be better off then. And I want to get married within the next two years.

"I don't regret any part of City Year but leaving. I don't regret anything I did in City Year. Anything they made me do. It's a chapter in my life. And it was a good one, while it lasted. I got my G.E.D. I learned a lot of stuff, about the homeless and stuff. Even though they may not think that I was good for it, it was still good for me.

"Right now I just want to work. Make money. And be respectable."

ROSA

Rosa completed her City Year by returning for another semester in the fall of 1991. Afterward, she began looking for a job, but found she lacked the qualifications for most positions. Her brother, who had been providing financial and emotional support, moved back to Puerto Rico. But Rosa had a new boyfriend who had a good job at a car dealership, and together they moved into an apartment in a three-decker house owned by her sister's husband in the Roslindale section of Boston, a racially mixed, working-class neighborhood. Within a few months of her graduation from City Year, Rosa was pregnant again, and this time she wanted to keep the baby. She and her boyfriend planned to get married.

I went to Rosa's house, and we talked in her dim, but comfortably furnished, first-floor living room. The house and apartment were modest, perhaps a little shabby, but the neighborhood was more pleasant than her old one. Rosa looked plump and happy. She dandled her healthy, two-month-old baby boy on her knees as we talked.

"I thought the team would be prejudiced against me because I was Puerto Rican, but they were friendly. If we had a problem, we talked to each other. They asked me things about P.R., the culture, stuff like that. We communicated real good. It was fun on the retreat, doing games and stuff. I learned a lot and I saw that City Year was going to be good. They teached me to work with hammers and with people, older people, and how to communicate with people. It was fun.

"I liked all the projects, except the one in Chelsea. Everybody was, like, you shouldn't be picking up the garbage, you should be working with the people. People need you.

"I liked working in the park, things that I never done before. Things that I never thought that I could learn to do. Man jobs. I thought those were man jobs. I never tried to do them.

"Tony teaches you a lot. He teaches you that things have to be right. Not just when you think, 'Oh, it's okay, it's okay to do it that way.' No; it has to be *right*. You can do better than okay. I learned a lot with Tony.

"After I got out of there, I started looking for a job like City Year. But there's nothing out there.

"I got a job selling perfume and cologne, house to house. But they told me in order for me to get paid I had to sell a certain amount of perfume. And they're real expensive. And I go house to house and nobody buys it.

"It's very hard. When you go outside, you expect people to be kind of understanding. How can you have experience if they don't let you work? They tell you there's something waiting for you outside, but there's nothing. Unless you go to school. Try to go to college. But then I got pregnant. So maybe I'll go to college later.

"I wanted this baby. Peter told me, we'll have a house, we'll have a family. It was different. I like this neighborhood. Quiet. People don't trouble you. I always wanted a quiet neighborhood. I would never change this.

"I think my decision to have an abortion was good because I had a lot of x-rays after my car accident that spring, when I didn't know I was pregnant. Also, I wasn't ready. I didn't have a steady place, I didn't have Peter, I didn't have nothing.

"The team really helped me out. I think that's really when I got close to them. It was like having a family that supported me a lot. I will not forget that.

"Sometimes I cry about it and I have to say to myself, 'I didn't kill nothing.' I pray to God to forgive me for what I did, but I think it was right. I didn't have a father, and I don't want for my son, any kid, not to have a father, either.

"In City Year, I learned to trust. I learned to trust Earl. I was so scared of him. I thought maybe he'd hit me or something. It was real scary, the way he looked at me. He was always drunk. I thought, what if I get in an argument with him? Maybe he'll hit me.

"And I asked him one day, would he do that? He smiled at me. We got to talking, and he was, like, 'You can trust me, I would never hurt you.' He started crying and I hugged him. I was so surprised.

"City Year is important. It keeps kids out of drugs. Out of trouble. It shows the kids how to be mature. How to take things out of life. You can take a moment and think about it. You can think, 'If you don't want to learn, why you in there?' When you're having a good time, you can take a moment and think about other people. City Year gives you that time."

TRACY

Tracy was working two jobs—home health aide and telemarketer/data entry person—and trying to find a third when I contacted her. She couldn't find time to meet with me when I was in Boston for a week doing these interviews, and I got the sense that she was not eager to spend time revisiting the events of the two years since graduation. But I did speak briefly with her on the phone.

"I got my own apartment now. I asked Mark to move out, and then he kicked *me* out. His name was on the lease. Anyway, I got my own apartment. It's a nice place, one bedroom. He's over with and I'm standing on my own two feet.

"I been at both these jobs almost a year. But I'm workin' too hard. I gotta find something better.

"About City Year? I tried to get back in. I reapplied the next year, but I never heard nothing.

"I don't like starting something without finishing it. I know I coulda done better."

TYRONE'S FAMILY

Tiajuana Gunn was in fragile health when I visited her. There had been two more deaths in her family since Tyrone was killed. In the spring of 1992 she was involved in a car accident while riding in a taxi, and a year later she was still having back problems related to the accident. To make matters worse, she was wearing a splint on her wrist due to a repetitive-movement injury brought on by her work as a typist. She said she often felt tired and drained.

Tyrone's sixteen-year-old brother Jeremy, she told me, had not been the same since Tyrone's death. Formerly a good student, he was now cutting school with some frequency. She didn't know what he did all day, and she worried about him. Her other sons still mourned Tyrone in different ways. Sparticus kept Tyrone's journal in his room and often reread it.

After two years, Tiajuana still spoke glowingly about City Year. She hoped Jeremy would join when he was old enough.

No one had ever been arrested for Tyrone's murder.

WILL

Will went straight to work for City Year as a member of the "alumni squad," a group of eight graduates who were invited back to spend a year working with the corps in various capacities, primarily as assistant team leaders. Many of the alumni were then expected to go off to college or other jobs, but since he already had a bachelor's degree, Will hoped after that to be made a team leader. Instead, he was asked to be Alan Khazei's assistant, a job that put him squarely at the center of events during a period when City Year was experiencing rapid growth. About six months later, in January of 1993, Will was promoted to program director, a new position that he described as being responsible for coordinating the efforts of the different departments: development, program delivery, community relations, and so on. By then City Year had 220 corps members (including the alumni staff) and a staff of more than seventy. When we spoke, Will expressed awe at his own rapid advance to a position of leadership and pride in his ever-increasing responsibilities. He said he hoped to stay with City Year for a while, perhaps helping to lead a replication effort in another city. We talked over coffee at a cafeteria around the corner from the City Year head-quarters.

"I remember walking in the first day and seeing the corps and my heart dropping, realizing that these people were not my age, very few looked like they'd graduated from college, and that this was a diverse group of people. I got very scared. I remember wanting to hold myself differently, not make jokes, thinking that maybe my words would be too long. I definitely didn't want anybody to know my background. Instinctively I knew I wanted to downplay the fact that I went to a private school, downplay that I drove a nice car.

"For the first couple months at least, when I was with the team, I held back, to see what kind of role I should play. I thought that I would be rejected by the group. I didn't know anybody that had come from the background I had, and it was the one background we never talked about. I sort of felt like everybody agreed that blacks had been oppressed and women are oppressed and blue-collar workers are oppressed and the common ground we would all share is that a rich family is disgusting and they're terrible people and I sort of felt like that was okay to bash.

"It made me look at my family in a different way. I never had realized before how much I had. I went through a lot. Coming in to work every day and then going home to Beacon Hill—and my roommate wants to talk about the country club. It sounds so stereo-typical but that's how it was. Two worlds. It's too weird. I remember the day would end sometimes and I'd say to myself, did I reveal too much? Because part of me felt like, if I grew up in Roxbury or wherever, and there was some guy on my team who had everything, I would resent it. I felt some guilt there.

"I remember the day that I felt I didn't hold back and was part of the team. We had to do a presentation. I came in with a script of how I thought it should go, and so I really put it out there, and when the team started to argue about it, I stepped forward and said, 'No! This is how I think it should go.' And that felt really good, that I could be myself and my teammates would listen to me like I listened to them. That was important to me—I suddenly felt very comfortable with them. And I stopped holding back, I started talking about my family and everything else. I was suddenly becoming me with a diverse group of people.

"The service projects—when we were in that shelter and dust was falling all over the place and we were climbing ladders, that was amazing. To look around and see Alison three floors down working with Chris, and I'm up here with Brendan using a nail gun, that was definitely cool. But what was cool about it was the way we would then be at lunchtime—exhausted but feeling accomplished. And the humor that would go on while you're on the work site.

"When I look back on the year, I think although service was great, it's all really part of working with a team. And it felt so good that it continues to feel very odd if I am in an environment where it's not diverse. Or when people aren't revealing themselves. It has totally changed the way I view relationships with friends. And it's changed my relationship with my family completely. When I was fifteen years old, I was this funny, fat, spoiled little snot. Little Lord Fauntleroy. And now my role is absolutely changed.

"People have the idea that young people doing service will be very good for the ex-gang member, but it's equally important and good for society to get somebody like myself turned around through it. I clearly will be a better person because of my experience here, and I will give back to the world in better ways. I view my family's role in society differently. They're very fortunate, they've got money, and I'm challenging my parents to start thinking of ways to give some of that money away, and they're taking that seriously. My father's taking the idea of being a businessman and giving back the way that corporate sponsors of City Year do. He's realizing through me and through City Year that he could play a similar role in the city he occupies. He employs two thousand people and he's saying, 'How can I get my employees doing service?'

"I spent my four years of college not being responsible for anything. And I felt owed, like I needed to have a BMW and a house and a condominium *soon*, and that I should be wearing a very nice suit to work. And that's so stupid now. These things might still happen, but I have to make it happen for myself. At Skidmore I never volunteered for a thing. And that's totally unacceptable to me now. I learned that through service.

"How can we improve City Year? I'd like to figure out how to engage the Earls better. I think there's clearly a place in the City Year community for at-risk youth, and they can gain a lot, but we've got to think it through a little bit more. They give a lot to the team. I gained a lot of perspective by having Earl on my team. But did Earl gain as much from me? I don't think so. We need to figure out why. Work that out better. Maybe it means providing housing so Earl is getting twenty-four hours of mentoring and role-modeling. Maybe you've got to do more intervention.

"National service should be like higher education. Higher education is taken very seriously in this country: there are community colleges, training programs, state schools, and private colleges, and if you want to educate yourself you can get a scholarship. This country believes that higher education is necessary. Likewise, I think there should be an opportunity for every young person to serve. There should be all kinds of different ways of serving. You would have millions of young people growing up knowing how important service is. Once you get them there they will all continue to give back, and they will see their role in society and in this country with a lot more ownership and responsibility."

TONY

The following year, Tony returned with City Year to Chelsea, and stayed there all year. Under a new organizational structure, he supervised different teams as they rotated through the small, impoverished city. He saw Chelsea as a kind of laboratory where City Year could experiment with new ways of aiding community development. Among other projects, Tony and the corps members oversaw the start-up of a community volunteer center, a soup kitchen, and an emergency food pantry, and expanded the neighborhood cleanup day. The year after that, with City Year twenty teams strong, Tony became a division manager, overseeing four teams in Chelsea. The teams remained in Chelsea all year. Tony was effusive about the project. "I think this is the best example at City Year of corps-member empowerment and partnerships with the community," he said. "We've got a really strong reputation for quality work." A number of Chelsea residents joined City Year to work in their own community.

Whenever graduates of our team, the original Chelsea team, came to visit, he would happily bend their ear about what had grown from the "seed" we planted in Chelsea. "The Wright brothers' airplane was up for only fifteen minutes," he would say, "but that was the basis for all the flight we have now."

Most team members stayed in touch with Tony to some degree, and he often helped them out with letters of recommendation and personal advice.

In the spring of 1993, Tony resigned his position at City Year to strike out on his own as an independent consultant to youth development organizations. He wanted to share what he had learned "outside the walls of City Year."

In Tony's end-of-year assessment memo, written after the Reebok Team's graduation in 1991, he said:

The most satisfying feeling for me at City Year is to go home at the end of the day knowing that the team put in an honest day of very hard work, that they were challenged and achieved results, and that we truly had done something that was helping someone else. I also enjoyed helping corps members to go beyond themselves, to find new strength and new confidence through their work; to help them deal with personal and experiential issues. When corps members begin to take initiative on their own and support each other actively without my telling them to, I feel proud and happy for them.

I relearned the lesson that you can lead a horse to water but you can't make him drink. This is something I learned painfully while dealing with the substance abuse of family and friends, but which my trials with Richie Dale drove painfully home.

I've relearned that young people respect fairness and consistency, and that they listen to what you do, not what you say.

Young people are both incredibly powerful and fragile. They are capable of moving mountains, but can be hurt or misled very easily by those whom they love, trust, and look up to.

We need to practice what we preach. While we stress the importance of diversity and inclusion, we have yet to achieve this in our staff. We speak often about respect being the key to service, yet we routinely make corps members wait for us to show up for meetings. City Year needs to be one place where young people can begin to regain faith in institutions that work.

Just after he announced his decision to leave City Year, I talked with Tony about the lessons he had learned, both during the year I was there and afterward, and about his feelings regarding national service.

"One thing I've learned is that it is very important that the decisions that get made that affect the whole organization should be made by people who are at the place where the rubber meets the road. I learned how important it is to be out on the front lines when deciding the direction an organization takes, how we allocate our resources, how we support people.

"One of the best selling points for City Year is that young people are here not as a recipient but as a resource to the community. But if you accept that way of framing the debate, which I have even used myself, you force people to choose. And I think it is a false choice.

"We need to provide more one-on-one support and development. The kinds of things that we were spending our time with on Fridays, like committees—I would have rather been spending that time with support-group stuff. Support groups on gender issues, or relationship issues. We were spending time with a yearbook committee and a prom committee, which are good things, too, but in terms of where some people were coming from . . .

"In my role as a supervisor I did a lot of counseling. I think I did a good job, but I am not professionally trained in it, and there are limits to what I can do. There's a strength that comes with doing that stuff, but I think that if you built in a support system, the efforts of the organization would have been better spent. For national service to succeed, it's going to need more and better quality support."

I asked him if he was discouraged that many team members had still not overcome their problems finding work, staying out of trouble, staying sober.

"You can't just put somebody through certain experiences, just as you would put a vegetable through a processor, and have them come out different at the other end. Human beings aren't like that. When you start with a young person coming into a program for a year, with twenty-two years of life behind them, you're not going to completely alter what came with them when they stepped in the door. You can't expect that every young person will suddenly turn around and excel.

"But you can expect that they make progress in all those areas. Progress should be the goal; to move as far along the path in all those areas as possible. One of the things people have to understand about national service, and youth service in general, is that they have to begin operating in a different paradigm. Youth service is not *the* solution. What it does is help us do the work that allows us to find the solution.

The work of diversity, the work of growing up, the work of taking personal responsibility, the work of learning how to follow directions, the work of citizenship, the work of building community.

"Tyrone's death totally woke the organization up to the flesh and bones of what we were doing. We got to see the invisible connections that we don't always see. We had been together only a month and already we had bonded to an extent we didn't realize. We suddenly felt our vulnerability.

"There's not been another event since then that had the same effect. Ever since then, City Year's single greatest strength has been our ability to build community. We became sensitized to how connected we are in doing this work, and we became more committed to building it and supporting it.

"Tyrone's funeral was a religious experience for me. In the three minutes that we carried his body from the hearse to the grave site, I felt that something powerful, something profound was happening. Only through City Year were so many people able to care so much for Tyrone and the Gunn family. I am convinced that we can help this society to transcend itself through the institution of service."

♦

When I tell people about my time in City Year, they usually ask me what my teammates are doing now, and in their hopeful faces I can see an expectation that I will tell them dramatic success stories, uplifting tales of lives turned around through service. Listeners are sometimes disappointed to learn that one of my teammates is in jail, that one is unemployed, one now has an out-of-wedlock child, and one still struggles with his drug and alcohol abuse. I, too, have felt discouragement at the trajectory of some of my former teammates' lives since leaving City Year.

But as Tony pointed out, life changes often happen slowly, incrementally. Small gains are sometimes more profound than they at first appear. And seeds planted at one time may not bear fruit until a month, a year, or even ten years later.

From these interviews I learned that the results of service and of membership in a diverse team may be serendipitous and unexpected. I was surprised and moved by much of what I heard.

My team faced challenges that went well beyond those confronted by most other City Year teams. Chance and hasty decisions combined to give the Reebok team a high concentration of members who were most at risk of dropping out: high school dropouts and people with criminal records or substance-abuse problems. The violent shock and grief of losing Tyrone disrupted the process of bonding and resulted in teamwide depression. In that context, it is not hard to understand why our completion rate (only half of the original team members finished the year) was so much lower than the overall City Year completion rate, which was close to 85 percent, and why some Reebok Team members still lead troubled lives.

But perhaps the extraordinary challenges the Reebok team faced make our experience even more instructive. I hope that advocates of national service will heed some of the warnings and criticisms my teammates offered: the need to avoid applying double standards for service participants from different backgrounds, for example, and the need to provide better counseling and support for those whose home lives, circumstances, disabilities, or histories are barriers to self-improvement and effective service. The need to continually examine what is being accomplished and what is not, and to recalibrate goals accordingly. The need to pay more attention to preparing people for the challenges they may face once their service year is over.

I also hope that those who seek to assess the value of national service will take note of the subtle and idiosyncratic results my teammates described, some of which are not likely to show up on five-year tracking surveys.

Richie, for instance, does not draw a specific link between his improving circumstances and his time in City Year, but the cherished respect he is now earning through honest work is something he first glimpsed while helping children at the Blackstone school. June does not yet know how to achieve what she wants, but she knows she misses the camaraderie she found in City Year, and she would like to recreate it in her life. Earl's claim that City Year taught him to "work eight hours without dying" is no small achievement; nor is Amy's claim that she "learned to feel" in City Year, nor Alison's discovery of a calling and a hidden talent in service, nor the trust and sense of family Rosa found within the team, nor Will's new awareness of his own privilege and his desire to give back to the community, nor Jackie's developing commitment to helping empower black and inner-city youth.

I was moved to see how team members have become vivid and important figures in one another's lives. For Earl, his connection to

Alison, to Tony, and others is a lifeline to a stabler world, something he reaches for in moments of crisis. Others on the team do not always communicate but are eager to know what one another are doing. Two years later, a sense of connection to each other is still strong for most team members.

I have often thought of an exchange I overheard between Brendan and David after a contentious team meeting at the beginning of the year. "We're never going to all like each other," Brendan said. "We're just too different. We're never even going to be able to work together!"

"Oh, yes we will," David replied. "I'm shooting for family."

Families are not always the best model. They fight a lot, and sometimes within a family, dire things go wrong. But siblings can love each other even when they don't like each other. And when something bad or good happens to the one, the others feel it. In a way, it happens to them all.

It was the same for us, the Reebok Team. Like a family, we became connected. For nine months we breathed the same dusty air, hefted the same tools, locked eyes across the same long pressure-treated boards. We tolerated the same hours, confronted the same obstacles, met the same people, relished the same successes, and suffered the same disappointments and losses. We made some small improvements in the city where we lived. We shared a history, an enterprise, a portion of each other's lives. And because we value that history, we value each other.

We had a team reunion in January 1993. The event was a small ceremony to honor Tyrone. Another youth organization was donating money to City Year in his remembrance, and Tony invited all of us to attend. Not everyone was there; Charles and Earl were in jail that day, David and Chris were too far away to come, and Richie's whereabouts were unknown at the time, but Brendan came, as did Amy, Rosa, Alison, Jackie, Tracy, Will, and June. It was a bittersweet gathering, and we promised one another we would do it again.

Communities are not built of friends, or of groups of people with similar styles and tastes, or even of people who like or understand each other. They are built of people who feel they are part of something that is bigger than themselves: a shared goal or enterprise, like righting a wrong, or building a road, or raising children, or living honorably, or worshiping a god. To build community requires only the ability to see value in others; to look at them and see a potential partner in one's enterprise.

National service offers an opportunity to build community, to create a sense of shared interest that crosses barriers of race, class, and culture—to create an understanding and respect for the essential humanity and individuality of others; a sense that trust and communication across racial and social boundaries are possible, and a willingness to try to open channels for that trust; a sense of optimism, that by putting our heads and hands to work, each of us has the power to effect change; a feeling of responsibility for one another.

In a country where poverty and racial alienation and inequality are still so strong that people are moved to riot and destroy even their own neighborhoods, there can be no more important goal.

Our triumphs as a group—the Reebok Team—were small. But multiply them: by ten, a hundred, or a hundred thousand. What if every seventeen- to twenty-two-year-old could join a City Year? What if every neighborhood could have a crew of energetic youths come in and provide the human power to meet pressing needs? What if every inner-city school could have a team of "City Years"?

What if every young person could experience belonging to a group that included people like Earl, like Alison, like Charles and Amy, Jackie, Will, all sharing an identity and a motive for their days? What if every person who ran for public office had known a Tyrone? Had tried to teach a child with learning disabilities? Had cleaned a street and seen it littered the next day? Had dug a hole in earth that drug dealers trod at night and plunged his hands into the soil to plant a rose? What would that mean for our society as generations of City Year graduates grew up and took their places in the ranks of adult citizens?

We'll never really know unless we try.

I f you are interested in learning more about national and community service opportunities in your area, contact:

American Alliance for Rights and Responsibilities
1725 K Street NW
Suite 1112
Washington, DC 20006
(202) 785–7844

Commission on National and Community Service
529 14th Street NW
Suite 452
Washington, DC 20045
(202) 724–0600

Communitarian Network
2130 H Street NW
Suite 714
Washington, DC 20052
(202) 994–7997

National Association of Service and Conservation Corps
666 Eleventh Street NW
Suite 500
Washington, DC 20001
(202) 737–6272

Points of Light Foundation
1737 H Street NW
Washington, DC 20006
(202) 223–9186

White House Office of National Service
Old Executive Office Building
Room 145
Washington, DC 20500-0145
(202) 456–6444

Youth Service America
1101 15th Street NW
Suite 200
Washington, DC 20005
(202) 296–2992

Acknowledgments

First, I would like to thank the members of the City Year Reebok Team of 1990–1991, who generously allowed me and my notebook into their lives and who became a kind of family to me during a challenging and unforgettable year. Their trust, openness, patience, and courage made this book possible. The team leaader, known here as Tony, made an especially vital contribution. He spent countless hours with me, sharing his thoughts and plans and fleshing out my understanding of events recounted here. The founders of City Year, Alan Khazei and Michael Brown, have long inspired me with their commitment to national service, and I am indebted to them for giving me the chance to be a part of City Year and to write about the experience.

I would never have undertaken, far less completed, this book without the loving support of my parents, William and Marianne Goldsmith. Their example and their faith in my ideas and ability gave me the confidence to leave a good job and begin this project, and fortified me at rough moments. Their generous financial assistance kept the lights on and the rent paid. They read and commented on the manuscript, draft after draft. This book is dedicated to them.

I would also like to thank Judy Lam, whose friendship made it possible for me to continue in times of uncertainty and whose insights often helped inform this work. Many family members and friends lived this project with me and contributed in essential ways, and I would especially like to thank Alex and Randy Forbes, Michael Goldsmith and Elline Hildebrandt, and Simin and Greg Curtis. I am grateful to Jon Amsterdam for his incisive editing assistance, which improved the book immensely, and for the photos he contributed.

Farr Carey, a member of the 1990–1991 City Year corps, took many of the beautiful photos that appear in this book. Many of our project sponsors and others we met during the year, as well as City Year corps and staff members, were generous with their time, their friendship, and their ideas, and if I had the space I would thank them all here.

I might have given up this project midway through were it not for a generous grant I received from the American Alliance for Rights and Responsibilities, a Communitarian public interest group. The AARR's help went far beyond financial aid, and I am indebted to the AARR staff: Executive Director Roger L. Conner, Patrick Burns, and Rob Teir. Their support and interest made me feel less alone in this undertaking, and their attention to my progress helped me stay on track. I am also grateful for the support of the Amelior Foundation.

Professor Alan Feldman and the members of my Radcliffe writing seminar both encouraged and inspired me, and their thoughtful comments helped me grapple with perplexing questions of style and approach. The Boston Writers' Room provided me with a quiet space to begin my work.

I have had many wonderful teachers in the course of my working life. In particular, I would like to thank Howard Husock, who first showed me how much a good story can tell, and whose annoyingly persistent question—"But Suzanne, what do you want to *say*?"—haunts me still. I am also grateful to my former colleagues and team members at the City Volunteer Corps, who taught me a good deal about respect, dedication, and common sense.

Finally, I would like to thank my literary agent, Rafe Sagalyn, copyeditor Ed Cohen, and my editor at the New Press, Diane Wachtell, who took an interest in this project from the very start, long before national service made its way into the spotlight.